EXPERIENCE, STRENGTH AND HOPE

OTHER BOOKS

ALCOHOLICS ANONYMOUS
The basic text for Alcoholics Anonymous

TWELVE STEPS AND TWELVE TRADITIONS
*An interpretive commentary on the A.A. program
by a co-founder*

ALCOHOLICS ANONYMOUS COMES OF AGE
A brief history of A.A.'s first two decades

AS BILL SEES IT
(formerly THE A.A. WAY OF LIFE)
Selected writings of A.A.'s co-founder

DR. BOB AND THE GOOD OLDTIMERS
*A biography, with recollections of early A.A.
in the Midwest*

PASS IT ON
*Bill W.'s life story; how the A.A. message
reached the world*

DAILY REFLECTIONS
A book of reflections by A.A. members for A.A. members

BOOKLETS

CAME TO BELIEVE . . .
Spiritual experiences of 75 A.A.s

LIVING SOBER
Practical suggestions heard at meetings

A.A. IN PRISON: INMATE TO INMATE
*Former Grapevine articles by people who found
A.A. in prison*

EXPERIENCE, STRENGTH AND HOPE

Stories from the First Three Editions of
Alcoholics Anonymous

ALCOHOLICS ANONYMOUS WORLD SERVICES, INC.
BOX 459, GRAND CENTRAL STATION
NEW YORK, NY 10163
2003

CONTENTS

Introduction   ix

Part One   1
  The Unbeliever   5
  A Feminine Victory   16
  A Business Man's Recovery   24
  A Different Slant   33
  The Back-Slider   35
  The Seven Month Slip   44
  My Wife and I   48
  A Ward of the Probate Court   57
  Riding the Rods   63
  The Salesman   76
  Fired Again   83
  Truth Freed Me!   90
  Smile with Me, at Me   93
  A Close Shave   101
  Educated Agnostic   103
  Another Prodigal Story   108
  The Car Smasher   114
  Hindsight   120
  On His Way   125
  An Alcoholic's Wife   128
  An Artist's Concept   130
  The Rolling Stone   135
  Lone Endeavor   140

Part Two	147
The Professor and the Paradox	151
His Conscience	157
New Vision for a Sculptor	166
Joe's Woes	179
There's Nothing the Matter With Me	193
Annie the Cop Fighter	203
The Independent Blonde	212
Part Three	219
He Had to Be Shown	221
He Thought He Could Drink Like a Gentleman	237
The European Drinker	248
The Vicious Cycle	256
The News Hawk	268
From Farm to City	278
Home Brewmeister	291
Too Young?	298
Those Golden Years	302
Lifesaving Words	310
A Teen-ager's Decision	313
Rum, Radio and Rebellion	316
Any Day Was Washday	328
A Flower of the South	332
Calculating the Costs	343
Stars Don't Fall	347
Growing Up All Over Again	364
Unto the Second Generation	367
A Five-Time Loser Wins	376
Promoted to Chronic	383
Join the Tribe!	393
Belle of the Bar	397

The Prisoner Freed   402
Desperation Drinking   406
The Career Officer   411
He Who Loses His Life   420

The Twelve Steps   432
The Twelve Traditions   433
The Twelve Concepts (Short Form)   434

INTRODUCTION

Since the first edition of the Big Book, *Alcoholics Anonymous,* came off press in 1939, there have been three revised editions—a second published in 1955, a third in 1976, and a fourth in 2001. In all four editions, the first 164 pages have remained unchanged, preserving A.A.'s message just as it was originally recorded by the founding members. The impetus for change has been the need for revisions to the section of personal stories, as suffering alcoholics of many different ages, occupations, lifestyles, and ethnic, racial, and religious backgrounds have learned about the Fellowship and come to knock on its doors.

The importance of these personal stories cannot be overstated. Co-founder Bill W. articulated it in a 1954 letter, written when he was immersed in collecting new stories for the second edition: "The story section of the Big Book is far more important than most of us think. It is our principal means of identifying with the reader outside of A.A.; it is the written equivalent of hearing speakers at an A.A. meeting; it is our show window of results. To increase the power and variety of this display to the utmost should be, therefore, no routine or hurried job. The best will be none too good. The difference between 'good' and 'excellent' can be the difference between prolonged misery and recovery, between life and death, for the reader outside A.A. . . . The main purpose of the revision is to bring the story section up to date, to portray more adquately a cross section of those who have found help—the audience for the book is people who are coming to Alcoholics Anonymous now."

As stories were added to new editions, others were removed. Difficult as it must have been to take out any A.A. story, hard decisions were integral to the process of making space for A.A. experience that reflected the growing diversity of the membership. And since there is no such thing as a "bad" A.A. story, every time a new edition came off press the General Service Office received calls and letters asking why some member's "favorite" had been removed.

The idea of developing a separate publication to make these slices of A.A. history and experience available once again came up periodically over the years, but for quite some time it did not receive substantial support. By 1997, however, when members of the General Service Conference called for preparation of a fourth edition of the Big Book, they asked concurrently for development of a volume of the stories that had been dropped from the first three editions. Alcoholics Anonymous had grown from the original struggling band of 100 members, living primarily in Ohio and New York, to a multifaceted, worldwide Fellowship, estimated at more than two million strong. Changes from the third edition to the fourth were the most extensive yet, and more than half the stories had to be taken out to make room for those of contemporary members. Thus, in the pages that follow, you will meet a large number and variety of A.A.s from earlier times, whose stories are no longer part of our basic text, but are most emphatically part of our common experience.

All but ten of the stories in this volume were published in either the first or the second edition of *Alco-*

holics Anonymous. As a collection, therefore, they greatly enrich our knowledge of "what we used to be like" as a Fellowship. Most of the A.A. writers got sober before the Twelve Traditions had been adopted, many of them in that chaotic period when A.A. was "flying blind" and learning from its many mistakes. For the most part, they stopped drinking, and stayed stopped, without the numerous A.A. meetings and other resources so readily available. Yet they demonstrate powerfully that A.A. experience is timeless. They tell us, as clearly as the speaker we heard last night, "what we are like now"—sober, grateful alcoholics who with the help of the A.A. program will continue to stay that one crucial drink away from a drunk.

PART ONE

The stories presented here were deleted when the second edition of Alcoholics Anonymous *was published, and the introductory material to this section provides information about A.A. as it was at that time.*

It was 1955, and thanks largely to the Big Book, A.A.'s membership had grown from a few struggling groups with a total of about 100 members to an estiated 6,000 groups with more than 146,000 members. Traveling A.A.s and those serving in World War II had carried the message throughout the U.S. and Canada, and into about 50 other nations. The Twelve Traditions had been adopted in 1950, establishing guiding principles for the formation and development of groups everywhere. And at the 1955 Convention in St. Louis, A.A.'s "coming of age," the Three Legacies of Recovery, Unity, and Service were turned over to the Fellowship as a whole by its founding members.

Given all these changes, the 1939 Big Book's personal stories section no longer adequately represented the membership, and co-founder Bill W. set out to broaden its scope in a revised edition. The Preface to the second edition explained: "When the book was first printed, we had scarcely 100 members all told, and every one of them was an almost hopeless case of alcoholism. This has changed. A.A. now helps alcoholics in all stages of the disease. It reaches into every level of life and into nearly all occupations. Our membership now includes many young people. Women, who were at first very reluctant to approach A.A., have come forward in large numbers. Therefore, the range of the story section has been broadened so that every alcoholic reader may find a reflection of him- or herself in it."

For the second edition, Bill restructured the story section in three parts: "Pioneers of A.A.," "They Stopped in Time," and "They Lost Nearly All." Only two stories from the first edition were retained intact; three were edited, one of which was retitled; two were completely rewritten, and 30 new stories were added. The completed section contained 38 stories, compared to 29 in the first edition (Dr. Bob's, along with 28 others).

The stories that follow, reprinted from the first edition, take us back to the "trial and error" days, and paint a fascinating picture of what the A.A. experience was in the formative years. The A.A.s we meet here had been sober for very short periods of time (Bill W. was sober only three and a half years, Dr. Bob about three). They were still a little unsure and afraid of this "thing" they had found, still groping for clear guidelines, still largely uneducated about their alcoholism. Much of the terminology is strange to us: they wrote of "former alcoholics," described their recovery as a "cure," and referred to alcohol in terms such as "John Barleycorn." There were only a handful of groups at the time, and many of these writers found A.A. more or less by accident—perhaps a friend or relative happened to hear about a group of former drunks who were staying sober, or some early members heard about their problem and made a Twelfth Step call.

Some of the rough edges found in the first edition stories (the use of profanity, for example, references to specific religious beliefs, and several rather disorganized stories) would be smoothed out in those chosen for later editions. When Bill W. began the revision, he laid out some general guidelines: "Since the audience for the book is likely to be newcomers, anything from the point of view of content or style that might offend or alienate those who are not familiar with the program should be carefully eliminated. . . . Profanity, even when mild, rarely contributes as much as it detracts. It should be avoided." In a letter to a prospective contributor, Bill set forth the framework he was seeking: "We are looking for straight personal narratives which describe the drinking history, how the newcomer arrived in Alcoholics Anonymous, how A.A. affected him, and what A.A. has since accomplished for him."

But with all their faults of style, the differences between the stories we hear today and those written in 1939 are not important. These writers were alcoholics, and their experience rings true to any A.A. member of any time or place.

THE UNBELIEVER

*D*ull . . . listless . . . semicomatose . . . I lay on my bed in a famous hospital for alcoholics. Death or worse had been my sentence.

What was the difference? What difference did anything make? Why think of these things which were gone—why worry about the results of my drunken escapades? What the hell were the odds if my wife had discovered the mistress situation? Two swell boys . . . sure . . . but what difference would a corpse or an asylum imprisoned father make to them? . . . thoughts stop whirling in my head . . . that's the worst of this sobering-up process . . . the old think tank is geared in high-high . . . what do I mean high-high . . . where did that come from . . . oh yes, that first Cadillac I had, it had four speeds . . . had a high-high gear . . . insane asylum . . . how that bus could scamper . . . yes . . . even then liquor probably poisoned me. What had the little doctor said this morning . . . thoughts hesitate a moment . . . stop your mad turning . . . what was I thinking about . . . oh yes, the doctor.

This morning I reminded Doc this was my tenth visit. I had spent a couple of thousand dollars on these trips and those I had financed for the plastered play girls who also couldn't sober up. Jackie was a honey until she got plastered and then she was a hellion. Wonder what gutter she's in now. Where was I? Oh . . . I asked the doctor to tell me the truth. He owed it to me for the amount of money I had spent. He faltered. Said I'd been drunk, that's all. God! Didn't I know that?

5

But Doc, you're evading. Tell me honestly what is the matter with me. I'll be all right did you say? But Doc, you've said that before. You said once that if I stopped for a year I would be over the habit and would never drink again. I didn't drink for over a year, but I did start to drink again.

Tell me what is the matter with me. I'm an alcoholic? Ha ha and ho ho! As if I didn't know that! But aside from your fancy name for a plain drunk, tell me why I drink. You say a true alcoholic is something different from a plain drunk? What do you mean . . . let me have it cold . . . brief and with no trimmings.

An alcoholic is a person who has an allergy to alcohol? Is poisoned by it? One drink does something to the chemical make-up of the body? That drink affects the nerves and in a certain number of hours another drink is medically demanded? And so the vicious cycle is started? An ever smaller amount of time between drinks to stop those screaming, twitching, invisible wires called nerves?

I know that history Doc . . . how the spiral tightens . . . a drink . . . unconscious . . . awake . . . drink . . . unconscious . . . poured into the hospital . . . suffer the agonies of hell . . . the shakes . . . thoughts running wild . . . brain unleashed . . . engine without a governor. But hell Doc, I don't want to drink! I've got one of the stubbornest will powers known in the business. I stick at things. I get them done. I've stuck on the wagon for months. And not been bothered by it . . . and then suddenly, incomprehensibly, an empty glass in my hand and another spiral started. How did the Doc explain that one?

He couldn't. That was one of the mysteries of true alcoholism. A famous medical foundation had spent a fortune trying to segregate the reasons for the alcoholic as compared to the plain hard, heavy drinker. Had tried to find the cause. And all they had been able to determine as a fact was that the majority of the alcohol in every drink taken by the alcoholic went to the fluid in which the brain floated. Why a man ever started when he knew those things was one of the things that could not be fathomed. Only the damn fool public believed it a matter of weak will power. Fear . . . ostracism . . . loss of family . . . loss of position . . . the gutter . . . nothing stopped the alcoholic.

Doc! What do you mean—nothing! What! An incurable disease? Doc, you're kidding me! You're trying to scare me into stopping! What's that you say? You wish you were? What are those tears in your eyes Doc? What's that? Forty years you've spent at this alcoholic business and you have yet to see a true alcoholic cured? Your life defeated and wasted? Oh, come, come Doc . . . what would some of us do without you? If even only to sober up. But Doc . . . let's have it. What is going to be my history from here on out? Some vital organ will stop or the mad house with a wet brain? How soon? Within two years? But, Doc, I've got to do something about it! I'll see doctors . . . I'll go to sanitariums. Surely the medical profession knows something about it. So little, you say? But why? Messy. Yes, I'll admit there is nothing messier than an alcoholic drunk.

What's that Doc? You know a couple of fellows that were steady customers here that haven't been drunk for about ten months? You say they claim they are cured? And they make an avocation of passing it on to others? What have they got? You don't know . . . and you don't believe they are cured . . .

well why tell me about it? A fine fellow you say, plenty of money, and you're sure it isn't a racket . . . just wants to be helpful . . . call him up for me will you, Doc?

How Doc had hated to tell me. Thoughts stop knocking at my door. Why can't I get drunk like other people, get up next morning, toss my head a couple of time and go to work? Why do I have to shake so I can't hold the razor? Why does every little muscle inside me have to feel like a crawling worm? Why do even my vocal chords quiver so words are gibberish until I've had a big drink? Poison! Of course! But how could anyone understand such a necessity for a drink that it has to be loaded with pepper to keep it from bouncing? Can any mortal understand such secret shame in having to have a drink as to make a person keep the bottles hidden all over the house. The morning drink . . . shame and necessity . . . weakness . . . remorse. But what do the family know about it? Little Doc was right, they know nothing. They just say "Be strong"—"Don't take that drink"—"Suffer it through."

What the hell do they know about suffering? Not sickness. Not a belly ache—oh yes, your guts get so sore that you cannot place your hands on them . . . oh sure, every time you go you twist and writhe in pain. What the hell does any non-alcoholic know about suffering? Thoughts . . . stop this mad merry-go-round. And worst of all, this mental suffering—the hating yourself—the feeling of absurd, irrational weakness—the unworthiness. Out that window! Use the gun in the drawer! What about poison? Go out in a garage and start the car. Yeah, that's the way out . . . but then people'll say "He was plastered." I can't leave that story behind. That's worse than cowardly.

Isn't there some one who understands? Thoughts . . . please, oh please, stop . . . I'm going nuts . . . or am I nuts now? Never . . . never again will I take another drink, not even a glass of beer . . . even that starts it. Never . . . never . . . never again . . . and yet I've said that a dozen times and inexplicably I've found an empty glass in my hand and the whole story repeated.

My Lord, the tragedy that sprang out of her eyes when I came home with a breath on me . . . and fear. The smiles wiped off the kids' faces. Terror stalking through the house. Yes . . . that changed it from a home into a house. Not drunk yet, but they knew what was coming. Mr. Hyde was moving in.

And so I'm going to die. Or a wet brain. What was it that fellow said who was here this afternoon? Damn fool thought . . . get out of my mind. Now I know I'm going nuts. And science knows nothing about it. And psychiatrists. I've spent plenty on them. Thoughts, go away! No . . . I don't want to think about what that fellow said this afternoon.

He's trying . . . idealistic as hell . . . nice fellow, too. Oh, why do I have to suffer with this revolving brain? Why can't I sleep? What was it he said? Oh yes, came in and told about his terrific drunks, his trips up here, this same thing I'm going through. Yes, he's an alcoholic all right. And then he told me he knew he was cured. Told me he was peaceful . . . (I'll never know peace again) . . . that he didn't carry constant fear around with him. Happy because he felt free. But it's screwy. He said so himself. But he did get my confidence when he started to tell what he had gone through. It was so exactly like my case. He knows what this torture is. He raised my hopes so high; it looked as though he had something. I don't know, I guess I was so sold that I expected him to spring some kind of a pill and I asked him desperately what it was.

And he said, "God."

And I laughed.

A ball bat across my face would have been no greater shock. I was so high with hope and expectation. How can a man be so heartless? He said that it sounded screwy but it worked, at least it had with him . . . said he was not a religionist . . . in fact didn't go to church much . . . my ears came up at that . . . his unconventionality attracted me . . . said that some approaches to religion were screwy . . . talked about how the simplest truth in the world had been often all balled up by complicating it . . . that attracted me . . . get out of my mind . . . what a fine religious bird I'd be . . . imagine the glee of the gang at me getting religion . . . phooey . . . thoughts, please slow down . . . why don't they give me something to go to sleep . . . lie down in green pastures . . . the guy's nuts . . . forget him.

And so it's the mad house for me . . . glad mother is dead, she won't have to suffer that . . . if I'm going nuts maybe it'd be better to be crazy the way he is . . . at least the kids wouldn't have the insane father whisper to carry through life . . . life's cruel . . . the puny-minded, curtain hiding gossips . . . "didn't you know his father was committed for insanity?" What a sly label that would be to hang on those boys . . . damn the gossiping, reputation-shredding busybodies who put their noses into other people's business.

He'd laid in this same dump . . . suffered . . . gone

through hell . . . made up his mind to get well . . .
studied alcoholism . . . Jung . . . Blank Medical Foundation . . . asylums . . . Hopkins . . . many said incurable disease . . . impossible . . . nearly all known cures
had been through religion . . . revolted him . . . made a
study of religion . . . more he studied the more it was
bunk to him . . . not understandable . . . self-hypnotism . . . and then the thought hit him that people had
it all twisted up. They were trying to pour everyone
into molds, put a tag on them, tell them what they had
to do and how they had to do it, for the salvation of
their own souls. When as a matter of fact people were
through worrying about their souls, they wanted action right here and now. A lot of tripe was usually
built up around the simplest and most beautiful ideas
in the world.

And how did he put the idea . . . bunk . . .
bunk . . . why in hell am I still thinking about him . . .
in hell . . . that's good . . . I am in hell. He said: "I
came to the conclusion that there is SOMETHING. I
know not what It is, but It is bigger than I. If I will acknowledge It, if I will humble myself, if I will give in
and bow in submission to that SOMETHING and
then try to lead a life as fully in accord with my idea of
good as possible, I will be in tune." And later the word
good contracted in his mind to God.

But mister, I can't see any guy with long white
whiskers up there just waiting for me to make a
plea . . . and what did he answer . . . said I was trying
to complicate it . . . why did I insist on making It human . . . all I had to do was believe in some power
greater than myself and knuckle down to It . . . and I
said maybe, but tell me mister why are you wasting
your time up here? Don't hand me any bunk about it

being more blessed to give than to receive ... asked him what this thing cost and he laughed. He said it wasn't a waste of time ... in doping it out he had thought of something somebody had said. A person never knew a lesson until he tried to pass it on to someone else. And that he had found out every time he tried to pass this on It became more vivid to him. So if we wanted to get hard boiled about it, he owed me, I didn't owe him. That's a new slant ... the guy's crazy as a loon ... get away from him brain ... picture me going around telling other people how to run their lives ... if I could only go to sleep ... that sedative doesn't seem to take hold.

He could visualize a great fellowship of us ... quietly passing this from alcoholic to alcoholic ... nothing organized ... not ministers ... not missionaries ... what a story ... thought we'd have to do it to get well ... some kind of a miracle had happened in his life ... common sense guy at that ... his plan does fire the imagination.

Told him it sounded like self-hypnotism to me and he said what of it ... didn't care if it was yoga-ism, self-hypnotism, or anything else ... four of them were well. But it's so damn hypocritical ... I get beat every other way and then I turn around and lay it in God's lap ... damned if I ever would turn to God ... what a low-down, cowardly, despicable trick that would be ... don't believe in God anyway ... just a lot of hooey to keep the masses in subjugation ... world's worst inquisitions have been practiced in His name ... and he said ... do I have to turn into an inquisitionist ... if I don't knuckle down, I die ... why the low-down missionary ... what a bastardly screw to put on a person ... a witch burner, that's what he is . . . the hell with him and all his damn theories . . . witch burner.

Sleep, please come to my door . . . that last was the eight hundred and eighty-fifth sheep over the fence . . . guess I'll put in some black ones . . . sheep . . . shepherds . . . wise men . . . what was that story . . . hell there I go back on that same line . . . told him I couldn't understand and I couldn't believe anything I couldn't understand. He said he supposed then that I didn't use electricity. No one actually understood where it came from or what it was. Nuts to him. He's got too many answers. What did he think the nub of the whole thing was? Subjugate self to some power above . . . ask for help . . . mean it . . . try to pass it on. Asked him what he was going to name this? Said it would be fatal to give it any kind of a tag . . . to have any sort of formality.

I'm going nuts . . . tried to get him into an argument about miracles . . . about Immaculate Conception . . . about stars leading three wise men . . . Jonah and the whale. He wanted to know what difference those things made . . . he didn't even bother his head about them . . . if he did, he would get tight again. So I asked him what he thought about the Bible. Said he read it, and used those things he understood. He didn't take the Bible literally as an instruction book, for there was no nonsense you could not make out of it that way.

Thought I had him when I asked about the past sins I had committed. Guess I've done everything in the book . . . I supposed I would have to adopt the attitude that all was forgiven . . . here I am pure and clean as the driven snow . . . or else I was to go through life flogging myself mentally . . . bah. But he had the answer for that one too. Said he couldn't call back the hellish things he had done, but he figured life might be a ledger page. If he did a little good here and there, maybe the score would be evened up some day. On the other hand, if he continued as he had been going there would be nothing but debit items on the sheet. Kind of common sense.

This is ridiculous . . . have I lost all power of logic . . . would I fall for all that religious line . . . let's see if I can't get to thinking straight . . . that's it . . . I'm trying to do too much thinking . . . just calm myself . . . quietly . . . quiet now . . . relax every muscle . . . start at the toes and move up . . . insane . . . wet brain . . . those boys . . . what a mess my life is . . . mistress . . . how I hate her . . . ah . . . I know what's the matter . . . that fellow gave me an emotional upset . . . I'll list every reason I couldn't accept his way of thinking. After laughing at this religious stuff all these years I'd be a hypocrite. That's one. Second, if there was a God, why all this suffering? Wait a minute, he said that was one of the troubles, we tried to give God some form. Make It just a Power that will help. Third, it sounds like the Salvation Army. Told him that and he said he was not going around singing on any street corners but nevertheless the Salvation Army did a great work. Simply, if he heard of a guy suffering the torments, he told him his story and belief.

There I go thinking again . . . just started to get calmed down . . . sleep . . . boys . . . insane . . . death . . . mistress . . . life all messed up . . . business. Now listen, take hold . . . what am I going to do? NEVER . . . that's final and in caps. Never . . . that's net no discount. Never . . . never . . . and my mind is made up. NEVER am I going to be such a cowardly low down dog as to acknowledge God. The two-faced, gossiping Babbitts can go around with their sanctimonious mouthings, their miserable worshipping, their Bible quotations, their holier-than-thou attitudes, their nicey-nice, Sunday-worshipping, Monday-robbing actions, but never will they find me acknowledging God. Let me laugh . . . I'd like to shriek with insane glee . . . my mind's made up . . . insane, there it is again.

Brrr, this floor is cold on my knees . . . why are the tears running like a river down my cheeks . . . God, have mercy on my soul!

A FEMININE VICTORY

*T*o my lot falls the rather doubtful distinction of being the only "lady" alcoholic in our particular section. Perhaps it is because of a desire for a "supporting cast" of my own sex that I am praying for inspiration to tell my story in a manner that may give other women who have this problem the courage to see it in its true light and seek the help that has given me a new lease on life.

When the idea was first presented to me that *I was an alcoholic,* my mind simply refused to accept it. Horrors! How disgraceful! What humiliation! How preposterous! Why, I loathed the taste of liquor—drinking was simply a means of escape when my sorrows became too great for me to endure. Even after it had been explained to me that alcoholism is a disease, I could not realize that I had it. I was still ashamed, still wanted to hide behind the screen of reasons made up of "unjust treatment," "unhappiness," "tired and dejected," and the dozens of other things that I thought lay at the root of my search for oblivion by means of whiskey or gin.

In any case, I felt quite sure that I was *not* an alcoholic. However, since I have faced the fact, and it surely is a fact, I have been able to use the help that is so freely given when we learn how to be really truthful with ourselves.

The path by which I have come to this blessed help was long and devious. It led through the mazes and perplexities of an unhappy marriage and divorce, and a dark time of separation from my grown children, and a readjustment of life at an age when most women feel pretty sure of a home and security.

But I *have* reached the source of help. I *have* learned to recognize and acknowledge the underlying cause of my disease: selfishness, self-pity and resentment. A few short months ago those three words applied to *me* would have aroused as much indignation in my heart as the word alcoholic. The ability to accept them as my own has been derived from trying, with the un-ending help of God, to live with certain goals in mind.

Coming to the grim fact of alcoholism, I wish I could present the awful reality of its insidiousness in such a way that no one could ever again fail to recognize the comfortable, easy steps that lead down to the edge of the precipice, and show how those steps suddenly disappeared when the great gulf yawned before me. I couldn't possibly turn and get back to solid earth again that way.

The first step is called—"The first drink in the morning to pull you out of a hangover."

I remember so well when I got onto that step—I had been drinking just like most of the young married crowd I knew. For a couple of years it went on, at parties and at "speakeasies," as they were then called, and with cocktails after matinees. Just going the rounds and having a good time.

Then came the morning when I had my first case of jitters. Someone suggested a little of the "hair of the dog that bit me." A half hour after that drink I was sitting on top of the world, thinking how simple it was to cure shaky nerves. How wonderful liquor was, in only a few minutes my head had stopped aching, my spirits were back to normal and all was well in this very fine world.

Unfortunately, there was a catch to it—I was an alcoholic. As time went on the one drink in the morning had to be taken a little earlier—it had to be followed by a second one in an hour or so, before I really felt equal to getting on with the business of living.

Gradually I found at parties the service was a little slow; the rest of the crowd being pretty happy and carefree after the second round. My reaction was inclined to be just the opposite. Something had to be done about that so I'd just help myself to a fast one, sometimes openly, but as time went on and my need became more acute, I often did it on the quiet.

In the meantime, the morning-after treatment was developing into something quite stupendous. The eye-openers were becoming earlier, bigger, more frequent, and suddenly, it was lunch time! Perhaps there was a plan for the afternoon—a bridge or tea, or just callers. My breath had to be accounted for, so along came such alibis as a touch of grippe or some other ailment for which I'd just taken a hot whiskey and lemon. Or "someone" had been in for lunch and we had just had a couple of cocktails. Then came the period of brazening it out—going to social gatherings well fortified against the jitters; next the phone call in the morning—"Terribly sorry that I can't make it this afternoon, I have an awful headache"; then simply forgetting that there were engagements at all; spending two or three days drinking, sleeping it off, and waking to start all over again.

Of course, I had the well known excuses; my husband was failing to come home for dinner or hadn't been home for several days; he was spending money which was needed to pay bills; he had always been a drinker; I had never known anything about it until I was almost thirty years old and he gave me my first drink. Oh, I had them all down, letter perfect—all the excuses, reasons and justifications. What I did not know was that I was being destroyed by selfishness, self-pity and resentment.

There were the swearing-off periods and the "goings on the wagon"—they would last anywhere from two weeks to three or four months. Once, after a very severe illness of six-weeks' duration (caused by drinking), I didn't touch anything of an alcoholic nature for almost a year. I thought I had it licked that time, but all of a sudden things were worse than ever. I found fear had no effect.

Next came the hospitalization, not a regular sanitarium, but a local hospital where my doctor would ship me when I'd get where I had to call him in. That poor man—I wish he could read this for he would know then it was no fault of his I wasn't cured.

When I was divorced, I thought the cause had been removed. I felt that being away from what I had considered injustice and ill-treatment would solve the problem of my unhappiness. In a little over a year I was in the alcoholic ward of a public hospital!

It was there that L—— came to me. I had known her very slightly ten years before. My ex-husband brought her to me hoping that she could help. She did. From the hospital I went home with her.

There, her husband told me the secret of his rebirth. It is not really a secret at all, but something free and open to all of us. He asked me if I believed in God or some power greater than myself. Well, I did believe in God, but at that time I hadn't any idea what He is.

As a child I had been taught my "Now I lay me's" and "Our Father which art in Heaven." I had been sent to Sunday School and taken to church. I had been baptized and confirmed. I had been taught to realize there is a God and to "love" him. *But though I had been taught all these things, I had never learned them.*

When B—— (L's husband) began to talk about God, I felt pretty low in my mind. I thought God was something that I, and lots of other people like me, had to worry along without. Yet I had always had the "prayer habit." In fact I used to say in my mind "Now, if God answers this prayer, I'll know there *is* a God." It was a great system, only somehow it didn't seem to work!

Finally B—— put it to me this way: "You admit you've made a mess of things trying to run them your way, are you willing to give up? Are you willing to say: 'Here it is God, all mixed up. I don't know how to unmix it, I'll leave it to you.'" Well, I couldn't quite do that. I wasn't feeling very well, and I was afraid that later when the fog wore off, I'd want to back out. So we let it rest a few days. L and B sent me to stay with some friends of theirs out of town—I'd never seen them before. The man out of that house, P—— had given up drinking three months before. After I had been there a few days, I saw that P—— and his wife had something that made them mighty hopeful and happy. But I got a little uneasy going into a perfect stranger's home and staying day after day. I said this to P—— and his reply was: "Why, you don't know how much it is helping me to have you here." Was that a surprise! Always before that when I was recovering from a tailspin I'd been just a pain in the neck to everyone. So, I began to sense in a small way just what these spiritual principles were all about.

Finally I very self-consciously and briefly asked God to show me how to do what He wanted me to do. My prayer was just about as weak and helpless a thing as one could imagine, but it taught me how to open my mouth and pray earnestly and sincerely. However, I had not quite made the grade. I was full of fears, shames, and other "bug-a-boos" and two weeks later an incident occurred that put me on the toboggan again. I seemed to feel that the hurt of that incident was too great to endure without some "release." So I forsook Spirit in favor of "spirits" and that evening I was well on the way to a long session with my old enemy "liquor." I begged the person in whose home I was living not to let anyone know, but she, having good sense, got in touch right away with those who had helped me before and very shortly they had rallied round.

I was eased out of the mess and in a day or two I had a long talk with one of the crowd. I dragged out all my sins of commission and omission, I told everything I could think of that might be the cause of creating a fear situation, a remorse situation, or a shame situation. It was pretty terrible, I thought then, to lay myself bare that way, but I know now that such is the first step away from the precipice.

Things went very well for quite a while, then came a dull rainy day. I was alone. The weather and my self-pity began to cook up a nice dish of the blues for me. There was liquor in the house and I found myself suggesting to myself "Just one drink will make me feel so much more cheerful." Well, I got the Bible and "Victorious Living" and sitting down in full view of the bottle of whiskey, I commenced to read. I also prayed. But I didn't say "I must not take that drink because I owe it to so and so not to." I didn't say "I won't take that drink because I'm strong enough to resist temptation." I didn't say "I must not" or "I will not" at all. I simply prayed and read and in half an hour I got up and was absolutely free of the urge for a drink.

It might be very grand to be able to say "Finis" right here, but I see now I hadn't gone all the way I was intended to go. I was still coddling and nursing my two pets, self-pity and resentment. Naturally, I came a cropper once more. This time I went to the telephone (after I had taken about two drinks) and called L to tell her what I had done. She asked me to promise that I would not take another drink before someone came to me. Well, I had learned enough about truthfulness to refuse to give that promise. Had I been living after the old pattern, I would have been ashamed to call for help. In fact I should not have wanted help. I should have tried to hide the fact that I was drinking and continued until I again wound up behind the "eight ball." I was taken back to B's home where I stayed for three weeks. The drinking ended the morning after I got there, but the suffering continued for some time. I felt desperate and I questioned my ability to really avail myself of the help that the others had received and applied so successfully. Gradually, however, God began to clear my channels so that real understanding began to come. Then was the time when full realization and acknowledgement came to me. It was realization and acknowledgement of the fact that I was full of self-pity and resentment, realiza-tion of the fact that I had not fully given my problems to God. *I was still trying to do my own fixing.*

That was more than a year ago. Since then, although circumstances are no different, for there are still trials and hardships and hurts and disappointments and disillusionments, self-pity and resentment are being eliminated. In this past year I haven't been tempted once. I have no more idea of taking a drink to aid me through a difficult period than I would if I had never drank. But I know absolutely that the minute I close my channels with sorrow for myself, or being hurt by, or resentful towards anyone, I am in horrible danger.

I know that my victory is none of my human doing. I know that I must keep myself worthy of Divine help. And the glorious thing is this: I am free, I am happy, and perhaps I am going to have the blessed opportunity of "passing it on." I say in all reverence—Amen.

A Business Man's Recovery

*T*he S.S. "Falcon" of the Red D. Line, bound
from New York to Maracaibo, Venezuela,
glided up the bay, and docked at the wharf in the port
of La Guayra on a hot tropical afternoon in early
1927. I was a passenger on that boat bound for the oil
fields of Maracaibo as an employee of the X Oil Company, under a two year contract at a good salary and
maintenance. There I hoped to buckle down to two
years of hard work, and save some money, but above
all to avoid any long, continued drinking that would
interfere with my work, because that had cost me too
many jobs in the past.

Not that I was going to give up drinking entirely;
no, such a step would be too drastic. But down here in
the oil fields with a bunch of hard working, hard
drinking good fellows, I, too, would learn how to handle my liquor and not let it get the best of me again.
Such an environment would surely do the trick, would
surely teach me to drink moderately with the best of
them and keep me away from those long, disastrous
sprees. I was still young, I could make the grade, and
this was my chance to do it. At last I had the real answer, and my troubles were over!

Red and I, who had become bosom shipboard
companions on the way down from New York, stood
at the rail watching the activity on the dock incident to
getting the vessel secured alongside. Red was also on
his way to Maracaibo to work for the same company,
and we agreed that so long as we were going to be

here overnight, we might as well go ashore together and look the town over.

Red was a swell fellow who might take a drink now and then, who might even get drunk once in a while, but he could handle his liquor and did not go to any great excesses. Thousands of other fellows like him, who have been my drinking companions from time to time, were in no way responsible for the way I drank, or what I did, or the way liquor affected me.

So off we went, Red and I, to do the town—and do it we did. After a few drinks we decided there wasn't much else to do in town except to make a round of the "cantinas," have a good time, get back to the ship early and get a good night's rest. So what harm would a little drinking do now, I reasoned. Especially with one full day and two nights ahead to get over it.

We visited every "cantina" along the straggling main street of La Guayra, and feeling high, wide and handsome, Red and I decided to return to the ship. When we rolled down to the dock we found that our ship had been berthed off from the wharf about thirty feet and that it was necessary to take a tender out to her. No such ordinary method would satisfy Red and myself, so we decided to climb the stern hawser hand over hand to get on board. The flip of a coin decided that I would go first; so off I started, hand over hand up the hawser.

Now even a good experienced sailor, perfectly sober, would never attempt such a foolhardy feat and, as was to be expected, about half way up the hawser I slipped and fell into the bay with a loud splash. I remember nothing more until the next morning. The captain of the boat said to me "Young man, it is true that God looks after drunken fools and little children.

You probably don't know it, but this bay is infested with man-eating sharks and usually a man overboard is a goner. How close you were to death, you don't realize, but I do."

Yes, I was lucky to be saved! But it wasn't until ten years later, after I had time and time again tempted Fate by going on protracted benders that I was really saved—not until after I had been fired from job after job, tried the patience of my family to the breaking point, alienated what might have been many, many good, lasting friendships, taken my dear wife through more sorrow and heartaches than any one woman should bear in a lifetime; after doctors, hospitals, psychiatrists, rest cures, changes of scenery and all the other paraphernalia that go with the alcoholic's futile attempts to quit drinking. Finally I dimly began to get the realization that during twenty years of continual drinking every expedient I had tried (and I had tried them all) had failed me. I hated to admit the fact even to myself, that I just couldn't lick booze. I was licked. I was desperate. I was scared.

I was born in 1900; my father was a hardworking man who did the very best he could to support his family of four on a small income. Mother was very good to us, kind, patient, and loving. As soon as we were old enough my mother sent us to Sunday School and it so happened that as I grew older I took quite an active interest, becoming successively a teacher and later Superintendent of a small Sunday School in uptown New York.

When the United States entered the World War in April 1917, I was under age but, like most other youngsters of that period, wanted very much to get into the fray. My parents, of course, would not hear of this but told me to be sensible and wait until I was eighteen. Being young and restless, however, and fired by the military spirit of the times, I ran away from home to join the Army in another city.

There I joined up. I didn't get into any of the actual hostilities at the front, but later, after the Armistice, served with the United States forces occupying the Rhineland, working my way up to a good non-commissioned rank.

While serving abroad I started to drink. This, of course, was entirely my own choice. Drinking by a soldier during those times was viewed with a degree of indulgence by both superiors and civilians. It seems to me, as I recall it now, that even then I wasn't satisfied to drink like the normal fellow.

Most of the United States Army of Occupation were sent back home in 1921 but my appetite for travel had been whetted, and having heard terrible stories of Prohibition in the United States, I wanted to remain in Europe where "a man could raise a thirst."

Subsequently I went to Russia, then to England, and back to Germany; working in various capacities, my drinking increasing and my drunken escapades getting worse. So back home in 1924 with the sincere desire to stop drinking and the hope that the Prohibition I had heard so much about would enable me to do it— in other words—that it would keep me away from it.

I secured a good position, but it wasn't long before I was initiated into the mysteries of the speakeasy to such an extent that I soon found myself once more jobless. After looking around for some time, I found that my foreign experience would help me in securing work in South America. So, full of hope once more, resolved that at last I was on the wagon to stay, I sailed for the tropics. A little over a year was all the company I then worked for would stand of my continual drinking and ever-lengthening benders. So they had me poured on a boat and shipped back to New York.

This time I was really through. I promised my family and friends, who helped me get along while looking for another job, that I would never take another drink as long as I lived—and I meant it. But alas!

After several successive jobs in and around New York had been lost, and it isn't necessary to tell you the cause, I was sure that the only thing that would enable me to get off the stuff was a change of scenery. With the help of patient, long-suffering friends, I finally persuaded an oil company that I could do a good job for them in the oil fields of Maracaibo.

But it was the same thing all over again!

Back to the United States. I really sobered up for a while—long enough to establish a connection with my present employers. During this time I met the girl who is now my wife. At last here was the real thing—I was in love. I would do anything for her. Yes, I would give up drinking. I would never, never do anything to even remotely affect the happiness that now came into my life. My worries were over, my problem was solved. I had sown my wild oats and now I was going to settle down to be a good husband and live a normal, happy life.

And so we were married.

Supported by my newfound happiness, my abstinence this time lasted about six months. Then a New Year's party we gave started me off on a long bender. The thing about this episode that is impressed on my mind is how earnestly and sincerely I then promised my wife that I would absolutely and positively this time give up drinking—and again I meant it.

No matter what we tried, and my wife helped me in each new experiment to the best of her ability and understanding, failure was always the result, and each time greater hopelessness.

The next step was doctors, a succession of them, with occasional hospitalization. I remember one doctor who thought a course of seventy-two injections, three a week, after two weeks in a private hospital, would supply the deficiency in my system that would enable me to stop drinking. The night after the seventy-second injection I was paralyzed drunk and a couple of days later talked myself out of being committed to the City Hospital.

My long-suffering employers had a long talk with me and told me that they were only willing to give me one last final chance because during my short periods of sobriety I had shown them that I could do good work. I knew they meant it and that it was the last chance they would ever give me.

I also knew that my wife couldn't stand it much longer.

Somehow or other I felt that I had been cheated— that I had not really been cured at the sanitarium even though I felt good physically. So I talked it over with my wife who said there must be something somewhere that would help me. She persuaded me to go back to the sanitarium and consult Dr. ——, which thank God I did.

He told me everything had been done for me that was medically possible but that unless I decided to quit I was licked. "But doctor," I said, "I have decided time and time again to quit drinking and I was sincere each time, but each time I slipped again and each time it got worse." The doctor smiled and said, "Yes, yes, I've heard that story hundreds of times. You really never made a decision, you just made declarations. You've got to decide and if you really want to quit drinking I know of some fellows who can help. Would you like to meet them?"

Would a condemned man like a reprieve? Of course I wanted to meet them. I was so scared and so desperate that I was willing to try anything. Thus it was that I met the band of life-savers, Alcoholics Anonymous.

The first thing Bill told me was his own story, which paralleled mine in most respects, and then said that for three years he had had no trouble. It was plain to see that he was a supremely happy man—that he possessed a happiness and peacefulness I had for years envied in men.

What he told me made sense because I knew that everything that I, my wife, my family and my friends had tried had failed. I had always believed in God even though I was not a devout church-goer. Many times in my life I had prayed for the things I wanted God to do for me, but it had never occurred to me that He, in His Infinite Wisdom knew much better than I what I should have, and be, and do, and that if I simply turned the decision over to Him, I would be led along the right path.

At the conclusion of our first interview, Bill suggested that I think it over and come back to see him within a few days if I was interested. Fully realizing the utter futility with which my own efforts had met in the past, and somehow or other sensing that delay might be dangerous, I was back to see him the next day.

At first, it seemed a wild, crazy idea to me, but because of the fact that everything else seemed so hopeless, and because it worked with these fellows who all had been through the same hell that I had been through, I was willing, at least, to have a try.

To my utter astonishment, when I did give their method a fair trial, it not only worked, but was so amazingly easy and simple that I said to them "Where have you been all my life?"

That was in February, 1937, and life took on an entirely different meaning. It was plain to see that my wife was radiantly happy. All of the differences that we seemed to have been having, all of the tenseness, the worry, confusion, the hectic days and nights that my drinking had poured into our life together, vanished. There was peace. There was real love. There was kindness and consideration. There was everything that goes into the fabric of a happy, normal existence together.

My employers, of course, the same as the writers of these stories, must remain anonymous. But I would be very thoughtless if I did not take this opportunity to acknowledge what they did for me. They kept me on, giving me chance after chance, hoping I suppose, that some day I would find the answer, although they themselves did not know what it might be. They do now, however.

A tremendous change took place in my work, in my relationship with my employers, in my association with my co-workers and in my dealings with our customers. Crazy as the idea seemed when broached to me by these men who had found it worked, God did come right into my work when permitted, as He had come into the other activities connected with my life.

With this sort of lubricant the wheels turned so much more smoothly that it seemed as if the whole machine operated on a much better basis than heretofore. Promotion that I had longed for previously, but hadn't deserved, was given to me. Soon another followed; more confidence, more trust, more responsibility and finally a key executive position in that same organization which so charitably kept me on in a minor position through the period of my drunkenness.

You can't laugh that off. Come into my home and see what a happy one it is. Look into my office, it is a happy human beehive of activity. Look into any phase of my life and you will see joy and happiness, a sense of usefulness in the scheme of things, where formerly there was fear, sorrow and utter futility.

A Different Slant

I probably have one of the shortest stories in this whole volume and it is short because there is one point I wish to get over to an occasional man who may be in my position.

Partner in one of this country's nationally known concerns, happily married with fine children, sufficient income to indulge my whims and future security from the financial standpoint should paint a picture in which there would be no possibility of a man becoming an alcoholic from the psychological standpoint. I had nothing to escape from and I am known as a conservative, sound business man.

I had missed going to my office several times while I tapered off and brought myself to sobriety. This time, though, I found I could not taper off, I could not stop and I had to be hospitalized. That was the greatest shock to my pride I ever had. Such a blow that I made the firm resolve to never again taste as much as one glass of beer. Careful thought and analysis went into this decision.

The doctor at this hospital told me vaguely of the work of men who called themselves Alcoholics Anonymous and asked if I wanted one of them to call upon me. I was sure I needed no outside help, but in order to be polite to the doctor and hoping he would forget it, I assented.

I was embarrassed when a chap called at my house one evening and told me about himself. He quickly sensed my slight resentment and made it plain to me that none of the crowd were missionaries, nor did they feel it their duty to try to help anyone who did not want help. I think I closed the talk by saying I was glad I was not an alcoholic and sorry he had been bothered by me.

Within sixty days, after leaving the hospital the second time, I was pounding at his door, willing to do anything to conquer the vicious thing that had conquered me.

The point I hope I have made is—even a man with everything from the material standpoint, a man with tremendous pride and the will power to function in all ordinary circumstances can become an alcoholic and find himself as hopeless and helpless as the man who has a multitude of worries and troubles.

THE BACK-SLIDER

*W*hen I was graduated from high-school the World War was on in full blast. I was too young for the army but old enough to man a machine for the production of the means of wholesale destruction. I became a machine-hand at high wages. Machinery appealed to me anyway, because I had always wanted to be a mechanical engineer. Keen to learn as many different operations as possible, I insisted on being transferred from one operation to another until I had a good practical knowledge of all machines in a standard machine shop. With that equipment I was ready to travel for broader experience and in seven years had worked in the leading industrial centers in the eastern states, supplementing my shop work with night classes in marine engineering.

I had the good times of the period but confined my drinking to weekends, with an occasional party after work in the evenings. But I was unsettled and dissatisfied, and in a sense disgusted with going from job to job and achieving nothing more than a weekly pay envelope. I wasn't particularly interested in making a lot of money, but I wanted to be comfortable and independent as soon as possible.

So I married at that time, and for a while it seemed that I had found the solution to my urge for moving around. Most people settle down when they marry and I thought I'd have the same experience, that my wife and I would choose a place where we could establish a home and bring up a family. I had the dream of wearing carpet slippers in a life of comparative ease by the time I was forty. It didn't work out that way. After the newness of being married had worn off a little the old wander business got me again.

In 1924 I brought my wife to a growing city in the middle west where work was always plentiful. I had been in and out of it several times before and I could always get a job in the engineering department of its largest industrial plant. I early acquired the spirit of the organization, which had a real reputation for constructive education of its workers. It encouraged ambition and aided latent talent to develop. I was keen about my work and strove always to place myself in line for promotion. I had a thorough knowledge of the mechanical needs of the plant and when I was offered a job in the purchasing department's mechanical section I took it.

We were now resident in sort of a worker's paradise, a beautifully landscaped district where employees were encouraged to buy homes from the company. We had a boy about two years after I started with the company and with his advent I began to take marriage seriously. My boy was going to have the best I could give him. He would never have to work through the years as I had done. We had a very nice circle of acquaintance where we lived, nice neighbors and my colleagues in the engineering department and later in purchasing were good people, many of them bent on getting ahead and enjoying the good things of life while they climbed. We had nice parties with very little drinking, just enough to give a little Saturday night glow to things—never enough to get beyond control.

Fateful and fatal came the month of October in the year 1929. Work slowed down. Reassuring statements from financial leaders maintained our confidence that industry would soon be on an even keel again. But the boat kept rocking. In our organization, as in many others, the purchasing department found its work lessened by executive order. Personnel was cut down. Those who were left went around working furiously at whatever there was to do, looking furtively at each other wondering who would be next to go. I wondered if the long hours of overtime with no pay would be recognized in the cutting down program. I lay awake lots of nights just like any other man who sees what he has built up threatened with destruction.

I was laid off. I took it hard, for I had been doing a good job, and I thought as a man often will, that it might have been somebody else who should get the axe. Yet there was a sense of relief. It had happened. And partly through resentment and partly from a sense of freedom I went out and got pretty well intoxicated. I stayed drunk for three days, something very unusual for me, who had very seldom lost a day's work from drinking.

My experience soon helped me to a fairly important job in the engineering department of another company. My work took me out of town quite a bit, never at any great distance from home, but frequently overnight. Sometimes I wouldn't have to report at the office for a week, but I was always in touch by the phone. In a way I was practically my own boss and being away from office discipline I was an easy victim to temptation. And temptation certainly existed. I had a wide acquaintance among the vendors to our company who liked me and were very friendly. At first I turned down the countless offers I had to take a drink, but it wasn't long before I was taking plenty.

I'd get back into town after a trip, pretty well organized from my day's imbibing. It was only a step from this daily drinking to successive bouts with absence from my route. I would phone and my chief couldn't tell from my voice whether I had been drinking or not, but gradually learned of my escapades and warned me of the consequences to myself and my job. Finally when my lapses impaired my efficiency and some pressure was brought to bear on the chief, he let me go. That was in 1932.

I found myself back exactly where I had started when I came to town. I was still a good mechanic and could always get a job as an hourly rated machine operator. This seemed to be the only thing which was offered and once more I discarded the white collar for the overalls and canvas gloves. I had spent more than half a dozen good years and had got exactly nowhere, so I did my first really serious drinking. I was good for at least ten days or two weeks off every two months I worked, getting drunk and then half-heartedly sobering up. This went on for almost three years. My wife did the best she could to help me at first, but eventually lost patience and gave up trying to do anything with me at all. I was thrown into one hospital after another, got sobered up, discharged, and ready for another bout. What money I had saved dwindled and I turned everything I had into cash to keep on drinking.

In one hospital, a Catholic Institution, one of the sisters had talked religion to me and had brought a priest in to see me. Both were sorry for me and assured me I would find relief in Mother Church. I wanted none of it. "If I couldn't stop drinking of my own free will, I was certainly not going to drag God into it," I thought.

During another hospital stay a minister whom I liked and respected came to see me. To me, he was just another non-alcoholic who was unable, even by the added benefit and authority of the cloth, to do anything for an alcoholic.

I sat down one day to figure things out. I was no good to myself, my wife, or my growing boy. My drinking had even affected him; he was a nervous, irritable child, getting along badly at school, making poor grades because the father he knew was a sot and an unpredictable one. My insurance was sufficient to take care of my wife and child for a fresh start by themselves and I decided that I'd simply move out of the world for good. I took a killing dose of bichloride of mercury.

They rushed me to the hospital. The emergency physicians applied the immediate remedies but shook their heads. There wasn't a chance, they said. And for days it was touch and go. One day the chief resident physician came in on his daily rounds. He had often seen me there before for alcoholism.

Standing at my bedside he showed more than professional interest, tried to buoy me up with the desire to live. He asked me if I would really like to quit drinking and have another try at living. One clings to life no matter how miserable. I told him I would and that I would try again. He said he was going to send another doctor to see me, to help me.

This doctor came and sat beside my bed. He tried to cheer me up about my future, pointed out I was still a young man with the world to lick and insisted that I could do it if I really wanted to stop drinking. Without telling me what it was, he said he had an answer to my problem and condition that really worked. Then he told me very simply the story of his own life, a life of generous tippling after professional hours for more than three decades until he had lost almost everything a man can lose, and how he had found and applied the remedy with complete success. He felt sure I could do the same. Day after day he called on me in the hospital and spent hours talking to me.

He simply asked me to make a practical application of beliefs I already held theoretically but had forgotten all my life. I believed in a God who ruled the universe. The doctor submitted to me the idea of God as a father who would not willingly let any of his children perish and suggested that most, if not all, of our troubles come from being completely out of touch with the idea of God, with God himself. All my life, he said, I had been doing things of my own human will as opposed to God's will and that the only certain way for me to stop drinking was to submit my will to God and let Him handle my difficulties.

I had never looked on my situation in that way, had always felt myself very remote indeed from a Supreme Being. "Doc," as I shall call him hereinafter, was pretty positive that God's law was the Law of Love and that all my resentful feelings which I had fed and cultivated with liquor were the result of either conscious or unconscious, it didn't matter which, disobedience to that law. Was I willing to submit my will? I said I would try to do so. While I was still at the hospital his visits were supplemented by visits from a young fellow who had been a heavy drinker for years but had run into "Doc" and had tried his remedy.

At that time, the ex-alcoholics in this town, who

have now grown to considerable proportions, numbered only Doc and two other fellows. To help themselves and compare notes they met once a week in a private house and talked things over. As soon as I came from the hospital I went with them. The meeting was without formality. Taking love as the basic command I discovered that my faithful attempt to practice a law of love led me to clear myself of certain dishonesties.

I went back to my job. New men came and we were glad to visit them. I found that new friends helped me to keep straight and the sight of every new alcoholic in the hospital was a real object lesson to me. I could see in them myself as I had been, something I had never been able to picture before.

Now I come to the hard part of my story. It would be great to say I progressed to a point of splendid fulfillment, but it wouldn't be true. My later experience points a moral derived from a hard and bitter lesson. I went along peacefully for two years after God had helped me quit drinking. And then something happened. I was enjoying the friendship of my ex-alcoholic fellows and getting along quite well in my work and in my small social circle. I had largely won back the respect of my former friends and the confidence of my employer. I was feeling fine—too fine. Gradually I began to take the plan I was trying to follow apart. After all, I asked myself, did I really have to follow any plan at all to stay sober? Here I was, dry for two years and getting along all right. It wouldn't hurt if I just carried on and missed a meeting or two. If not present in the flesh I'd be there in spirit, I said in excuse, for I felt a little bit guilty about staying away.

And I began to neglect my daily communication

with God. Nothing happened—not immediately at any rate. Then came the thought that I could stand on my own feet now. When that thought came to mind—that God might have been all very well for the early days or months of my sobriety but I didn't need Him now—I was a gone coon. I got clear away from the life I had been attempting to lead. I was in real danger. It was just a step from that kind of thinking to the idea that my two years training in total abstinence was just what I needed to be able to handle a glass of beer. I began to taste. I became fatalistic about things and soon was drinking deliberately knowing I'd get drunk, stay drunk, and what would inevitably happen.

My friends came to my aid. They tried to help me, but I didn't want help. I was ashamed and preferred not to see them come around. And they knew that as long as I didn't want to quit, as long as I preferred my own will instead of God's will, the remedy simply could not be applied. It is a striking thought that God never forces anyone to do His will, that His help is ever available but has to be sought in all earnestness and humility.

This condition lasted for months, during which time I had voluntarily entered a private institution to get straightened out. On the last occasion when I came out of the fog, I asked God to help me again. Shamefaced as I was, I went back to the fellowship. They made me welcome, offered me collectively and individually all the help I might need. They treated me as though nothing had happened. And I feel that it is the most telling tribute to the efficacy of this remedy that during my period of relapse I still knew this remedy would work with me if I would let it, but I was too stubborn to admit it.

That was a year ago. Depend upon it that I stay mighty close to what has proven to be good for me. I don't dare risk getting very far away. And I have found that in simple faith I get results by placing my life in God's hands every day, by asking Him to keep me a sober man for 24 hours, and trying to do His will. He has never let me down yet.

THE SEVEN MONTH SLIP

*A*t fourteen years of age, when I should have been at home under the supervision of my parents, I was in the United States Army serving a one year enlistment. I found myself with a bunch of men none too good for a fourteen year old kid who passed easily for eighteen. I transferred my hero-worshipping to these men of the world. I suppose the worst damage done in that year in the army barracks was the development of an almost unconscious admiration for their apparently jolly sort of living.

Once out of uniform I went to Mexico where I worked for an oil company. Here I learned to take on a good cargo of beer and hold it. Later I rode the range in the Texas cow country and often went to town with the boys to "whoop it up on payday." By the time I returned to my home in the middle west I had learned several patterns of living, to say nothing of a cock-sure attitude that I needed no advice from anyone.

The next ten years are sketchy. During this time I married and established my own home and everything was lovely for a time. Soon I was having a good time getting around the law in speakeasies. Oh yes, I outsmarted our national laws but I was not quite successful in evading the old moral law.

I was working for a large industrial concern and had been promoted to a supervisional job. In spite of big parties, I was for three or four years able to be on the job the next morning. Then gradually the hangovers became more persistent and I found myself not only needing a few shots of liquor before I could go to work at all, but finally found it advisable to stay at home and sober up by the taper-off method. My bosses tried to give me some good advice. When that didn't help they tried more drastic measures, laying me off without pay. They covered up my too frequent absences many times in order to keep them from the attention of the higher officials in the company.

My attitude was that I could handle my liquor whenever I wanted to go about it seriously, and I considered my absences no worse than those of other employees and officials who were getting away with murder in their drinking.

One does not have to use his imagination much to realize that this sort of drinking is hard on the matrimonial relationship. After proving myself neither faithful nor capable of being temperate, my wife left me and obtained judicial separation. This gave me a really good excuse to get drunk.

In the years 1933 and 1934 I was fired several times, but always got my job back on my promises to do better. On the last occasion I was reduced to the labor gang in the plant. I made a terrific effort to stay sober and prove myself capable of better things. I succeeded pretty well and one day I was called into the production chief's office and told I had met with the approval of the executive department and to be ready to start on a better job.

This good news seemed to justify a mild celebration with a few beers. Exactly four days later I reported for work only to find that they too knew about the "mild" celebration and that they had decided to check me out altogether. After a time I went back and was assigned one of the hardest jobs in the factory. I was in bad shape physically and after six months of this, I quit, going on a drunk with my last paycheck.

Then I began to find that the friends with whom I had been drinking for some time seemed to disappear. This made me resentful and I found myself many times feeling that everybody was against me. Bootleg joints became my hangouts. I sold my books, car, and even clothing in order to buy a few drinks.

I am certain that my family kept me from gravitating to flophouses and gutters. I am eternally thankful to them that they never threw me out or refused me help when I was drinking. Of course I didn't appreciate their kindness then, and I began to stay away from home on protracted drinking spells.

Somehow my family heard of two men in town who had found a way to quit drinking. They suggested that I contact these men but I retorted "If I can't handle my liquor with my own will power then I had better jump over the viaduct."

Another of my usual drinking spells came on. I drank for about ten days with no food except coffee before I was sick enough to start the battle back to sobriety with the accompanying shakes, night sweats, jittery nerves, and horrible dreams. This time I felt that I really needed some help. I told my mother she could call the doctor who was the center of the little group of former drinkers. She did.

I allowed myself to be taken to a hospital where it took several days for my head to clear and my nerves to settle. Then, one day I had a couple of visitors, one a man from New York and the other a local attorney. During our conversation I learned that they had been as bad as myself in this drinking, and that they had found relief and had been able to make a come-back.

Later they went into more detail and put it to me very straight that I'd have to give over my desires and attitudes to a power higher than myself which would give me new desires and attitudes.

Here was religion put to me in a different way and presented by three past-masters in liquor guzzling. On the strength of their stories I decided to give it a try. And it worked, as long as I allowed it to do so.

After a year of learning new ways of living, new attitudes and desires, I became self-confident and then careless. I suppose you would say I got to feeling too sure of myself and Zowie! First it was a beer on Saturday nights and then it was a fine drunk. I knew exactly what I had done to bring myself to this old grief. I had tried to handle my life on the strength of my own ideas and plans instead of looking to God for the inspiration and the strength.

But I didn't do anything about it. I thought "to hell with everybody. I'm going to do as I please." So I floundered around for seven months refusing help from any quarter. But one day I volunteered to take another drunk on a trip to sober him up. When we got back to town we were both drunk and went to a hotel to sober up. Then I began to reason the thing out. I had been a sober, happy man for a year, living decently and trying to follow the will of God. Now I was unshaven, unkempt, ill-looking, bleary-eyed. I decided then and there and went back to my friends who offered me help and who never lectured me on my seven month failure.

That was more than a year ago. I don't say now that I can do anything. I only know that as long as I seek God's help to the best of my ability, just so long will liquor never bother me.

MY WIFE AND I

*C*oming from a farm boyhood with the common education of the little red schoolhouse, I had worked
during the war and afterwards for seven years at high
wages in a booming industrial town, had saved considerable money and finally married an able, well-edu-
cated woman who had an unusual gift of common
sense and far more than the average business vision, a
true helpmate in every way.

In our early twenties, we were both ambitious and
had boundless faith in our ability to succeed. We
talked over the future all the time, exchanged ideas
and really planned our way in life. Just working in a
factory, even at highly-paid piece work, and saving out
of my wages, did not seem to us to be the best way to
do. We talked things over and decided to strike out for
ourselves. Our first venture, a neighborhood grocery
store, prospered. Another neighborhood store, in an
ideal location at a nearby summer resort, looked good
to us. We bought it and started in to make it go. Then
came a business slump affecting the whole country.
With fewer customers I had lots of time on my hands
and was getting to like high-powered home brew and
the potent liquors of prohibition days entirely too
well. That didn't help the business. We finally shut up
shop.

Jobs were scarce, but by persistence I again found
a factory job. In a few months the factory closed
down. We had again accumulated a small stake and
since the job situation showed no improvement, we
thought we would try business again.

This time we opened a restaurant in a semi-rural section and for a time all went well. My wife opened up in the morning, did all the baking and cooking and waited on trade. I relieved her later in the day and stayed open late to catch every possible bit of business. Our place became a regular hang-out for groups of late-comers who showed up with a bottle every now and then.

I told myself that I was one man who could handle my liquor because I was always on my feet at closing time. I talked knowingly about spacing my drinks, about taking only a measured shot, and about the folly of gulping down big drinks. Yes sir, I was never going to be one of those "rummies" who let liquor get the best of them. Young and strong, I could throw off the effects of the previous night's drinking and stand the nausea the following morning, even abstaining from taking a drink until the afternoon. But before long the idea of suffering for a few hours didn't seem so good.

The morning drink became the first act of the daily routine. I had now become a "regular." I had my regular remedy—a stiff shot to start the day and no waiting till a specified time. I used to wait for the need; soon I was craving the stuff so much that I didn't wait for that. My wife could see that it was gripping me. She warned me, gently at first, with quiet seriousness. Was I going to pave the way to losing this business just when it needed to be nursed along? We began to run behind. My wife, anxious for the goal we had set out to reach, and seeing the result if I didn't brace up, talked straight from the shoulder. We had words. I left in a passion.

Our separation lasted a week, I did a lot of thinking, and went back to my wife. Quieter, somewhat remorseful, we talked things over. Our situation was worse than I had anticipated. We got a buyer for the place and sold out. We still had some money left.

I had always been a natural mechanic, handy with tools. We moved back into town with a slim bankroll and, still determined never to be a factory hand again, I looked around and finding a workshop location with a house adjacent I started a sheet-metal shop. I had chosen a very difficult time to start up. My business practically vanished on account of the depression.

There were no jobs of any kind. We fell far behind on our rent and other obligations. Our cupboard was often bare. With every penny needed for food and shelter, and wearing old clothes with nothing new except what our two youngsters needed, I didn't touch a drop for two years. I went after business. I slugged doorbells all over the town asking for jobs. My wife rang bells with me, taking one side of the street while I worked the other. We left nothing undone to keep going, but we were still far behind, so far that at the low point we could see eviction and our belongings in the street.

I braced myself to talk to our landlord who was connected with a large real estate firm managing many properties. We were behind six months in our rent and they saw that the only way to get their back rent was to give me a couple of small jobs. My wife learned to use the tools to shape and fashion material when I was doing the installation work. The real estate firm liked my work and began to give me more jobs. In those grim days, with babies to feed, I couldn't spend what little money came in for drink. I stayed sober. My wife and I even started back to church, began paying our dues.

They were thin years, those depression years. For three years in succession, Christmas in our little family was just the 25th of December. Our customers saw us as two earnest young people trying to get along and as times improved a little, we began to get better jobs. Now we could hire some competent workmen and bought a car and a few small trucks. We prospered and moved into a better-equipped house.

My pockets, which hadn't jingled for years, now held folding money. The first greenbacks grew into a roll with a rubber band around it. I became well-known to real estate firms, business men, and politicians. I was well-liked, popular with everyone. Following a prosperous season came a quiet period. With time on our hands I had a drinking spell. It lasted for a month, but with the aid of my wife, I checked myself in time. "Remember how we lost the store! Remember our restaurant!" my wife said. Yes, I could remember. Those times were too recent and their memory too bitter. I solemnly swore off and once more climbed aboard the wagon, this time for nine long months.

Business kept up. It became evident that by careful handling we might eventually have something pretty good, a sufficient income to provide a good living for us all and ensure a good education for our children.

My business is seasonal. Fall and early winter are rush times. The first few months of the year are quiet. But though business slackened, I got around making contracts, lining up future work and meeting people who would be able to put work in my way. Not yet sensing any great danger, in spite of past experiences, I seldom refused the invitations of business friends to have a drink. In a short time I was drinking every day and eventually much more than I had ever done before, for I always had a roll in my pocket.

At first I was even more jolly than usual when I came home in the evening to my wife and family. But the joking good fellow who was the husband and father they had known, gave place to a man who slammed the door when he came in. My wife, genuinely alarmed now as week after week went past without any sign that I was going to quit, tried to reason with me, but the old arguments didn't work this time.

Summer came on with its demand for roof repairs and spouting installations. My wife often started the men to work in the morning, did shop jobs, kept the books, and in addition, ran the house and looked after the family.

For eight months my daily routine was steady drinking. Even after slumping in bed late at night in a semi-stupor, I would get up at all hours and drive to some all-night spot where I could get what I wanted. I was going to have a good time in spite of hell and high water.

I became increasingly surly when at home. I was the boss. I was master in my own house, wasn't I? I became morose, with few lucid moments between drinks. I would listen to no arguments and certainly attempts to reason with me were futile. Unknown to me, my wife influenced some of my friends and business associates to drop in casually. They were mostly non-drinkers and generally ended up by mildly upbraiding me.

"A fine lot of Job's comforters," I would say. I felt that everybody was against me, thought bitterly of my wife as being of little help and told myself I wasn't getting the breaks, that everybody was making a mountain out of a molehill and so, to hell with everything! I still had money and with money I could always buy bottled happiness. And still my wife kept trying. She got our pastor to talk to me. It was no good.

Drinking and staying drunk without cessation, even my splendid constitution began to give way. My wife called doctors who gave me temporary relief. Then my wife left me after a bitter quarrel, taking the children with her. My pride was hurt and I began to regard myself as an injured husband and an unappreciated father who, deep in his heart, just doted on his children. I went to see her and demanded to see them. I up and told her that I didn't care whether she came back or not, that I wanted the children. My wife, wise woman, thought she still had a chance to save me, save our home for the children. She threw aside her sense of injury, spoke right up to me and said she was coming back, that forbidding her the house wouldn't work, that she had helped me get what I had and was going to cross its threshold and resume its management. She did just that. When she opened the door she was appalled at the sight of it, curtains down, dishes and utensils unwashed, dirty glasses and empty bottles everywhere.

Every alcoholic reaches the end of the tether some day. For me there came a day when, physically and mentally, I was unable to make my way to a saloon for a drink. I went to bed. I told my wife for the first time that I wanted to quit drinking, but couldn't. I asked her to do something for me; I had never done this before. I realized that I needed help. Somehow in talking with a lady doctor, my wife had heard of another doctor who in some mysterious ways had stopped drinking after thirty years and had been successful in helping a few other alcoholics to become sober men. As a last resort, my wife appealed to this doctor, who insisted on a certain situation before he could help; his experience had taught him that unless that situation existed nothing could be done for the alcoholic.

"Does your husband want to stop drinking, or is he merely temporarily uncomfortable? Has he come to the end of the road?" he asked my wife.

She told him that for the first time I had expressed a desire to quit, that I had asked her in desperation to try to do something—anything, to help me stop. He said he would see me the following morning.

With every part of my being craving a drink, I could hardly sit still when I got up to await the visit from the man she had talked to on the phone, but something kept me in the house. I wanted to hear what this fellow had to offer and since he was a medical man I had some preconceived notions ready for him when he came. I was pretty jittery when my wife opened the door to admit a tall, somewhat brusque professional man who, from his speech, was obviously an Easterner. I don't know what I had expected, but his salutation, designed to shake me up, I can see now, had almost the same effect as the hosing with cold water in a turkish bath.

"I hear you're another 'rummy,'" he said as he smiled and sat down beside me. I let him talk. Gradually, he drew me out until what I did tell him gave him a picture of my experience. And then he put it to me plainly. "If you are perfectly sure that you want to quit drinking for good, if you are serious about it, if you don't merely wish to get well so that you can take up drinking again at some future date, you can be relieved," he said.

I told him that I had never wanted anything as much in my life as to be able to quit using liquor, and I meant every word of it.

"The first thing to do with your husband," he said, turning to my wife, "is to get him to a hospital and have him 'defogged.' I'll make the necessary arrangements."

He didn't go into any further explanation, not even to my wife. That evening I was in a hospital bed. The next day the doctor called. He told me that several former alcoholics were dry as a result of following a certain prescribed course of action and that some of them would be in to see me. My wife came to see me faithfully. She, too, had been learning, perhaps more quickly than I was doing, through talking with the doctor who by this time was getting down to brass tacks with me. My friend was the human agency employed by an all-wise Father to bring me into a pathway of life.

It is an easy matter to repeat and orally affirm a faith. Here were these men who visited me and they, like myself, had tried everything else and although it was plain to be seen none of them were perfect, they were living proof that the sincere attempt to follow the cardinal teachings of Jesus Christ was keeping them sober. If it could do that for others, I was resolved to try it, believing it could do something for me also.

I went home after four days, my mind clear, feeling much better physically and, what was far more important, with something better than just will power to aid me. I got to know others of these alcoholics whose human center was my doctor. They came to our home. I met their wives and families. They invited my wife and myself to their homes. I learned that it would be well to begin the day with morning devotion, which is the custom in our house now.

It was almost a year when I began to get a little careless. One day I hoisted a few drinks, arriving home far from sober. My wife and I talked it over, both knowing it had happened because I had stopped following the plan. I acknowledged my fault to God and asked His help to keep to the course I had to follow.

Our home is a happy one. My children no longer hide when they see me coming. My business has improved. And—this is important—I try to do what I can for my fellow alcoholics. In our town there are some 70 of us, ready and willing to spend our time to show the way to sobriety and sanity to men who are like what we used to be.

A WARD OF THE
PROBATE COURT

*A*t about the time of my graduation from high school, a state university was established in our city. On the call for an office assistant, I was recommended by my superintendent, and got the position. I was rather his choice and pride, but a few years later, I met him in a nearby city and "panhandled" him for two "bucks" for drinks.

I grew with the institution and advanced in position. I took a year off for attendance at an engineering college. At college I refrained from any hilarious celebrating or drinking.

War was declared. I was away from home on business at the State Capitol where my mother couldn't raise objections and I enlisted. Overseas I was on five fronts from Alsace up to the North Sea. Upon relief from the lines—back in the rest-area, "vin rouge" and "cognac" helped in the let down from trying circumstances. I was introduced to the exhilaration of intoxication. The old spirit, "What the hell? Heinie may have you tagged," didn't help toward any moderation in drinking then. We had many casualties but one of the real catastrophes was the loss of a pal, a lieutenant who died from the D.T.'s over there, after it was all over. This didn't slow me up, and back in the States I had a big fling before returning home.

My plans were to cover up with my mother and the girl I was to marry, that I had become addicted to alcohol. But I exposed the fact on the day our engagement was announced. On the way I met a training camp buddy, got drunk and missed the party. Booze had got over its first real blow on me. I saw her briefly that night but didn't have the guts to face her people. The romance was over.

To forget, I engaged in super-active life in social, fraternal, and civic promotion in my community. This all outside my position in the President's Office of the State University. I became a leader—the big flash in the pan. I organized and was first commander of the American Legion Post—raised funds and built a fine memorial Club House. Was Secretary of Elks, Eagles, Chamber of Commerce, City Club, and active as an operator and officer in political circles. I was always a good fellow and controlled my drinking, indulging only in sprees in private clubs or away from home.

I was deposed from the executive position at the college by a political change in the governorship of the State. I knew the sales manager of the Securities Division of a large Utility corporation in Wall Street, and started to sell securities. The issues and the market were good and I had a fine opportunity. I was away from home and I began to drink heavily. To get away from my drinking associates, I managed to be transferred to another city, but this didn't help. Booze had me, my sales and commissions diminished, I remained almost in a continuous stupor on my drawing account until I was released.

I braced up, got sober, and made a good connection with a steamship agency, a concern promoting European travel and study at most all important universities in Europe. Those were the bath-tub gin days and for drinking in and about my office, I held out in this position for only a year.

I was now engaged to be married and fortunately I

got another position as a salesman for a large corporation. I worked hard, was successful, and drinking became periodic. I was married and my wife soon learned that I was no social drinker. I tried hard to control it, but could not. There were many separations and she would return home. I would make pledges and a sincere effort and then my top would blow off again. I began here to take sanitarium treatments to satisfy my wife and my folks.

I had a great capacity for drink and work. With the help of turkish baths, bromo-seltzer and aspirin, I held to the job. I became top-notcher in the entire sales force of the country. I was assigned to more special territory and finally into the market of keenest competition. I was top rate in salary, won bonus awards and was bringing in the volume. But there was always the drawback my excessive drinking made at times. I was called in once, twice, and warned. Finally I wasn't to be tolerated any longer, although I was doing a good job. I had lasted five and a half years.

I lost my wife along with my job and fine income. This was a terrible jolt. I tried for a hook-up, but I had a black eye marring a good record. I became discouraged and depressed. I sought relief with booze. There began the four black years of my life.

I had returned home to the community where I had been so prominent. These were dry days still and I hung out at the clubs with bars. I got so I would last on a job but a few days, just until I could get an advance for drinks. I began to get entangled with the law—arrested for driving while intoxicated and drunken and disorderly conduct.

My folks heard of the cure at the State Hospital. I was picked up drunk and sent there by the Probate

Court. I was administered paraldehyde and came to in a receiving ward among lunatics. I was transferred to another ward of less violent cases and I found a little group of alcoholics and "junkers" (dope addicts). I learned from them the seriousness of being a ward of the Probate Court. I felt then if I ever got released the old devil alcohol would never get me in a jam like this again. In times of great distress such as this, I would pray to God for help.

I was fortunate and was released after eleven days and nights barred up in the laughing academy—"bughouse." That was enough. I wanted no more of it. I took a job as manager of a club and put myself to the old acid test. I was going to really assert my will power. I even tended bar part of the time, but never imbibed a bit. This lasted about three months.

I went to an annual convention of my overseas division and came to locked up in a cheap hotel room, new shoes, suit coat, hat and purse missing. I must have slipped badly.

Then followed much drinking and trouble. After a few arrests for intoxication, the law decided another sojourn to the State Hospital would tame me. They jumped the stay this time from eleven days to eleven weeks. It was getting tough for me. I came out in good physical condition and held a fear of getting probated again, thinking the siege might be eleven months. I got another job and stayed dry for about two months and off to the races again.

I became terribly weak—couldn't eat and tried to get nourishment from booze and mostly only bootleg at that. One time, I just made it into a hospital and another time a police patrol took me to the hospital instead of the jail. I suffered badly from insomnia. As many as three shots in the arm had no effect.

I would get in shape and back at it again. I was going to battle to the finish. The time came when I was to be paid my soldier's bonus. I had the limit or maximum coming. Friends advised my folks to send me to a Veterans Hospital before I got this money in my hands. I was probated again, held in a county jail for two weeks and sent again to the asylum. This was my summer resort for three months. I was on the waiting list for the Veterans Hospital but I got into such wonderful physical condition from eating and working out of doors that I was released.

I reached home full of resentment against my folks for their having my money tied up under a guardianship. I went out and got saturated and landed in jail—I had been free from the asylum for about eight hours. Behind the bars again so soon—this was bad. However, I was freed again the next day and this was my last confinement with the law. I began to use my head, I continued to drink but kept under cover or hid in the "jungles" with the bums.

In a few months an old friend came along. He located me a few times in saloons. We had been drinking pals in the early days, particularly at the club houses. He had heard of my predicament. He himself had quit drinking and looked fine. He encouraged me to visit him in a nearby city.

I wanted to quit drinking, but hadn't much faith in ever getting away from it. I agreed to go into a hospital as a patient of a doctor who had been an alcoholic for many years and was now a new man.

It is almost uncanny—in just eight days I left there a different person. This doctor in plain words was a wonderful guy—he spent many hours with me telling me his experience with alcohol. Others of his band, which was then small, visited me—told me their stories. They were all strangers to me, but treated me as a friend. I was impressed with their interest and fellowship. I learned the secret. They had a religious experience. I was willing, and renewed my acquaintance with God and acknowledged Him as a reality.

I found it easy. I came to life and have been free now for two years. I hope never to take another drink. I am building up a reputation again and nearly every day am complimented on my appearance.

I have a new outlook on life. I look forward to each day with happiness because of the real enjoyment it is to me to be sane, sober, and respectable. I was existing really from one drink until the next, with no perception about circumstances, conditions, or even nature's elements. My acquaintance with God—lost and forgotten when I was a young man—is renewed. God is all-loving and all-forgiving. The memories of my past are being dimmed by the life I now aspire to.

RIDING THE RODS

*F*ourteen years old and strong, I was ready—an American Whittington who knew a better way to get places than by walking. The "clear the way" whistle of a fast freight thundering over the crossing on the tracks a mile away was a siren call. Sneaking away from my farm home one night, I made my way to the distant yards. Ducking along a lane between two made-up trains that seemed endless, I made my way to the edge of the yards. Here and there I passed a silent, waiting figure. Then a little group talking among themselves. Edging in, I listened eagerly. I had met my first hoboes. They talked of places I had never heard of. This town was good. A fellow could get by on the Bowery all winter if he knew the ropes; that other town was "hostile"; thirty days for "vag" awaited you in another if you didn't hit the cinders before the road "bulls" fine-combed the train.

Then they noticed me. Somehow a new kid is always an object of interest to the adventurers of the rails. "Where ya makin' for, kid?"

I had heard one of them mention "Dee-troit" and it seemed as good an answer as any. I had no plans, just wanted to get away—anywhere—just away!

"The Michigan Manifest will be along any minute now; I think she's moving." The tall hobo who had spoken grabbed me by the arm. "Come on, kid. We'll help you."

Suddenly I felt big. I had gotten away! The two hoboes talked, the tall one about getting work in Detroit, the other arguing for staying on the road. Then the one who had boosted me up began to quiz me. I told him I had run away from the farm. In a sort of halting way he told me not to get the train habit or it would get me until I would always want to be moving. The rocking motion of the car as the train increased speed became a cradle song in my ears. I fell asleep.

It was way past dawn when I awoke. My two companions were already sitting up and talking. The day wore on. We passed through small towns. Soon the train was threading its way between factories and huge warehouses, crossing tracks with brisk clatter, coming into a railway yard. Brakes went on. They helped me off. We were in Detroit.

My hobo friends parted at a street corner. The tall one took me along right into town and got a room for both of us with "Mother Kelly," a kindly Irish landlady if ever there was one. "Sit tight, kid," he said. "I'll see you through as much as I can. Me to find a job."

He got a job. For almost two years he looked after me. He was always vigilant, steering me past the snares and pitfalls that are always in the path of a growing boy. This hobo, Tom Casey, who never talked much about himself or his experiences except as a warning illustration of "What not to do," made me start a bank account and keep it growing. It is to him I owe the fact that I didn't become a "road kid," that I never became a hobo. Came a day when he left me. The road was calling him, he explained, although that never seemed to me to be the reason. I never saw Tom Casey again, but from this man I received my first lesson in the guiding and compelling principle of the Good Life. "Love thy neighbor as thyself."

I was city-wise by this time, uncontaminated to be

sure, thanks to my friend. No longer a "boy rube in the big town," I found a job quickly enough but I missed Tom. I began to hang around pool rooms and it was inevitable that I soon learned to handle a schooner of beer and an occasional "shot." Jobs were plentiful. If I didn't feel right in the morning after a night with the "corner gang" I didn't go to work. I lost jobs. My bank account dwindled, disappeared entirely. My new barroom friends were little help. I was broke.

It was summer and the park benches, hard and uncomfortable as they were, appealed to me more than the squalid "flops" of the city's slums. So I slept out a few nights. Young and full of energy, I hunted for work. The war was on and work was easy to get. I became a machine-shop hand, progressing rapidly from drillpress to milling machine to lathe. I could quit a job one day and have a new one the next with more money. Soon I again had a good boardinghouse, clothes and money. But I never started another bank account. "Plenty of time for that," I thought. My weekends were spent in my conception of "a good time," finally becoming regular carousals and debauches over Saturday and Sunday. I had the usual experiences of being slipped a "Mickey Finn" and getting slugged and rolled for my money. These had no deterrent effect. I could always get jobs and live comfortably again in a few weeks. Soon, however, I tired of the weary routine of working and drinking. I began to dislike the city. Somehow my boyhood days on the farm didn't seem so bad at a distance.

No, I didn't go home, but found work not too far away. I still drank. I soon got restless and took a freight for a Michigan city, arriving there broke late at night. I set out to look for friends. They helped me find work. Slowly, I began to climb the industrial ladder once more and eventually achieved a responsible position as a machine setter in a large plant. I was sitting on top of the world again. The sense of accomplishment I had now told me that I had earned the right to have enjoyable weekends once more. The weekends began to extend to Tuesday and Wednesday until I frequently worked only from Thursday to Saturday with the bottle always in my mind. In a vague sort of way I had set a time to quit drinking but that was at least fifteen years away and "What the hell!" I said to myself. "I'm going to have a good time while I'm young."

Then I was fired. Piqued, I drank up my last paycheck and when I got sober found another job—then another—and another in quick succession. I was soon back on the park benches. And once more I got a break when everything seemed dark. An old friend volunteered to get me a job driving a bus. He said he would buy me a uniform and give me the hospitality of his home if I would promise to quit drinking. Of course I promised. I had been working about three days when the bus line superintendent called me into his office.

"Young fellow," he said, "in your application you state that you don't use alcoholic liquors. Now, we always check a man's references and three of the firms you have worked for say you're a highly capable man, but you have the drink habit."

I looked at him. It was all true, I admitted, but I had been out of work such a long time that I welcomed this job as an opportunity to redeem myself. I told him what I had promised my friend, that I was sincerely doing my best and not drinking a drop. I asked him to give me a chance.

"Somehow I think you are in earnest," he said. "I believe you mean it. I'll give you a chance and help you to make good."

He shook my hand in friendship and encouragement. I strode from his office with high hope. "John Barleycorn will never make a bum out of me again," I told myself with determination.

For three months I drove my route steadily with never a hitch. My employers were satisfied. I felt pretty good. I was really on the wagon this time, wasn't I?

Yes indeed, I was on the wagon for good.

I soon repaid my debt to my friend for his stake in me and even saved a little money. The feeling of security increased. It was summer and, hot and tired at the end of the day, I began to stop at a speakeasy on my way home. Detroit beer was good then, almost like old-time pre-Prohibition stuff. "This is the way to do it," I would say to myself. "Stick to beer. After all, it's really a food and it sure hits the spot after a trick of wheeling that job around in this man's town. It's that hard liquor that gets a man down. Beer for mine."

Even with all the hard lessons of bitter experience behind me I did not realize that thinking along that line was a definite red light on my road in life—a real danger signal.

The evening glass of beer led, as usual, to the night when I didn't get away from the bar until midnight. I began to need a bracer in the morning. Beer, I knew from experience, was simply no good as a bracer—all right as a thirst quencher perhaps, but lacking action and authority the next morning. I needed a jolt.

The morning jolt became a habit. Then it got to be several jolts until I was generally pretty well organized when I started to work. Spacing my drinks over the day I managed not to appear drunk, just comfortable as I drove along the crowded thoroughfares of the city. Then came the accident.

On one of the avenues a man darted from between parked cars right in my path. I swung the bus sharply over to keep from hitting him but couldn't quite make it. He died in the hospital. Passenger and sidewalk witnesses absolved me completely. Even if I had been completely sober I couldn't have cleared him. The company investigation immediately after the accident showed me blameless but my superiors knew I had been drinking. They fired me—not for the accident—but for drinking on the job.

Well, once more I felt I had enough of city life and found a job on an upstate farm. While there I met a young schoolteacher, fell in love with her and she with me. We were married. Farm work was not very remunerative for a young couple so we went successively to Pontiac, Michigan, and later to an industrial city in Ohio. For economy's sake we had been living with my wife's people, but somehow we never seemed to be able to get ahead. I was still drinking but not so much as formerly, or so it seemed to me.

The new location seemed ideal—no acquaintances, no entanglements, no boon companions to entice me. I made up my mind to leave liquor alone and get ahead. But I forgot one boon companion, one who was always at my elbow, one who followed me from city to farm and back to city. I had forgotten about John Barleycorn.

Even so, the good resolutions held for a time—new job, comfortable home and understanding helpmate, they all helped. We had a son and soon came another. We began to make friends and moved in a small social circle of my fellow-workers and their wives and families. Those were still bootleg days. Drinks were always available but nobody seemed to get very drunk. We just had a good time, welcome surcease after a week of toil. Here were none of the rowdy debauches that I had known. I had discovered "social drinking," how to "drink like a gentleman and hold my liquor." There is no point in reiterating the recurrence of experience already described. The "social drinking" didn't hold up. I became the bootlegger's first morning customer. How I ever managed to hold the job I had now I don't know. I began to receive the usual warnings from my superiors. They had no effect. I had now come to an ever-deepening realization that I was a drunkard, that there was no help for me.

I told my wife that. She sought counsel of her friends and my friends. They came and talked with me. Reverend gentlemen, who knew nothing of my problem, pointed me to the age-old religious formula. I would have none of it. It left me cold. Now, with hope gone, I haunted the mean thoroughfares of speakeasy districts, with my mind on nothing but the next drink. I managed to work enough to maintain a slim hold on my job. Then I began to reason with myself.

"What good are you!" I would say. "Your wife and children would be better off if they never saw you again. Why don't you get away and never come back? Let them forget about you. Get away—get away anywhere—that's the thing to do."

That night, coatless and hatless, I hopped a freight for Pittsburgh. The following day I walked the streets of the Smoky City. I offered to work at a roadside stand for a meal. I got the meal, walked on, sat down by the roadside to think.

"What a heel I've turned out to be!" I soliloquized. "My wife and two kids back there—no money—what can they do? I should have another try at it. Maybe I'll never get well, but at least I can earn a dollar or two now and then—for them."

I took another freight back home. Despite my absence, my job was still open. I went to work, but it was no go. I would throw a few dollars at my wife on payday and drink up what was left. I hated my surroundings, hated my job, my fellow-workers—the whole town. I tried Detroit again, landing there with a broken arm. How I got it I'll never know, for I was far gone in drink when I left. My wife's relatives returned me to my home in a few days. I became morose, mooning around the house by myself. Seeing me come home, my wife would leave me a little money on the table, grab the children and flee. I was increasingly ugly. Now, all hope was gone entirely. I made several attempts on my life. My wife had to hide any knives and hammers. She feared for her own safety. I feared for my mind—feared that I was breaking—that I would end up insane. Finally the fear got so terrible that I asked my wife to have me "put away" legally. There came a morning when, alone in my room, I began to wreck it, breaking the furniture, destroying everything in sight. Desperate, my wife had to employ the means I had suggested to her in the depths of alcoholic despair. Loath to have me committed to the state asylum, still trying to save something from the wreckage of my life and hers, she had me placed in a hospital, hoping against hope to save me.

I was placed under restraint. The treatment was

strenuous—no alcohol—just bromides and sleeping potions. The nights were successions of physical and mental agony. It was weeks before I could sit still for any length of time. I didn't want to talk to anyone and cared less to listen. That gradually wore off and one day I fell into casual conversation with another patient—another alcoholic. We began to compare notes. I told him frankly that I was in despair, that no thinking I had ever been able to do had shown me a way of escape, that all my attempts to try will power (well meaning persons had often said, "Why don't you use your will power?—as if will power were a faculty one could turn on and off like a faucet!) had been of no avail.

"Being in here and getting fixed up temporarily," I told him bitterly, "is no good. I know that only too well. I can see nothing but the same old story over again. I'm simply unable to quit. When I get out of here I'm going to blow town."

My fellow-patient and newfound acquaintance looked at me a long time and finally spoke. From the most unexpected quarter in the world, from a man who was in the same position I was in, from a fellow-alcoholic, came the first ray of hope I had seen.

"Listen, fellow," he said, looking at me with ten times the earnestness of the many good citizens and other well-intentioned persons who had tried their best to help me. "Listen to me. I know a way out. I know the only answer. And I know it works."

I stared at him in amazement. There were several mild mental cases in the place and, little as I knew about their exhibitions of tendencies, I knew that even in a normal conversation, strange ideas might be expected. Was this fellow perhaps a little balmy—a wee bit off? Here was a man, an admitted alcoholic like myself, trying to tell me he knew the remedy for my situation. I wanted to hear what he had to suggest but made the reservation that he was probably a little "Nutty." At the same time I was ready to listen, like any drowning man, to grasp at even a straw.

My friend smiled, he knew what I was thinking. "Yes," he continued. "Forget that I'm here. Forget that I'm just another 'rummy.' But I had the answer once—the only answer."

He seemed to be recalling his very recent past. Looking at me earnestly, his voice impressive in its sincerity, he went on. "For more than a year before coming here I was a sober man, thoroughly dry. I wasn't just on the wagon. I was dry! And I would still be dry if I had stuck to the plan which kept me sober all that time."

Let me say here that he later went back to the very plan he told me about and has been sober for more than a year for the second time.

He told me his story briefly and went on to tell me of a certain cure for alcoholism—the only certain cure. I had anticipated hearing of some new treatment, some newly discovered panacea that I had not heard of, something which no doubt combined drugs and mental healing. But it was neither one nor the other; it was certainly not a mixture of any kind.

He spoke of a group of some 30 men in my town who were ready to take me by the hand and call me by my first name. They would be friends without canting or ranting. He told me they met once a week to talk over their experiences, how they tried to help each other, how they spent their time in helping men like me.

"I know it sounds strange, incredible maybe," he said. "I slipped, got drunk after being sober for a year, but I'm going back to try again. I know it works."

Helpless, without faith in myself or anyone else, entirely doubtful that the fellow really had something, I began to ask questions. I had to be interested or go crazy.

"How do you go about this—where do I have to go?" I asked.

"You don't have to go anywhere," he said. "Someone will come to you." He didn't go into any detail, just told me that much and little more. I did some thinking that afternoon. Calling one of the nurses I asked her to get in touch with my wife and have her come to see me that evening.

She came during visiting hours. She expected, I know, to hear me plead for instant release from the place. I didn't talk about that. In my lame way I told her my story. It made little impression.

"It doesn't sound right," she said. "If this plan—and for the life of me I don't quite get it from what you've told me—if this plan is successful, why is this fellow back here himself?"

I was stumped. I was too ignorant about the thing myself to be capable of explaining it clearly to her. "I don't know," I said. "I'll admit it sounds queer, the way this fellow is and all that, but somehow I feel there's something to it. Anyhow, I want to know more about it."

She went away skeptically. But the next day I had a visitor, a doctor who had himself been an alcoholic. He told me a little more about the plan. He was kindly, didn't offer any cut and dried formula to overcome my life-long difficulty. He presented no religious nostrums, suggested no saving rituals. Later he sent some of the other ex-alcoholics to see me.

A few days later my fellow-alcoholic was released, and shortly afterward I was allowed to go home also. Through the man who first told me of the plan I was introduced to several other members of the group of former alcoholics. They told me their experiences. Many were men of former affluence and position. Some had hit even lower levels than I had.

The first Wednesday evening after my release found me a somewhat shame-faced but intensely curious attendant at a meeting in a private home in this city. Some forty others were present. For the first time I saw a fellowship I had never known in actual operation. I could actually feel it. I learned that this could be mine, that I could win my way to sobriety and sanity if I would follow a few precepts, simple in statement, but profound and far-reaching in their effect if followed. It penetrated to my inner consciousness that the mere offering of lip-service wasn't enough. Still ignorant, still a little doubting, but deadly in earnest, I made up my mind to make an honest effort to try.

That was two years ago. The way has not been easy. The new way of life was strange at first, but all my thoughts were on it. The going was sometimes slow; halting were my steps among the difficulties of the path. But always, when troubles came, when doubts assailed and temptation was strong and the old desire returned, I knew where to go for aid. Helping others also strengthened me and helped me to grow.

Today I have achieved, through all these things, a measure of happiness and contentment I had never known before. Material success has mattered little. But I know that my wants will be taken care of.

I expect to have difficulties every day of my life; I expect to encounter stops and hindrances, but now there is a difference. I have a new and tried foundation for every new day.

THE SALESMAN

I learned to drink in a workmanlike manner when the law of the land said I couldn't, and what started out as a young man's fun became a habit which in its later existence laid me by the heels many a time and almost finished my career.

'Teen years were uneventful with me. I was raised on a farm but saw little future in farming. I was going to be a businessman, took a business college course, acquired a truck and stand in the city market of a nearby town, and started off. I brought produce from my folks' place and sold it to city customers and there were plenty of them with bulging pocketbooks.

Back of me was the normal life of a farmer's son. My parents were unusually understanding people. My father was a life-long comrade till the day of his death. The business theory I had learned in college was now being practiced and I was equipped beyond many of my competitors to be materially successful. Soon I had expanded until I was represented in all the city markets and also in another city. In 1921 we had the forerunner of the later depression and my customers disappeared. Successively I had to close my stands and was finally wiped out altogether. Being a young man of affairs, I had begun to do a little business and social drinking and now with time on my hands, I seemed to do more of it.

Following a year of factory work, during which time I got married, I got a job with a grocer as clerk. My grocer-employer was an expert wine-maker and I had free access to his cellar. The work was monotonous in the extreme, behind a counter all day when I had been used to driving around attending to business, meeting people and building for what I thought was a great future. I mark, too, as a milestone, the death of my father, whom I missed greatly.

I kept hitting the wine, with just occasional use of liquor. Leaving the grocery I went back into the produce business and out among people, went back to liquor again and got my first warning to quit before it got me.

I was anxious to get with a concern which would give me an opportunity to build up again, and landed a job with a nationally known biscuit company. I was assigned to a good business region, covering several important towns, and almost at once began to earn real money. In a very short time I was the star salesman of the company, winning a reputation as a business-getter. Naturally I drank with my better customers, for on my route I had many stops where that was good business. But I had things rather well under control and the early days on this job I seldom wound up my day's work with any visible effects of drinking.

I had a private brewery at home which was now producing 15 gallons a week, most of which I drank myself. It is typical of the attitude I had toward alcohol at that time that, when a fire threatened total destruction of my home and garage, I rushed to the cellar and rescued my most precious possessions—a keg of wine and all the beer I could carry, and got pretty indignant when my better half suggested that I had better get some of the needed effects out of the house before it burned down.

My home-brewing gradually became a bore and I began to carry home bottles of powerful bootleg whiskey, starting with half a pint every night and winding up with a quart as my daily after-supper allowance. For a time I kept on the job spacing my drinks en route and very little of them in the morning hours. I just couldn't wait until I got home to drink. In a very short time I became an all-day drinker.

Chain-store managers and quantity buyers were both my guests and hosts and every now and then we had prodigious parties. Finally, in a re-organization shake-up resulting in new district managers with a pretty poor territory deal for me, I gave the company two weeks notice and quit. I had bought a home but in the year and a half following I had little income and finally lost that. I became satisfied with just enough to live on and buy the liquor I wanted. Then I landed in the hospital when my car was hit by a truck. My car was ruined entirely. That loss and my injuries plus the recriminations of my wife sort of sobered me up. When I got out of the hospital I stayed sober for six weeks and had made up my mind to quit.

I went back in the business where I had been a successful salesman, but with another company. When I started with this concern I talked things over with my wife and made her some very solemn promises. I wasn't going to touch another drop of liquor.

By this time prohibition was a thing of the past and saloons and clubs where I was well known as a good customer and a good spender became my patrons. I rolled up business until I was again a star, but after the first four months on the new job I began to slip. It is not unusual in the drinking experience of any man that after a time of sobriety he comes to the conclusion that he "can handle it." In no time at all liquor again became the most important thing in my life and every day became like another, steady drinking in every saloon and club on my route. I would get to headquarters every night in a top-heavy condition, just able to maintain equilibrium. I began to get warnings and was repeatedly fired and taken on again. My wife's parents died about this time in unfortunate circumstances. All my troubles seemed to be piling up on me and liquor was the only refuge I knew.

Some nights I wouldn't go home at all and when I did go home I was displeased when my wife had supper ready and equally angry when she didn't. I didn't want to eat at all and frequently when I underestimated my consumption of the amount of liquor I brought home, I made extra trips back to town to renew the supply. My morning ration when I started out was five double whiskies before I could do any business at all. I would go into a saloon, trembling like a leaf, tired in appearance and deathly sick, I would down two double whiskies, feel the glow and become almost immediately transformed. In half an hour I would be able to navigate pretty well and start out on my route. My daily reports became almost illegible and finally, following arrest for driving while intoxicated and on my job at that, I got scared and stayed sober for several days. Not long afterward I was fired for good.

My wife suggested I go into my old home in the country, which I did. Continued drinking convinced my wife I was a hopeless case and she entered suit for divorce. I got another job, but didn't stop drinking. I kept on working although my physical condition was such as to have required extensive hospitalization. For years I hadn't had a peaceful night's sleep and never knew a clear head in the morning. I had lost my wife, and had become resigned to going to bed some night and never waking again.

Every drunkard has one or two friends who haven't entirely given up hope for him, but I came to the point where I had none. That is, none but my Mother, and she, devoted soul, had tried everything with me. Through her, people came to me and talked, but nothing they said—some were ministers and others good church members—helped me a particle. I would agree with them when they were with me and as fast as they went away, I'd go after my bottle. Nothing suggested to me seemed to offer a way out.

I was getting to a place where I wanted to quit drinking but didn't know how. My Mother heard of a doctor who had been having marked success with alcoholics. She asked me if I'd like to talk to him and I agreed to go with her.

I had known, of course, of the various cures and after we had discussed the matter of my drinking fairly thoroughly, the doctor suggested that I go into the local hospital for a short time. I was very skeptical, even after the doctor hinted there was more to his plan than medical treatment. He told me of several men whom I knew who had been relieved and invited me to meet a few of them who got together every week. I promised I would be on deck at their next meeting but told him I had little faith in any hospital treatments. Meeting night, I was as good as my word and met the small group. The doctor was there but somehow I felt quite outside of the circle. The meeting was informal, nevertheless I was little impressed. It is true they did no psalm singing, nor was there any set ritual, but I just didn't care for anything religious. If I had thought of God at all in the years of drinking, it was with a faint idea that when I came to die I would sort of fix things up with Him.

I say that the meeting did not impress me. However, I could see men whom I had known as good, hard-working drunkards apparently in their right minds, but I just couldn't see where I came into the picture. I went home, stayed sober for a few days, but was soon back to my regular quota of liquor every day.

Some six months later, after a terrific binge, in a maudlin and helpless state, I made my way to the doctor's home. He gave me medical treatment and had me taken to the home of one of my relatives. I told him I had come to the point where I was ready for the remedy, the only remedy. He sent two of the members to see me. They were both kindly to me, told me what they had gone through and how they had overcome their fight with liquor. They made it very plain that I had to seek God, that I had to state my case to Him and ask for help. Prayer was something I had long forgotten. I think my first sincere utterance must have sounded pretty weak. I didn't experience any sudden change, and the desire for liquor wasn't taken away overnight, but I began to enjoy meeting these people and began to exchange the liquor habit for something that has helped me in every way. Every morning I read a part of the Bible and ask God to carry me through the day safely.

There is another part I want to talk about—a very important part. I think I would have had much more difficulty in getting straightened out if I hadn't been almost immediately put to work. I don't mean getting back on my job as salesman. I mean something that is necessary to my continued happiness. While I was still shakily trying to rebuild my job of selling, the doctor sent me to see another alcoholic who was in the hospital. All the doctor asked me to do was tell my story. I told it, not any too well perhaps, but as simply and as earnestly as I knew how.

I've been sober for two years, kept that way by submitting my natural will to the Higher Power and that is all there is to it. That submission wasn't just a single act, however. It became a daily duty; it had to be that. Daily I am renewed in strength and I have never come to the point where I have wanted to say, "Thanks God, I think I can paddle my own canoe now," for which I am thankful.

I have been reunited with my wife, making good in business, and paying off debts as I am able. I wish I could find words to tell my story more graphically. My former friends and employers are amazed and see in me a living proof that the remedy I have used really works. I have been fortunate to be surrounded with friends ever ready to help, but I firmly believe any man can get the same result if he will sincerely work at it God's way.

FIRED AGAIN

*I*t seems to me that I never did do things normally. When I learned to dance I had to go dancing every night in the week if possible; when I worked or studied I wanted no interruptions or distractions. Wherever I worked I wanted to be the highest paid man in the place or I was irritated; and of course when I drank I could never seem to stop until I was saturated. I was usually hard to get along with as a boy; if the others wouldn't play my way I'd go home.

The town we lived in when I was a child was rather new and raw, peopled largely by immigrants who seemed to be constantly getting married with free drinks and eats for anybody who cared to come. We kids usually managed to get to these celebrations, and although supposed to have soda pop we could get ourselves one or two beers. With this sort of background and more money than was good for me, it was fairly easy to start getting drunk before I was sixteen.

After I left home I earned rather decent salaries but was never satisfied with my position, salary, or the treatment accorded me by my employer. I very seldom stayed on one job for more than six months until I was married at the age of 28, at which time I had already begun to lose jobs because of my drinking. Whenever things went wrong I knew that a few drinks would make everything rosy, my fears, doubts and worries would vanish and I would always promise myself that the next time I would stop short of getting plastered. Somehow things seldom worked out that way though.

I was irritated by the efforts of so many doctors,

ministers, lawyers, employers, relatives and friends who remonstrated with me, none of whom knew from personal experience what I was up against. I'd fall down, get up, work a while, get my debts paid (at least the most pressing ones), drink moderately for a few days or weeks, but eventually get myself so messed up in tanglefoot that I'd lose another job. In one year (1916) I quit two jobs because I thought I'd be discharged anyhow and was fired outright from five more, which is more jobs than many men have in a lifetime. Had I remained sober, any one of them would have led to advancement because they were with growing companies and in my chosen field of engineering.

After being discharged for the fifth time that year, I drank more than ever, cadging drinks and meals where I could, and running up a large rooming-house account. My brother took me home and my folks talked me into going to a sanitarium for thirty days. This place was operated by a physician who was a personal friend of the family and I was his only patient at the time. The doctor did his best, saw that I got into good physical condition, tried to straighten out the mental quirks he thought partly responsible for my drinking, and I left with the firm resolve never to drink again.

Before I left the sanitarium I answered an advertisement for an engineer in a small Ohio town and after an interview, obtained the position. In three days after leaving the sanitarium I had a job I liked at a satisfactory salary in a small town with basic living costs (board, room and laundry) amounting only to about 15% of my salary. I was all set, sober, working in a congenial atmosphere for a firm that had more profitable business than they knew what to do with. I made some beautiful plans. I could save enough in a few years to complete my formal education and there were no saloons in the town to trip me up. So what? So at the end of the week I was drunk again for no particular reason at all that I could understand. In about three months I was out of a job again, but in the meantime two things of major importance had happened. I had fallen in love and war had been declared.

I had learned my lesson. I knew definitely that I couldn't take even one drink. I wanted to get married, so I planned very earnestly to get another job, stay sober, and save some money. I went to Pittsburgh on Sunday, called on a manufacturer of rolling-mill equipment and on Monday, got a position and went to work. I was first paid at the end of the second week, was drunk before the end of the day and couldn't be bothered with going to work the next Monday.

Why did I take that first drink? I honestly don't know. Anyhow I nearly went crazy that summer and really developed some sort of mental disturbance. The night clerk of the small hotel where I was staying saw me go out about three in the morning in pajamas and slippers and had a policeman take me back into my room. I suppose he was used to screwy drunks or he would have taken me to jail instead. I stayed there a few days and sweated the alcohol out of my system, went to the office to collect the balance of my salary, paid my room rent, and found I had just enough money to get home. So home I went, sick, broke, discouraged and despairing of ever attaining a normal, happy life.

After two or three weeks of idleness at home, I obtained a subordinate position with a former employer, doing the lowest grade of drafting work on an hourly basis. I kept reasonably sober for several months, went to see my fiancée one or two weekends, was advanced rapidly in salary and responsibility, had a date set for the wedding and then inadvertently learned that one of the men working under my direction was receiving about forty dollars more per month than I was, which burnt me up to such an extent I quit after an argument, took my money, packed my personal effects, left them at the corner drugstore, and went downtown and got plastered. Knowing that I would be greeted with tears, sorrowful sympathy and more grief when I got home, I stayed away until I was again destitute.

I was really worried sick about my drinking, so father again advanced the money for treatment. This time I took a three-day cure and left with the firm resolve never to drink again, got a better position than I'd had before and actually did keep sober for several months, saved some money, paid my debts and again made plans to get married. But the desire for a drink was with me constantly after the first week or two, and the memory of how sick I had been from liquor and the agonies of the treatment I had undergone faded into the background. I had only begun to restore the confidence of my associates, family, friends and myself before I was off again, without any excuse this time. The wedding was again postponed and it looked very much as though it would never take place. My employer did not turn me loose but I was in another nice jam nevertheless. After considerable fumbling around mentally as to what to do I went back to the three-day cure for the second time.

After this treatment I got along a little better, was married in the spring of 1919 and did very little drinking for several years. I got along very well with my work, had a happy home life, but when away from home with little likelihood of being caught at it, I'd go on a mild binge. The thought of what would happen if my wife caught me drinking served to keep me reasonably straight for several years. My work became increasingly more important. I had many outside interests and drinking became less of a factor in my life, but I did continue to tipple some during my out-of-town trips and it was because of this tendency that things finally became all snarled up at home.

I was sent to New York on business and later stopped at a nightclub where I had been drunk before. I certainly must have been very tight and it is quite likely that I was "Mickey Finned," for I woke up about noon the next day in my hotel without a cent. I had to borrow money to get home on but didn't bother to start back till several days later. When I got there I found a sick child, a distracted wife and had lost another job paying $7,000 a year. This, however, was not the worst of it. I must have given my business card to one of the girls at the nightclub for she started to send me announcements of another clip-joint where she was employed and writing me long-hand "come on" notes, one of which fell into my wife's hands. I'll leave what happened after that to the reader's imagination.

I went back into the business of getting and losing jobs and eventually got to the point where I didn't seem to have any sense of responsibility to myself or to my family. I'd miss important family anniversaries, forget to come home for Christmas and in general wouldn't go home until I was exhausted physically and flat broke. About four years ago I didn't come home on Christmas Eve but arrived there about six o'clock on Christmas morning, minus the tree I had promised to get, but with an enormous package of liquor on board. I took the three-day cure again with the usual results but about three weeks later I went to a party and decided a few beers wouldn't hurt me; however I didn't get back to work for three days and a short while later had lost my job and was again at the bottom of things. My wife obtained employment on a relief basis and I finally got straightened out with my employer who placed me in another position in a nearby city which I also lost by the end of the year.

So it went until about a year ago when a neighbor happened to hear me trying to get into the house and asked my wife whether I had been having some drinking difficulties. This, of course, disturbed my wife but our neighbor was not just inquisitive. She had heard of the work of an ex-alcoholic doctor who was busily engaged in passing on the benefits he had received from another who had found the answer to his difficulties with liquor. As a result of this my wife saw the doctor. Then I talked with him, spent a few days in a local hospital and haven't had a drink since.

While in the hospital about twenty men called on me and told me of their experiences and the help they had received. Of the twenty I happened to know five, three of whom I had never seen completely sober. I became convinced then and there that if these men had learned something that could keep them sober, I also could profit from the same knowledge. Before leaving the hospital, two of these men, convinced of my sincerity of purpose, imparted to me the necessary knowledge and mental tools which have resulted in my complete sobriety for thirteen months, and an assurance that I need never, so long as I live, drink anything of an alcoholic nature if I kept on the right track.

My health is better, I enjoy a fellowship which gives me a happier life than I have ever known, and my family joins me in a daily expression of gratitude.

TRUTH FREED ME!

*I*n May 1936, after a prolonged period of alcoholism, my friends, my associates, my superiors, and those people who really loved me in spite of embarrassments too numerous to mention, finally left me because they had come to the conclusion that I didn't have any idea of doing or trying to do the right thing.

I was a spineless individual who didn't care a rap for anyone or anything—I was hopeless and knew it—and then in my extremity, The Divine Comforter, "Truth" came to me in a barroom where I had spent the major portion of six weeks.

The Divine Comforter, in my experience, came in the guise of a former drinking companion whom I had assisted home on several occasions. Because of physical infirmities brought about by alcoholic excess, he had been unable to walk a distance of three blocks to his home unassisted, when I last saw him. Now he approached me, and to my amazement he was sober and appeared greatly improved in physical condition.

He induced me to take a ride with him, and as we rode along told me of the marvelous thing that had come into his life. He had more than a practical idea of my difficulties, he also had a logical and practical idea as to how they might be overcome.

He started the conversation by explaining acute alcoholism and stated very bluntly that I was an alcoholic. This was news to me in spite of the fact that I had promised everybody east of the Mississippi, if they would take time to listen, that I was through with drink. At the time I made these promises, I honestly wanted to quit drinking, but for some unknown reason hadn't seemed able to. He told me why I failed.

He then suggested that I accompany him to a local doctor who had been helpful to him. It took forty-eight hours of persuasion and quite a few drinks to fortify myself, but I finally agreed to go. The doctor turned out to be one who had been an alcoholic himself, and in gratitude for the release he had found and because he understood the true meaning of the phrase "Brotherly Love" was spending a great portion of his time helping unfortunate individuals like myself.

With the help and advice of these two individuals and two or three associates, I was able, for the first time in two and a half years, to stay sober for six weeks, and then disastrously tried the beer experiment. For some time I couldn't get hold of myself, but gradually came out of hiding and exposed myself again to this influence which had been so helpful.

July 2, 1936, I again contacted the two individuals, and since that day I have never had a drink. However, because of the difficulties I encountered as the result of the beer experiment, I was unable for some time to find reality in this new way of life. I was doubtful, fearful, full of self-pity, afraid to humiliate myself.

This unreality lasted until December 11th, when I was faced with the absolute necessity of raising a sum of money. For the first time came the realization that I was faced with a difficulty from which I seemed unable to extricate myself. Of course, I took time out to bemoan the fact that "after all I'd done, this had to happen to me" but on the advice of my wife, I reluctantly went to a banker.

I told him my story completely. I went to him believing that my need was money. I went there as a last resort to attempt to pry it loose to meet my needs. My need was not money, but again I had been led to the proper source. After having related my story to the banker, who knew my reputation not only as an alcoholic but as an individual who didn't pay his bills, he said, "I know something of what you are trying to do, and I believe you are on the right track. Are you right with the Father who knows your needs before you ask? If so, you are not dependent upon this bank or any individual in it, or any rules by which we operate, because your help comes from an ever present and all powerful Father. I am going to do everything I can to secure this loan for you. However, I don't want anything that happens here to throw you off the track, I want you to leave here feeling that you have done everything you could to secure these funds, and go about your business with God's work. I don't know whether that calls for you to go and collect a bill, sell some new contract, or to sit quietly and pray, but your Father knows and if you will but permit Him, He will direct you."

I had again found reality. My needs were met from another entirely unexpected source.

The manifestations of this ever present Power in my experience since 1936 are too numerous to mention. Let it suffice to say that I am profoundly grateful for the opportunities I have had of seeing and knowing "TRUTH."

SMILE WITH ME, AT ME

*A*t the age of eighteen I finished high school and during my last year there my studies were dropping away to be replaced by dancing, going out nights, and thinking of a good time as most of the boys of my age did. I secured a job with a well known telegraph company which lasted about a year, due to the fact I thought I was too clever for a $7.00 a week job which did not supply me with enough money for my pleasures, such as taking girls out, etc. I was not at all satisfied with my small wages.

Now, I was a very good violinist at the time and was offered jobs with some well known orchestras, but my parents objected to my being a professional musician although my last year in high school was mostly spent playing for dances and giving exhibition dances at most of the fraternity affairs. Now naturally I was far from satisfied with my $7.00 a week wages, so when I came across a boy neighbor of mine on the subway one night (by the way I read in the newspaper that this same boy died four days ago), he told me he was a host in a celebrated Restaurant and Cabaret, and that his salary ran $14.00 per week and he made $50.00 a week in tips. Well, think of being paid for dancing with the carefree ladies of the afternoon and receiving all that sum, and me working for only $7.00 per. The following day I went straight uptown to Broadway and never did go back to my old job.

This was the beginning of a long stretch of high-flying as I thought, only to find out when I was forty-one years old to be very low-flying. I worked in this restaurant until I was twenty-one, then we went into the world war. I joined the navy. My enlistment pleased the owner of my cabaret so much that he offered me a good job at the end of my federal service.

The day I walked in to his establishment with my release from active duty, he said, "You are my assistant manager from now on." Well, this pleased me as you can imagine and my hat from then on would not fit.

Now, all this time my taste for liquor was constantly growing although it was no habit and I had no craving. In other words, if I had a date and wanted a drink with the girl friend I would, otherwise I would not think of it at all.

In six months time I found I was too good for this job and a competitive restaurateur, a chain of the best well-known nightclubs offered me a better position which I accepted. This night life was starting to tell and show its marks and together with the slump in that sort of business at the time, I decided to apply for a job with a well known ballet master who drilled many choruses for Broadway shows.

I was this man's assistant and I really had to work very hard for the little money I received, sometimes twelve hours or more a day, but I got the experience and honor which was just what I was looking for. This was one time when my work interfered with my drinking. This job came to an end one evening when I was drinking quite heavily. A certain prominent actress inquired of Professor X, my boss, if I would be interested to sign an eighty week contract for a vaudeville tour. It seems she could use me as a partner in her act. Now, a very nice woman, Miss J. who was office clerk and pianist for the boss, overheard the conversation and told both Mr. X and Miss Z that I would not be interested.

On hearing this I went out and drank enough to cause plenty of trouble, slapping Miss J. and doing an all round drunk act in the studio.

This was the end of my high-flying among the white lights. I was only twenty-four years old and I came home to settle down; in fact I had to. I was broke both financially and in spirit.

Being a radio operator in the navy, I became interested in amateur radio. I got a federal license and made a transmitting radio set and would often sit up half the night trying to reach out all over the country. Broadcasting radio was just in its infancy then, so I began to make small receiving sets for my friends and neighbors. Finally I worked up quite a business and opened a store, then two stores, with eleven people working for me.

Now here is where Old Barleycorn showed his hidden strength. I found that in order to have a paying business I had to make friends, not the kind I was used to, but ordinary, sane, hard working people. In order to do this I should not drink, but I found that I could not stop.

I will never forget the first time I realized this. Every Saturday, my wife and I would go to some tavern. I would take a bottle of wine, gin, or the like, and we would spend an evening dancing, drinking, etc. (This was fourteen years ago.)

I was practically a pioneer in the radio business and that must account for people putting up with me as they did. However, within three years time I had lost both stores, I won't say entirely due to my drinking, but at least if I had been physically and mentally fit, I could have survived and kept a small business going.

Now from this time up to about a year ago, I drifted from one job to another. I peddled brushes, did odd jobs such as painting, and finally got established with a well known piano company as assistant service manager.

Then came the big crash of 1929 and this particular company abolished their radio department. For two years I worked for one of my old competitors who owned a radio store. He put up with my drinking until I was in such a physical breakdown that I had to quit.

All this time my troubles at home were getting worse. My whole family blamed my failure on the alcoholic question and so the usual arguments would start the instant I came in the house. This naturally made me go out and drink some more. If I had no money, I would borrow, beg, or even steal enough for a bottle.

My wife fortunately went to business which was our only salvation. Our little boy was six years old at the time and due to the fact we needed someone to care for him during the day we moved in with my family. Now the trouble did start, because I not only had my wife to face every evening, but three of the elders of the family.

My wife did everything for me she possibly could. First she got in touch with a well known psychiatrist and I went faithfully to him for a few months. This particular doctor was such a nervous individual, I thought he had the St. Vitus' dance and I really thought he needed some kind of treatment more than I did. He advised hospitalization from three months to a year.

Well, this was all out of order as far as I was concerned. In the first place I had an idea that my wife wanted to put me away in a state institution where maybe I would be stuck for the rest of my life. In the second place, I wanted to go, if anywhere, to a private institution and that was far beyond our financial means. In the third place, I knew that that would be no cure, because I reasoned that it would be like taking candy out of a young child's reach. The instant I would come out a free man I would go right back to old Alky again. In this one thing I found out later I was perfectly right.

What I thought and wanted at the time was "not to want, to want to take a drink." This phrase is a very important link in my story. I knew this could only be done by myself, but how could I accomplish it? Well, this was the main question.

The point was always that when I did drink, I wanted all the time not to, and that alone wasn't enough. At the time I felt like a drink, I did not want to take it at all, but I had to it seemed. So if you can grasp what I mean, I wished I would not want that drink. Am I nuts, or do you get me?

To get back to the doctor. If anything, these visits made me worse, and worst of all, everyone told me I wanted to drink and that was all there was to that. After going to as many as six or eight other doctors, some of my own friends advised my wife to make her plans for the future as I was a hopeless case, had no backbone, no will power, and would end up in the gutter.

Well, here I was, a man with much ability, a violinist, a radio engineer, a ballet master, and at this point took up hair dressing, so that added one more to the list. Can you beat it? I knew there must be some way out of all this mess. Everyone told me to stop my drinking, but none could tell me how, until I met a friend and believe me he turned out to be a true friend, something I never had until this past year.

One morning, after one of my escapades, my wife informed me I was to go with her to a public hospital or she would pack up and leave with our boy. My father, being a physician for forty years, put me in a private New York hospital. I was there ten days and was put in physical shape, and above everything else put on the right path to recovery and happiness.

My friend first asked me if I really wanted to stop drinking, and if I did, would I do anything no matter what it was in order to? I knew there was only one thing left to do if I wished to live and not enter an insane asylum where I knew I would eventually wind up.

Making up my mind that I would, he said, "Fine." And went on to explain the simple steps to take. After spending an hour or two with me that day he returned two days later and went into the subject more thoroughly. He explained he had been in the same hospital with the same malady and, after taking these steps after his discharge, had not taken a drink in three years and also there were about sixty others that had this same experience. All these fellows got together on Sunday evenings and brought their wives and everybody spent a very pleasant time together.

Well, after I met all these people, I was more than surprised to find a very interesting, sociable, and friendly crowd. They seemed to take more interest in me than all of my old fraternity brothers or Broadway pals had ever done.

There were no dues or expenses whatsoever. I went

along for about fourteen weeks, partly keeping these ideas, and so one afternoon I thought it would do no harm to take a couple of drinks and no more. Saying to myself, "I have this thing in hand now, I can be a moderate drinker." Here I made a fatal mistake. After all my past experience, again I thought I could handle the situation only to find out one week later it was the same old thing. I repeated the same thing over again and another week again.

Finally I was back at the hospital, although I went under protest. My wife had expected to take two weeks vacation in the country with me, but instead had to use this money for hospital expenses. During my one week stay, I held this as a grudge against her. The result was I got drunk three days after I was discharged from the hospital. And she left me for two weeks. During this period of time I drank heavily, being upset not only over her absence, but perfectly at sea as to how I could ever get back on my feet and make a new start again.

There was no mistake about it, there was something that I failed to do in those simple steps. So I carefully went over each day as I could since my first drink after the fourteen weeks of sobriety, and found I had slipped away from quite a few of some of the most important things which I should do in order to keep sober.

Certainly I was down now—ashamed to face my new friends—my own family giving me up as lost and everyone saying, "The system didn't work, did it?"

This last remark was more than too much for me. Why should this fellowship of hard working fellows be jeopardized by me? It worked for them. As a matter of fact, not one who had kept faithfully to it has ever slipped.

One morning, after a sleepless night worrying over what I could do to straighten myself out, I went to my room alone—took my Bible in hand and asked Him, the One Power, that I might open to a good place to read—and I read. "For I delight in the law of God after the inward man. But I see a different law in my members, warring against the law of my mind and bringing me into captivity under the law of sin which is in my members. Wretched man that I am! Who shall deliver me out of the body of this death?"

That was enough for me—I started to understand. Here were the words of Paul, a great teacher. What then if I had slipped? Now, I could understand.

From that day I gave and still give and always will, time every day to read the word of God and let Him do all the caring. Who am I to try to run myself or anyone else?

A CLOSE SHAVE

The year 1890 witnessed my advent as the youngest of five sons to a fine Christian mother and a hard working blacksmith father. At the age of eight my father used to send me after his pail of beer and it was by lapping the foam off the beer that I first discovered that the taste was much to my liking. By the time I was fourteen, at which time I quit school, I had found that wine and hard cider were also pleasing to my palate. The next six years I spent learning the art of barbering and by the end of this period I had become both a proficient barber and an earnest drinker.

During the next 10 to 12 years I was able to acquire several lucrative shops, some with poolrooms and restaurants attached. It seemed quite impossible however for me to stand prosperity, so I would drink myself out of one situation, get myself together a bit, develop another, and then repeat the performance.

The time came when I could no longer refinance myself, so I began to float about the country, getting a job here and there as I could, but invariably I got fired in a short time because of my unreliability.

My marriage, which occurred in 1910 about the time I started my successful ownership of shops, resulted in our having a family of ten children who were usually desperately in need because I used my slender income for booze instead of providing for them.

I finally secured a job in a shop in a town of about 4,500 people, where I now live. My reputation for drinking soon became more or less generally known. About this time a deacon and the pastor of one of the local churches used to come in the shop for their work and were constantly inviting me to church and Bible classes, which invitations irritated me very much. I earnestly wished they would mind their own business.

I finally did accept one or two invitations to social functions at the home of one of these men, and was received so cordially that the barrier between us was partially lowered.

I did not stop drinking however, though my feeling toward these men was kindly. They at last persuaded me to go to a nearby town to have a talk with a doctor who had had a great deal of experience with this type of trouble. I listened to the man for two hours, and although my mind was quite foggy, I retained a good deal of what he said. I feel that the combined effort of these three Christian gentlemen made it possible for me to have a vital spiritual experience. This occurred in March 1937.

For about six years previous to this time I was never at any time completely free from the influence of liquor.

Since that time I have regained the love of my family and the respect of the community, and can truthfully say that the past two years have been the happiest of my life.

I have busied myself a great deal during these two years in helping others who were afflicted as I was, and the combined efforts of the deacon, the pastor, and myself, have resulted in nine other men finding a way out of difficulties which were identical with mine. I feel this activity has played an important part in my mastery of this most devastating habit.

EDUCATED AGNOSTIC

*W*hy go into the drinking pattern that is so much the same with all of us? Three times I had left the hospital with hope that I was saying goodbye forever. And here I was again.

The first day there I told the kindly doctor that I was a thoroughly hopeless case and would probably continue to return as long as I could beg, borrow, or steal the money to get in. On the second day he told me that he knew of something that would keep me off liquor for life. I laughed at him. Yes, indeed, I would do anything or take anything that would produce such results, but there wasn't anything. On the third day a man came to talk with me. He was an alcoholic who had stopped! He talked about alcoholism and a spiritual way of life. I was deeply impressed by his seriousness, but nothing that he said made sense to me. He spoke about God, and a power greater than one's self. I remember being very careful not to say anything that might shake his faith in whatever it was he believed! I was deeply grateful to him for taking the trouble to talk with me, but what he had was not for me. I had thought much about religion and had come to rather definite conclusions. There was no God. The universe was an inexplicable phenomenon. In spite of my sorry state and outlook, there were many beautiful things in life, but no beauty. There were truths discoverable about life, but no truth. There were people who were good, kind, considerate, but no such thing as goodness. I had read rather extensively, but when people began to talk in such ultimates I was lost. I could find in life no eternal purpose nor anything that might be labeled "divine guidance." War, illness, cruelty, stupidity, poverty and greed were not and could not be the product of any purposeful creation. The whole thing simply didn't make sense.

About this I felt no deep emotion. I had struggled with the problem during late adolescence, but had long since ceased to give it anxious thought. Many people believe in a god of some sort and worship him various ways. That was excellent. I thought it nice that so many people, poor misguided souls, could find so simple a solution to their problems. If this world proved too hopelessly disillusioning they could always seek comfort in a more pleasant existence promised in a world to come, where wrongs would be righted and justice tempered with tender mercy would prevail. But none of that was for me. I had enough courage and intellectual honesty to face life as I saw it without recourse to a self-erected deity.

The next day another man visited me. He, too, had been an alcoholic and stopped drinking. He pointed out that I had found myself unable to handle my liquor problem by myself. He had been in the same position, yet he hadn't had a drink in over three years! He told me of other men who had found sobriety through the recognition of some power beyond themselves. If I cared to I was to consider myself invited to a gathering the following Tuesday where I would meet other alcoholics who had stopped.

With the knowledge I now have, it is hard for me to recall how screwy the whole thing sounded—the blind leading the blind, a union of drunks, all banded together in some kind of a spiritual belief! What could be more idiotic! But . . . These men were sober! Nuts!

I returned to my despairing wife with this incoherent story of a bunch of drunks who had found a cure for their alcoholism through some kind of spiritual exercise and who held regular meetings where, as far as I could figure out, they went through some kind of spiritual exercise! She was very nearly convinced that my mental balance had now been completely and probably permanently destroyed. The only rational support I could find for giving it a try was that it was vouched for by the kindly doctor who she had met on several occasions at the hospital. That and the fact that nothing else worked.

May I stop at this point and address a few sentences direct to agnostic or atheistically inclined alcoholics: You can't take less stock in the references made to God in this book than I would have if this book had been available to me at this time. To you those references have no meaning. They have simply used a name that people give to a fond delusion. All your life, except possibly in early childhood, when you conceived of an enormous figure with a flowing white beard somewhere beyond the clouds, it has meant nothing. You have now too much intelligence and honesty to allow of such delusions. Even if you could, you are too proud to affirm a belief now that you are in desperate trouble, that you denied when things were rosy. Or, you might possibly persuade yourself to believe in some creative force, or algebraic "X," but what earthly good would an "X" be in solving such a problem as you face? And, even admitting, from your knowledge of psychology, it is possible you might acquire such delusions, how could you possibly believe in them if you recognized them as delusions? Some such thinking must have been going on in your mind as you have weighed these incredible experiences against your own inability to cope with a problem that is gradually destroying your personality. Rest assured that such questions were in my mind. I could see no satisfactory solution to any of them. But I kept hard to the only thing that seemed to hold out any hope, and gradually my difficulties were lessened. I have not given up my intellect for the sake of my soul, nor have I destroyed my integrity to preserve my health and sanity. *All I had feared to lose I have gained and all I feared to gain I have lost.*

But to conclude my story: The following Tuesday, hardly daring to hope and fearful of the worst, my wife and I attended our first gathering with former alcoholic slaves who had been made free through the rediscovery of a power for good, found through a spiritual attitude toward life. I know that I have never before been so inspired. It was not anything that happened. Because nothing happened. Nor yet by anything that was said, but more by an atmosphere created by friendliness, sincerity, honesty, confidence, and good cheer. I couldn't believe that these men could have been drunks, and yet gradually I learned their stories, alcoholics every one!

That was, with me, the beginning of a new life. It would be difficult, if not impossible, for me to put into words the change that has taken place in me. I have since learned that with many members the change has been almost instantaneous. This was not the case with me. I was tremendously inspired at first, but my basic thinking was not altered that evening nor did I expect any profound change. I felt that while the spiritual aspect of what these men had was not for me, I did believe strongly in the emphasis they put on the need to help others. I felt that if I could have the inspiration of these gatherings and if I could have an opportunity to try to help others that the two together would re-enforce my own will power and thus be of tremendous assistance. But gradually, in a manner I cannot explain, I began to re-examine the beliefs I had thought beyond criticism. Almost imperceptibly my whole attitude toward life underwent a silent revolution. I lost many worries and gained confidence. I found myself saying and thinking things that a short time ago I would have condemned as platitudes! A belief in the basic spirituality of life has grown and with it belief in a supreme and guiding power for good.

In the process of this change I can recognize two immensely significant steps for me. The first step I took when I admitted to myself for the first time that all my previous thinking might be wrong. The second step came when I first consciously wished to believe. As a result of this experience I am convinced that to seek is to find, to ask is to be given. The day never passes that I do not silently cry out in thankfulness, not merely for my release from alcohol, but even more for a change that has given life new meaning, dignity, and beauty.

ANOTHER PRODIGAL STORY

"Hello, Pal."

"Hello, Buddy!"

"Have a drink?"

"Got one!"

"Come over on the next stool. I'm lonesome. Hell of a world."

"You said it, brother—hell of a world."

"You taking rye? Mine's gin. God, I'm up against it now!"

"How's 'at?"

"Oh, same old hell—hell—hell. She's going to leave me now!"

"Your wife?"

"Yeah. How am I going to live? Can't go home like this; too damn drunk to stay out. Can't land in jail—will if I stay out—ruin my business—business going anyway—break her heart. Where is she you ask? She's at the store, working I guess, probably eating her heart out waiting for me. What time is it? Seven o'clock? Store's been closed an hour. She's gone home by now. Well, what the hell. Have one more—then I'll go."

That is a hazy recollection of my last debauch. Nearly a year ago now. By the time my new "bar fly friend" and I had soaked up several more, I was shedding tears and he, in the tender throes of drunken sympathy, was working out a guaranteed plan whereby my wife would greet me with great joy and out-spread arms as soon as "we" got home.

Yes "we" were going to my home. He was the

finest fixer in the world. He knew all about how to handle wives. He admitted that!

So, two drunks, now lifetime buddies, stumbled out arm in arm headed up the hill towards home.

A draft of cool air cleared some of the fog away from my befuddled brain. "Wait a minute, what's this so-and-so plan of yours? I got to know about it," I said. "I got to know what you're going to say and what I say."

The plan was a honey! All he had to do was to lead me up to the apartment, ring the bell, ask my wife if I was her husband, and then tell her he had found me down at the river about to jump from the bridge and had saved my life.

"That's all there is to it," he kept mumbling over and over, "works every time—never fails."

On up the hill we staggered, then my "life saver" got a better idea that would clinch the deal. He'd have to go home first and put on clean linen. Couldn't let the nice lady see a dirty shirt.

That sounded all right. Maybe he'd have a bottle at his home. So we stumbled up to his place, a dreary third floor back room, on a third rate street.

I have a hazy recollection of that place, but have never been able to find it since. There was a photograph of a quite pretty girl on his dresser. He told me it was a picture of his wife and that she had kicked him out because he was drunk. "You know how women are," he said.

Some fixer!

He did put on a clean shirt all right and then reached into a drawer and pulled out a .38 calibre revolver. That gave me quite a sobering shock. I reached for the gun, realizing in a hazy way that here was trouble.

He began to pull the trigger and every moment I expected to hear an explosion, but the gun was empty. He proved it!

Then he got a new idea. To reconcile my wife and make her happy, he would tell her the gun was mine, that I stood on the bridge, with the gun at my head and that he snatched it away just in time to save my life.

God almighty must have, at this moment, granted me a flash of sanity. I quickly excused myself while he was completing his toilet and, on the pretext of phoning my wife, rushed noisily down the stairs and ran down the street with all my might.

Some blocks away I came to a drug store, bought a pint of gin, and drank half of it in several large gulps, staggered on up to my apartment, and tumbled into bed, fully dressed and dead drunk.

This wasn't any new terror for my wife. This sort of thing had been going on for several years, only I was getting worse and worse with each drunken spree and more difficult to handle.

Only the previous day I had been in an accident. A Good Samaritan saw my condition and got me away quickly, before the police came, and drove me back to my home.

I was dreadfully drunk that day and my wife consulted a lawyer as preliminary to entering divorce action. I swore to her that I wouldn't drink again and within 24 hours, here I was in bed dead drunk.

Several months previously I had spent a week in a New York hospital for alcoholics and came out feeling that everything would be all right. Then I began to think that I had the thing licked. I could practice a little controlled drinking. I knew I couldn't take much but just one drink before dinner. That went all right, too. Sure I had it licked now! The next step was to take one quick one at noon and cover it up with a milk shake. To make it doubly sure, I'd have ice cream put into the milk shake, and then, so help me, I don't know what the next step down was, but I surely landed at the bottom with an awful, heartbreaking thud.

The next morning was June 7th. I recall the date so well because the sixth is my daughter's birthday. And that, by the grace of God, was my last spree.

That morning I was afraid to open my eyes, surely my wife would have kept her promise and left me. I loved my wife. It is a paradox I know, but I did and do.

When I did stir, there she was sitting at my bedside.

"Come on," she said, "get up, bathe, shave and dress. We're going to New York this morning."

"New York!" I said, "To the hospital?"

"Yes."

"I haven't any money to pay a hospital."

"I know you haven't," she said, "but I arranged it all last night over long distance and I'm going to give you the one chance, once again. If you let me down this time, that's all there is."

Well, I went into the hospital again feeling like a whipped cur. My wife pleaded with the doctor to please do something to save her husband, to save her home, to save our business, and our self-respect.

The doctor assured us that he really had something for me this time that would work and with that faint hope, we separated; she to hurry back home, 150 miles away, and carry on the work of two people and I to sit trembling and fearful there in what seemed to me, a shameful place.

Four days later a man called on me and seemed interested to know how I was coming along. He told me that he, too, had been there several times but had now found relief.

That night another man came. He, too, had suffered the same trouble and told how he and the other fellow and several more had been released from alcohol.

Then the next day a fine fellow came, and in a halting but effective way, told how he had placed himself in God's hand and keeping. Almost before I knew it, I was asking God to clean me up.

I suppose there are many who feel a strong resentment against such a spiritual approach. Some of Alcoholics Anonymous whom I have met since that day tell me they had difficulty in accepting a simple, day to day, plan of faith. In my case I was ripe for such an opportunity, perhaps because of early religious training. I have always, it seems, had a keen sense of the fact and presence of God.

That, too, like loving my wife and at the same time hurting her so dreadfully, is paradoxical, but it's a fact. I knew that God was there with infinite love and yet, somehow, I kept on drifting further and further away. But now I do feel that my heart and mind are "tuned in" and by His grace there will be no more alcoholic "static."

After making this final agreement (not just another resolution) to let God be first in my life, the whole outlook and horizon brightened up in a manner which I am unable to describe except to say that it was "glorious."

The following day was Monday and my ex-alcoholic friend insisted that I check out from the hospital and come over to his home in 'Jersey. I did that and there I found a lovely wife and children all so "happy about the whole thing."

The next night I was taken to a meeting at the home of an ex-alcoholic in Brooklyn, where to my surprise, there were more than 30 men like myself, telling of a liberty of living unmatched by anything I had ever seen.

Since returning to my home, life has been so different. I have paid off the old debts, have money enough now for decent clothes and some to use in helping others, a thing which I enjoy doing but didn't do when I had to contribute so generously to alcohol.

I am trying to help other alcoholics. At this writing there are four of us working, all of whom have been kicked around dreadfully.

There is no "cocky" feeling about this for me. I know I am an alcoholic and while I used to call on God to help me, my conclusion is that I was simply asking God to help me drink alcohol without its hurting me, which is a far different thing than asking him to help me not to drink at all.

So here I stand, living day to day, in His presence, and it is wonderful—This prodigal came home.

THE CAR SMASHER

*D*uring the first week of March 1937, through the grace of God, I ended 20 years of a life made practically useless because I could not do two things.

First, I was unable to not take a drink.

Second, I was unable to take a drink without getting drunk.

Perhaps a third as important as the other two should be added: my being unwilling to admit either of the first two.

With the result I kept trying to drink without getting drunk, and kept making a nightmare of my life, causing suffering and hardship to all those relatives and friends who tried so hard to help me and whom, when I was sober, I took the greatest pleasure in pleasing.

The first time I drank anything strong, or in greater quantity than a glass of beer, I got disgustingly drunk and missed the dinner which had been arranged for me in honor of my coming marriage.

I had to be taken home and remained in bed the following day, more sick than I thought a human could be and live. Yet, until two years ago I periodically did the same thing.

Making money was always pretty easy when I was sober and worked.

All right when sober—absolutely helpless with a drink aboard. But I seemed to have had the idea that making money or a living was something to take or let alone.

I got into the real estate business—began to neglect business, sometimes with four houses under construction, wouldn't see any of them for a week or even longer—sometimes paid good money for an option, then forgot to exercise it. I made and lost plenty of money in the market.

Understand, I wasn't actually drunk all of this time but there seemed always to be an excuse to have a drink, and this first one, more and more often led to my becoming drunk. As time went on, periods between drunks got shorter and I was full of fear; fear that I wouldn't be able to do anything I agreed to do; fear of meeting men; worrying about what they might know of my drinking and its results; all of which made me quite useless whether I was sober or drunk.

Thus I drifted. Breaking promises to my wife, my mother, and a host of other relatives and friends who stood more from me and tried harder than humans should be expected to, to help me.

I always seemed to pick the most inopportune time for a binge. An important business deal to be closed might find me in another city. Once when entrusted to purchase for a large customer, I agreed to meet his representative in New York. I spent the time waiting for a train in a bar; arrived in New York tight; stayed tight the week; and came home by a route twice the distance from New York.

Worked weeks, by long distance, wire, letters, and personal calls, to contact possible business connections under proper conditions and finally succeeded, only to show up tight or get tight and insult the man whose friendship, or respect, meant so much.

Each time there was the feeling of regret, inability to understand why, but a firm determination that it would never happen again—but it did—in fact the periods between became increasingly shorter, and the duration of each binge longer.

During the aforementioned period, I had spent thousands of dollars, my home was broken up; half a dozen cars smashed up; I had been picked up by police for driving while intoxicated—plain drunk; had sponged and borrowed money; cashed rubber checks; and made such a general nuisance of myself that I lost all the friends I had. At least they felt unwilling to be a party to financing me while I made a more complete ass of myself. And I, on my side was ashamed to face any of them when I was sober.

My friends secured jobs for me; I made good on them for a time. I advanced quickly to night superintendent in a factory but it wasn't long until I was missing, or worse, turning up drunk; was warned—warned again; finally fired. I was later rehired as a factory hand and mighty glad to have it—advance again—then back to the bottom—always the same process.

I drank continuously and when I drank, sooner or later, and generally sooner, I got drunk and threw everything away.

During the early part of 1935 my brother secured my release from the city jail. On that day, by sincere but non-alcoholic friends, I was shown what might be done about my drinking with the help of God.

I asked for this help, gratefully accepted it, and in addition to losing my desire for drink, asked for and received the same help in other matters. I began to earn my living and in my newfound security, was unashamed to meet people I had avoided for years with happy results.

Things continued well. I had two or three advancements to better jobs with greater earning power. My every need was being met as long as I accepted and acknowledged the Divine Help which was so generously given.

I find now, as I look back, that this period covered about six or eight months, then I began to think how smart I was, to wonder if my superiors realized what they had in me, if they were not pretty small about the money they paid me; as these thoughts grew, my feeling of gratefulness grew less. I was neglecting to ask for help—when I received it as I always did, I neglected to acknowledge it. Instead I took great credit for the non-drinking too—it came to me strongly that I had conquered the drinking habit myself—I became convinced of my great will power.

Then someone suggested a glass of beer—I had one. This was even better than I thought—I could take a drink and not get drunk. So another day, another beer until it was regular every day. Now I was indeed in the saddle concerning drink—could take it or leave it alone. Just to prove it to myself, I decided to march right past the place I usually stopped for beer, and I felt pretty good as I went to the parking lot for my car. The longer I drove the greater was my pride that I had finally licked liquor. I was sure I had—so sure in fact that I stopped and had a beer before I went home. In my smugness I continued to drink beer and began occasionally to drink liquor.

So it went until inevitably, "as darkness follows the sun," I got drunk and was right back where I had been fifteen years before, slipping into a binge every now and then—never knowing when they would come— nor where I would wind up.

That lasted about eight months—I didn't miss much time from work—did spend one ten day stretch in the hospital after a beating I got while drunk—was warned a few times by my superiors—but was "getting by."

In the meantime I had heard of some men who, like myself, were what I had always scoffed at being—alcoholics. I had been invited to see them, but after twenty years of drinking, I felt there was nothing wrong with me. *They* might need it; *they* might be queer; but not me. I wasn't going to get drunk again.

Of course I did, again and again, until these men not only contacted me but took me under their wing.

After a few days of "degoofing" in a hospital, these men came to me one by one and told me of their experiences. They didn't lecture—didn't tell me I should quit. But they did tell me *how* to quit. THAT WAS IMPORTANT and simple too.

Their suggestion was that we simply acknowledge we had made a pretty dismal failure of our lives, that we accept as truth and act upon what we had always been taught and known, that there was a kind and merciful God, that we were His children, and that if we would let Him, He would help us.

I had certainly made a mess of my life. From the age of 20 I had thrown aside everything God had seen fit to endow me with. Why not avail myself of this all wise, ever-present help?

This I did. I ask for, accept, and acknowledge this help, and know that so long as I do, I shall never take a drink and what is more important, though impossible without the first, all other phases of my life have been helped.

There are, it seems to me, four steps to be taken by one who is a victim of alcoholism.

First: Have a real desire to quit.

Second: Admit you can't. (This is the hardest.)

Third: Ask for His ever-present help.

Fourth: Accept and acknowledge this help.

HINDSIGHT

*F*ired! Still, I got a new and better job. One which gave me more time to relax and where drinking was permitted during working hours. People were beginning to criticize my drinking habits and I scoffed at them. Hadn't I earned ten thousand dollars that year? And wasn't this the middle of the depression? Who were they to say that I couldn't handle my liquor? A year of this and I was fired.

Other jobs followed with the same net result. After each experience of this kind I would sit down and figure out the reason why it happened. I always found a good reason, and usually people accepted it and gave me another chance. For weeks, sometimes months, I wouldn't touch a drop and because I could do this, I reasoned that there was a real excuse for that last bender, and since that excuse no longer existed I could start to drink moderately again.

I usually did—for a while. Then I would step up the consumption about one glass per day until I reached the stage where all of the past unhappy experiences associated with drinking were brought back to my mind. Soon I was crying in my beer, full of self-pity, and off again to a flying start toward a floundering finish.

How many times this happened, I don't know. I don't even want to know. I do know that during this period I completely smashed nine new automobiles and was never scratched. Even this didn't convince me that there might be a God who was looking out for me in answer to the prayers of others. I made many friends and abused them terribly. I didn't want to, but when it was a question of a friendship or a drink, I usually took the drink.

In a final effort to escape, I went to New York thinking I could leave my reputation and troubles behind me. It didn't work. I was hired by eight nationally known organizations and fired just as quickly when they had checked my references. The world was against me. They wouldn't give me a chance. So I continued my drinking and took any mediocre job I could get.

Occasionally I dropped into a church half hoping that I might absorb something, anything, that might help a little bit. On one of these visits I saw and met a girl who I felt could be the answer to all of my problems. I told her all about myself and how I felt sure that with her friendship and love everything could and would be different. Although born in New York she was "from Missouri." I would have to show her first. She had seen other girls try to reform men by marrying them and she knew it didn't work.

She suggested praying and having faith and a lot of things that seemed silly at the time, but I really got down to business and started doing some serious bargaining with God. I prayed and prayed. In all earnestness I said, "If You will get this girl for me then I'll stop drinking for You." And "If You will only get me my original job back, I'll drink moderately for You."

I soon found out that God didn't work that way because I didn't get the girl or the job.

Six months later I was sitting in a small hotel on the west side of New York full of remorse and desperate because I didn't know what would happen next. A middle-aged man approached me and said in a very sincere voice, "Do you really want to stop drinking?" Immediately I answered, "Yes," because I knew that was the correct answer. He wrote down a name and address and said "When you are sure you do, go and see this man." He walked away.

I began to think, "Did I really want to quit? Why should I? If I couldn't have this girl and I couldn't ever have a good job again, why in the hell should I quit?" I tucked the address into my pocket along with a nickel for subway fare, just in case I ever decided to really quit. I started drinking again, but could get no happiness or release regardless of the number of drinks.

Occasionally I would check up to see if the address and the nickel were still safe, because I was being tortured with one thought this girl had given to me. "You must be decent for your own sake. And because you want to be decent, not because someone else wants you to be."

A week later I found myself in the presence of the man whose address was in my pocket. His story was incredible. I couldn't believe it, but he had the proof. I met men whose stories convinced me that in the ranks of men who had been heavy drinkers I was an amateur and a sissy.

What I heard was hard to believe but I wanted to believe it. What's more I wanted to try it and see if it wouldn't work for me.

It worked, and is still working. For weeks I was bitter against society. Why didn't someone put me wise to this before? Why did I have to go on like that for years making my parents unhappy, abusing friends, and passing up opportunities? It wasn't fair that I should be the instrument to make people unhappy.

I believe now that I was given this experience so that I might understand and be of use in helping others to find a solution to this and other problems.

When I decided to do something about my problem, I was reconciled to the fact that it might be necessary for me to wash dishes, scrub floors, or do some menial task for possibly many years in order to re-establish myself as a sober, sane, and reliable person. Although I still wanted and hoped for the better things in life, I was prepared to accept whatever was due me.

Once I became sincere, good things began to happen to me. My first experience in overcoming fear was three weeks later when I applied for a position with a national organization. After numerous questions I was finally asked why I had left the company I had been with six years. I replied that I had been fired for being a drunk. The manager was flabbergasted and so completely astounded by the truth that he refused to believe me. I referred him to my former employer but he refused to write him—but he did give me the job.

It has been three and a half years since I made that decision. Those years have been the happiest years of my life. The little girl, who was big enough to tell me the nasty truth when I needed it, is now my wife.

Eight months ago I went to another city to set up a new business. I had sufficient money to last me several months. What I wanted to accomplish could have been done under ordinary circumstances in about two weeks. The obstacles I have encountered and overcome are hard to enumerate. At least twenty times I have been sure that I would be doing business within the next twenty-four hours and at least twenty times something has happened which later made it seem that the business never would get started.

While I am writing this I happen to be at the low point for the twenty-first time. Money is exhausted. All recent developments have been unfavorable, everything seems on the surface to be wrong. Yet I am not discouraged. I am not blue. I feel no bitterness toward these people who have tried to obstruct the progress of the business, and somehow I feel because I have tried hard, played square, and met situations, that something good will come from this whole experience. It may not come the way I want it, but I sincerely believe that it will come the way that it is best.

On His Way

*I*n early youth I believe I had some of the tendencies which lead to alcoholism. I refer to attempted escapes from reality.

At fifteen and sixteen, although free at home to drink small amounts of beer and wine, I drank considerable quantities of stronger liquors at school and other places. Not enough to cause serious worry, but enough apparently to give me occasionally what I thought I wanted. Escape? A feeling of superiority? I do not know.

I then decided I'd had enough of school, which decision was probably shared by the schools. The next few years were spent in civil engineering work, travel, sports, and a little idleness, and I seem to have avoided alcoholic difficulties of the more pronounced kind.

Immediately before marriage and in the short time before sailing for France, alcohol began to take a real part in my life. A year and a half in war time France postponed the inevitable and the post war period of hopes and plans brought me nearer and nearer to the point where I eventually found myself to be an alcoholic. Not that I would have admitted it then, having the alcoholic's usual facility for deception, both to self and others.

Divorced, sometimes suspecting that drinking was the basis for most of my troubles but never admitting it, I had enough left in health, interests of various kinds, and luck to carry on with considerable success.

About this time I stopped all social drinking. I became a periodic drunkard, the sprees lasting from three days to three weeks and dry intervals lasting from three weeks to four months.

During one of the best years, I made a happy marriage and the age of thirty-five found me with the following: a beautiful little home presided over by a kind, understanding, and lovely wife; a partnership in a firm I had helped to found years before; more than a comfortable income; many luxuries and many friends; opportunity to follow my interests and hobbies; a love of my work; pride in my success; great health; optimism; and hope on the credit side. On the other hand, I had a growing, gnawing fear of my recurring trouble.

I slipped by far too easy stages to the bottom in less than eight years. Not a pleasant place, the bottom. Sometimes I slept in a cheap hotel or rooming house, sometimes a flophouse, sometimes the back room of a police station and once in a doorway; many times in the alcoholic ward at a hospital, and once in a subway toilet. Sometimes decently fed, clothed, and housed, I worked at my business on commission with a large firm; sometimes I dared not appear there cold, hungry, with torn clothes, shaking body and muddled brain advertising what I had become. Helpless, hopeless, bitter.

Sometimes I was apparently on the way back, and sometimes writhing in bed for days at a time, terrorized by the fear of insanity and by the specters of people without faces, people with horrible faces, people grimacing and laughing at me and my misery. Tortured by dreams from which I would awake with a scream of agony and bathed in cold sweat. Tortured by daydreams of what might have been, dreams of the kindness, faith and love that had been heaped upon me.

Due to this last however, and to what little remained of my former self and perhaps to some lingering power of spiritual faith, I became somewhat better. Not well, but better.

This helped me to talk stock and to try to do some clear thinking. I found my inventory somewhat mixed, but as my thoughts became clearer, I grew much better and at last arrived at the point where for the first time in several years I could see some light and hope ahead of me. Through a haze of doubt and skepticism I began to realize, partly at least, many things in myself which had greased the path I had pursued, and some vague thoughts and ideas came to me that are now crystallizing with the help of the men I have been happy to join.

What thoughts and ideas? The answer is short, although the road to it is long and tedious.

My intelligence, instead of drawing me further away from spiritual faith, is bringing me closer to it. I no longer react in quite the same way when my will and desires are apparently frustrated.

The simple words "Thy Will Be Done" and the simple ideas of honesty and of helping others are taking on a new meaning for me. I should not be surprised to find myself coming to the astounding conclusion that God, whoever or whatever He may be, is eminently more capable of running this universe than I am. At last I believe I am on my way.

AN ALCOHOLIC'S WIFE

I have the misfortune, or I should say the good fortune, of being an alcoholic's wife. I say misfortune because of the worry and grief that goes with drinking, and good fortune because we found a new way of living.

My husband did not drink, to my knowledge, for several years after we were married. Then we started on an occasional Saturday night party. As I drank nothing except an occasional highball I soon became what was called a "wet blanket." The parties became more frequent and more often I was left at home.

I would sit up and wait for him. As each car passed the house I would return to walking the floor and crying and feeling so sorry for myself, thinking, "Here I am left at home to take care of the baby, and him out having a good time."

When he did return sometimes on Sunday and sometimes a week later, it usually called for a scene. If he was still drunk I would put him to bed and cry some more. If he was sober it would mean I would say all the things I had been thinking and cry some more. He usually got drunk again.

I finally went to work, as the bills worried me. I thought if I worked and got the bills paid he would quit drinking. He had no money in the bank but would write checks as he knew I would pay them for the boy's sake and in the hopes that each time would be the last.

I thought I should have a lot of credit, as I was paying his bills, taking care of the house and baby, besides my work, making as much money as he was, doing without things I wanted so he could have a good time.

I always went to church and thought I was living a Christian life. After my husband came in contact with Alcoholics Anonymous I thought our troubles were over as I was sure all our trouble was his drinking.

I soon found out that there was a lot wrong with me. I was selfish with my money, time, and thoughts. I was selfish about my time because I was always tired and had no time left for my family's pleasure or to do God's work. All I did was go to Sunday School and Church on Sunday with the boy and thought that was all God wanted me to do. I would be irritable and lose my temper and say all manner of things which usually called for another drunk and my pitying myself all over again.

Since giving my husband's problem to God I have found a peace and happiness. I know that when I try to take care of the problems of my husband I am a stumbling block as my husband has to take his problems to God the same as I do.

My husband and I now talk over our problems and trust in a Divine Power. We have now started to live. When we live with God we want for nothing.

An Artist's Concept

"There is a principle which is a bar against all information, which is proof against all arguments and which can not fail to keep a man in everlasting ignorance— that principle is contempt prior to investigation."

—Herbert Spencer

*T*he above quotation is descriptive of the mental attitudes of many alcoholics when the subject of religion, as a cure, is first brought to their attention. It is only when a man has tried everything else, when in utter desperation and terrific need he turns to something bigger than himself, that he gets a glimpse of the way out. It is then that contempt is replaced by hope, and hope by fulfillment.

In this personal story I have endeavored to relate something of my experience in the search for spiritual help rather than a description of the neurotic drinking that made the search necessary. After all, the pattern of most alcoholic experiences fits a pretty general mold. Experiences differ because of circumstances, environment, and temperament, but the after effects, both physical and mental, are almost identical. It makes but little difference how or why a man becomes an alcoholic once this disease manifests itself. The preventive measures adopted for alcoholic tendencies in the future will have to be found in a more progressive program of mental hygiene and medical research than is now obtainable. It is important that at present we believe there is only one sure pathway to recovery for any alcoholic.

In my own case I was not entirely ignorant of the

causes that led me into excessive drinking. In a desperate effort to eliminate these causes, to find a means to better mental and physical health, I investigated the alcoholic problem from every angle. Medicine, psychology, psychiatry, and psychoanalysis absorbed my interest and supplied me with a great deal of general and specific information. It led me in the end, however, to the fact that for me here was a mental and physical disease that science had placed in the category of "incurables." Briefly, all that this study and research ever did for me was to show something about WHY I drank. It substantiated a fact I had known all along, that my drinking was symptomatic. It did point out a road to better mental health but it demanded something of me in return that I did not have to give. It asked of me a *power* of self-will but it did not take into consideration that this self-will was already drugged with poison—that I was very sick. Intuitively I also knew that a person constrained to temperance by the domination of will is no more *cured* of his vice than if he were locked up in prison. I knew that somehow, some way, the mental stream, the emotions, must be purified before the right pathway could be followed.

It was about this same time that I began "flirting" with religion as a possible way out. I approached the subject in a wary, none too reverent, attitude. I believed in an omnipotent God or Deity, but the orthodox approach through the church, with its dogma and ritual, left me unmoved. The more I struggled to gain an intelligent grasp upon spiritual development, the more confused I became. On the other hand a purely materialistic viewpoint that postulated a "mechanical order of things" seemed too negative even to entertain. As an artist I had spent too much time communing with nature—trying to place upon canvas or paper my emotional feelings, not to know that a tremendous spiritual power was back of the universe. There was, however, so much that seemed illogical or sentimental about religion in general—so many doubts assailed me, so many problems to be confronted—yet there was within myself a strong and urgent desire for spiritual satisfaction. The occasional periods in which I felt a spirtual emotion, I immediately examined with all the ardor of the inveterate analyst. Was this emotion just a form of religious ecstasy? Was it fear? Was it just blind belief or had I tapped something?

"Most men," wrote Thoreau, "lead lives of quiet desperation." It was the articulation of this despair that led to my drinking in the beginning. Religion, so far, had only added to my desperation. I drank more than ever.

A seed had been planted, however, and a short time afterward I met the man who has for the past five years devoted a great deal of time and energy to helping alcoholics. Looking back on that meeting, the simplicity of his talk with me is amazing. He told me very little but what I already knew, in part, but what he did have to say was bereft of all fancy spiritual phraseology—it was simple Christianity imparted with Divine Power. The next day I met over twenty men who had achieved a mental rebirth from alcoholism. Here again it was not so much what these men told me in regard to their experiences that was impressive, as it was a sense of feeling that an invisible influence was at work. What was it this man had and these other men exemplified without their knowing? They were human everyday sort of people. They certainly were not pious. They had no "holier than thou" attitude. They were not reformers, and their concepts of religion in some cases were almost inarticulate. But they had *something*! Was it just their sincerity that was magnetic: Yes, they certainly were sincere, but much more than that emanated from them. Was it their great and terrible need, now being fulfilled, that made me feel a vibratory force that was new and strange? Now I was getting closer and suddenly, it seemed to me, I had the answer. These men were but instruments. Of themselves they were nothing.

Here at last was a demonstration of spiritual law at work. Here was spiritual law working through human lives just as definitely and with the same phenomena expressed in the physical laws that govern the material world.

These men were like lamps supplied with current from a huge spiritual dynamo and controlled by the rheostat of their souls. They burned dim, bright, or brilliant, depending upon the degree and progress of their contact. And this contact could only be maintained just so long as they obeyed that spiritual law.

These men were thinking straight—therefore their actions corresponded to their thoughts. They had given themselves, *their minds,* over to a higher power for *direction.* Here, it seemed to me, in the one word "Thought"—was the crux of the whole spiritual quest. That "As a man thinketh in his heart, so is he" and so is his health, his environment, his failure, or his success in life.

How foolish I had been in my quest for spiritual help. How selfish and egotistical I had been to think that I could approach God *intellectually.* In the very struggle to obtain faith I had lost it. I had given to the term faith a religious significance only. I had failed to see that faith was "our common everyday manner of thinking." That good and evil were but end results of certain uniform and reliable spiritual laws. Obviously, my own thinking had been decidedly wrong. Normal most of the time, it was abnormal at the wrong times. Like everyone's thinking, it was a mixture of good and bad, but mainly it was uncontrolled.

I had been sticking my chin out and getting socked by spiritual law until I was punch drunk. If one could become humble, if he could become *"as a little child"* before this powerful spiritual thought force, the pathway could be discovered.

The day I made my first efforts in this direction an entire new world opened up for me. Drinking as a vicious habit was washed completely out of my consciousness. I have never even been tempted to take a drink since. As a matter of fact there are so many other things within myself that need correction that the drink habit looks silly in comparison. Please do not assume that all this is but an exposition of spiritual pride. A chart of my spiritual progress would look like the "graph" of a business that had been hit by everything but an earthquake. But there has been progress. It has cured me of a vicious habit. Where my life had been full of mental turmoil there is now an ever-increasing depth of calmness. Where there was a hit or miss attitude toward living there is now new direction and force.

The approaches of man to God are many and varied. My conception of God as Universal Mind is after all but one man's approach to and concept of the Supreme Being. To me it makes sense, opens up a fascinating field of endeavor and is a challenge, the acceptance of which can make of life the "Adventure Magnificent."

THE ROLLING STONE

*A*fter the breaking up of our home, my Father went west and took up his work and became fairly successful.

Then it was decided that I should be sent to a preparatory school, so to a midwestern school I was sent. It didn't last long, for I got into a jam and left.

I went to Chicago, wrote my Father and he sent me fare to come on west, which I did. I started in to High School after I got there, but I had no companionship, for my Father was away most of the day and when he came in he always spent the evenings reading and studying.

This all caused me to become very bitter towards anything religious, because I felt that I was only in his way when he wanted to read his religious books and he took only enough interest in me to leave a dollar on the dresser each morning to buy my meals with. It caused me to become so hostile towards anything religious that I formed hatred against religion which I was to carry for years.

During the time which I spent by myself, I had found that I could buy wine and loaf around saloons and it wasn't long before I had formed a taste for drink. I was only about fourteen years old then, but I looked eighteen.

When vacation time came I wanted to go to San Francisco. My father willingly let me go and after seeing the sights of that city I decided I wanted to go to sea and see the world, so it was only a short time before I found myself signed as an apprentice at sea and leading a new life.

In the meantime my mother had married again. I knew she was well taken care of so my letters were few and my visits home were years apart, and through the selfish interest I had taken in myself I never gave a thought to how worried she might be over me. I had become a person wrapped up in my own life only and giving no thought of anyone else.

Starting to sea out of San Francisco brought me in and out of port there a great deal, so I considered San Francisco my home, and as I had arrived there about 1905 I knew the old San Francisco of before the earthquake where the lid was off and vice flourished at all times.

In my young life I saw all and knew all and considered myself well able to play the game as others did.

I developed into a steady drinker and, when going to sea, was sure I took enough liquor along to take care of me for the trip. When we arrived at a foreign port we would go ashore and proceed to see the sights which mostly started at the first saloon. If American liquor was not to be had or was too high in cost then we would drink their native drink, and as I look back it hardly seems possible that I have a brain left to remember with for I have done about everything possible to destroy it by over-indulgence in alcohol.

I have been to most of the ports in this world; have stayed in some for some time; have put in a winter in Alaska; lived in the tropics; but no time did I ever find a place where I could not get liquor.

I quit the sea when I was just past 20. I had become interested in construction work, also had studied some art and learned the Fresco decorating trade.

Eventually I went into the building trade and have followed that ever since.

I had always made good wages or made good at contracting, but was ever a rolling stone, never staying in one place long and drinking just the same as in my seafaring days.

I had always a certain respect for myself and I carried my liquor well for years; knew enough not to make a show of myself and stopped when I had enough.

Then came the war. I was 29 years old and was in Texas when I went into the army and went overseas from there. After leaving Texas I found out that we were stopping in my home town for an hour and I received permission to call my mother when we arrived there, so fortunately I was able to get her down to the train before I left. I had not been home in 11 years and I told her if I came back alive I would come home to stay.

I had not been in the service long before I was a high ranking non-commissioned officer, for I had learned army discipline years before in the army transport service and while in this country and when behind the lines in France this gave me a chance to get my liquor when my buddies couldn't.

But when we got to the front lines it was the first time in years that I was unable to get my daily share of alcohol but, when it was possible, I never missed.

On into Germany for six months where I made up for lost time. "Schnapps" was barred to American Troops but I got mine. After coming back to the U.S. I received an honorable discharge and came back to my home and mother.

Then I started trying to break away from liquor

but it did not last. The last few years found me in all kinds of mixups for I had at last developed into an alcoholic.

When I drank I would get to the state where it required a doctor to straighten me out. The times I have had to rely upon doctors are numerous. I even tried sanitariums for relief. I had plenty of suffering thrown in but still I would drift back again to that first drink and off again I went.

I wanted to quit but each time I drank it was worse than before. The misery that my mother went through was unbelievable, for I had become her sole support. I was willing to try anything if I could only get a release from this curse. I knew it was breaking up my home and I was losing everyone that was dear to me.

For a few months I was successful in discontinuing drinking. Then all of a sudden I fell again. I lost my position and thought I was through.

When I was told of a doctor who had been successful in overcoming alcohol and was asked to go and see him in a nearby city, I consented but with a feeling that it was just another cure.

From him and a number of other men, however, I found it was possible to become a man again. He suggested my entrance into a hospital to clear my mind and build me up. Meals had become a thing of the past for me. I had lost all appetite for food but forced myself to eat a little to survive.

This doctor told me that unless I was sincere in wanting to quit drinking, I would be wasting his time and mine and also money in doing this. My answer was I would try anything that would release me.

I went into the hospital and started to build my body up again through proper nourishment, and my mind through a different method than I had ever known of.

A religious awakening was conveyed to me through some unseen force. I at one time would have laughed at such a possibility because I had tried it and failed because I had not applied it properly. I, at last, was shown the way by those men to whom I am now most grateful.

I am now 50 years old, unmarried, have become sane and sensible again, have made my mother happy and brought back those who were dear to me, have made many new friends, mix where I never mixed before, received back my old position. I have the respect of my fellow men and have learned how to actually live and really enjoy life. It has been nearly a year and a half since I have found this new life and I know as long as I do the few things that God requires me to do, I never will take another drink.

LONE ENDEAVOR*

$\mathcal{A}$s a mother looked idly through a small medical journal, an article written by a doctor on alcoholism caught her attention. Anything in reference to this subject was worthy of perusal, for her son, an only child, had been drinking uncontrollably for years. Each year of his drinking had added new heartaches, though every small ray of hope had been investigated, though he had tried desperately to stop. But little had been accomplished. He was occasionally able to remain sober for short periods at a time, but things constantly became worse.

So this mother read the short medical article with heavy heart, for she was constantly on the alert to find something which might prove helpful to her son.

The article gave only a vague hint of the solution found by many alcoholics, which is fully covered in this book, but the mother immediately wrote to the doctor explaining her heart-breaking problem, and requesting further information. She felt there must be help somewhere, and surely if other men had recovered from alcoholism, her son also had a chance.

The doctor turned her letter over to Alcoholics Anonymous. It ended as follows:

> "God knows if you can help my son, it will bring happiness to many of us who love him and ache with him in his futile efforts to overcome his problem. Please accept my gratitude

---

*This story appeared only in first printing of first edition.

140

for whatever you may be able to do and let me hear from you."

A few days later the following letter was sent to this mother. It was our initial effort to help others through the book alone.

"About a hundred men, here in the east, have found a solution for alcoholism that really works. We are now preparing a book hoping to help others who suffer in the same way, and are enclosing a rough copy of the first two chapters. As soon as possible we will forward rough copy of the rest of the proposed book."

We received no answer for some time, and later wrote again:

"We are sending you a pre-publication multilith copy of 'ALCOHOLICS ANONYMOUS.' We would appreciate hearing about your son's condition and his reaction to this volume, as this is the first time we have had an opportunity of trying to help an alcoholic at long distance. Won't you please write us?

Sincerely,
Alcoholics Anonymous"

After another period of silence from the far west, during which time we began to think this book was inadequate without personal contact, we received a long letter from the son himself. A letter which we feel will be of tremendous help to others who live in distant places, who feel alone and totally unable to work this program out by themselves. A letter which encompasses a man's solitary effort to take what we had to offer and carry the program through alone. Alone except for one book and the help which printed pages could give; alone until he had tried our program of recovery and found spiritual comfort and help.

He wrote as follows:

"I want to thank you from the bottom of my heart for your letters and for 'ALCOHOLICS ANONYMOUS.' I have read this book from cover to cover and it is really the first time I have read anything dealing with alcoholism that made sense and showing understanding of the problems of the alcoholic.

I found the personal stories very accurate as pertaining to my own experience; any one of them might have been my own story.

I started drinking in 1917 when I was 18. I enlisted in the army, soon became a non-commissioned officer, went overseas as a sergeant. I associated with older men, drank, gambled, and ran around with them, sampling everything France had to offer.

Upon my return from France I continued drinking. At the time I could get plenty tight at night, get up in the morning and go to work feeling O.K. The following fifteen years were one drunk after another which, of course, as they got worse, meant one job after another. Police Department, truck driving, etc. Then in an attempt to get away from it all I enlisted in the U.S. Marine Corps. In 13 months time I drank very little and was promoted to Gunnery

Sergeant, a rank that usually takes 10 or 12 years to obtain, if ever. I started drinking again. In six months I was reduced to Line Sergeant. I transferred to get away from my former associates.

Then came several years in China. China of all places for a man who wanted to stay away from booze. My four years over, I did not re-enlist.

Came more jobs selling automobiles, real estate, etc. Then down to odd jobs. I was drinking so much no one could take a chance by giving me a steady job, such as I could easily have handled if I left the liquor alone. I married and the booze split that up. My mother was a nervous wreck. I was getting arrested for drinking three or four times a year. I had myself committed on two different occasions to State Hospitals, but soon after discharge, I was back at it again. Two years ago I went to a private hospital for a liquor cure. A week after getting out I was curious as to what would happen if I took a drink. I took it—nothing happened. I took another—why go further. I went back to the private hospital, came out and was O.K. for a few months—then at it again.

Now previous to this and at the time of these cures, I was working at a State Hospital for the insane. I saw continually the effects of liquor but did it help me to leave it alone? No—it did not. But it did make me realize that if I did not, I would end up in the 'bughouse' and someone else would be carrying the keys.

After several years of working at mental institutions always in a violent ward, on account of my 6 feet 2 inches and 210 lbs., I realized there was too much nervous tension and every couple of months I would 'blow up' and be off drunk for a week or ten days. I left mental work and got a job at the County General Hospital where I am now in a medical ward. We get quite a few patients with D.T.s, all broken out with wine sores, etc. I steadied down a bit, but not enough. I was off 'sick' for several days every six or eight weeks.

I married again. A good Catholic girl whose people were used to having liquor, especially wine around the house always. She of course could not understand about my drinking—as far as that's concerned, neither could I. And all this time my poor mother and wife became more and more worried.

Mother had heard of your wonderful work and wrote a doctor. You answered with letters, and finally the book. Before the book arrived and after reading the chapters I knew that the only way to combat this curse was to ask the help of the greater Power, God. I realized it even though I was then on a binge!

I contacted a friend of mine who is liaison officer of the Disabled Veterans of the World War. He made arrangements for my care in a State Sanitarium which specializes in alcoholism. I wanted to get the liquor out of my system and start this new idea right. I explained my absence as 'Flu' and under the care of the head psychiatrist spent most of the time, from Sept. 1, 1938 till Jan. 15, 1939, at the hospital having my appendix removed and a ventral hernia fixed up.

Six weeks ago I returned from the sanitarium and your book was here waiting for me. I read, more than that I pored over it so as not to miss anything. I thought to myself, yes this is the only way. God is my only chance. I have prayed before but I guess not the right way. I have followed out the suggestions in the book. I am happier this moment than I have been in years. I'm sure I have found the solution, thanks to ALCOHOLICS ANONYMOUS.

I have had talks with another man, an attorney, who was at the sanitarium when I was. He has my book now and he is very much enthused.

I go down to the sanitarium every week for a check-up and medicine which they give me, just a tonic, no sedatives. The manager has asked me to contact some of his patients along our line. How I told him I would appreciate his letting me do so!

Would you put me in touch with some 'A.A.s' out here? I know it would help me and help me to help others.

I hope you can make sense out of this letter. I could write so much more but this I have written just as it popped into my head.

Please let me hear from you."

This man's lone struggle was impressive. Wouldn't this story of his solitary recovery be helpful to many others who would have to start out by themselves with only this book to aid them?

So we immediately sent him a wire:

> JUST RECEIVED LETTER. MAY WE HAVE YOUR PERMISSION TO USE LETTER ANONYMOUSLY IN BOOK AS FIRST EXAMPLE OF WHAT MIGHT BE ACCOMPLISHED WITHOUT PERSONAL CONTACT. IMPORTANT YOU WIRE THIS PERMISSION, AS BOOK IS GOING TO PRINTER.
>
> ALCOHOLICS ANONYMOUS

His wire arrived next day:

> PERMISSION GRANTED WITH PLEASURE. LOTS OF LUCK.

PART TWO

The stories that follow were taken out of Alcoholics Anonymous *when the third edition was prepared in 1976. As stated in the introduction to the preceding section, the background here does not pertain entirely to the stories themselves, but to changes in A.A.*

By the time the third edition was published, its Foreword could report that "the total worldwide membership of Alcoholics Anonymous was conservatively estimated at more than 1,000,000, with almost 28,000 groups meeting in over 90 countries. Surveys of groups in the United States and Canada indicate that A.A. is reaching out, not only to more and more people, but to a wider and wider range. Women now make up more than one-fourth of the membership . . . [and] seven percent of the A.A.'s surveyed are less than 30 years of age—among them, many in their teens." The Fellowship had become well known to the general public. Professionals who worked with suffering alcoholics were increasingly knowledgeable about us, and many newcomers reached A.A. at the urging of a doctor or other professional or via an alcoholism treatment center. And a new phenomenon, specialized groups for young people, gay members, lawyers, doctors, and others, were becoming a part of the A.A. scene.

Clearly, it was time to revise the personal stories section. Under the supervision of an ad hoc committee of the trustees' Literature Committee, staff members from the General Service Office and two editors, all of whom had known or worked with Bill W. (who died in 1971), undertook the task. The number of stories was increased to 42. While the section entitled "Pioneers of A.A." remained unchanged, new material added to the other two sections included the experience of two teen-agers, two retirees, a Native American, two ex-convicts, and a number of others taken from a variety of occupations and lifestyles. The subcommittee sought material from the Fellowship at large, and also tapped the resources of "our meeting in print," the A.A. Grapevine, for 12 of the new stories.

The stories in the following pages show that Bill W.'s guidelines concerning style and structure, mentioned in Part One, were followed. Their writers avoided the use of profanity, and for the most part adhered to the now-familiar framework of "what we used to be like, what happened, and what we are like now." These A.A.s paint a picture of the Fellowship in the 1950s, a more mature, established society than we were in the preceding section. They have been sober longer, and they view the program and its effect on their lives as a familiar path to sobriety, rather than as unknown, unexplored territory. The process of finding Alcoholics Anonymous is no longer quite so haphazard—most tell of attending group meetings or being directed to a clubhouse. And the groups now have the luxury of instituting some procedures that would never have been an option in earlier times (witness the A.A. who wasn't allowed to do any twelfth stepping with less than three months of sobriety, and compare that to 1939, when three months was considered quite a long time).

But whatever the changes may have been in group customs and practices, the core of these stories was unchanged from the days of the founders—drinking, getting sober, and most importantly, living sober.

THE PROFESSOR
AND THE PARADOX

Says he, "We A.A.'s surrender to win;
we give away to keep; we suffer to get well,
and we die to live."

I am in the public information business. I use that
phrase or designation because if I say I am a college professor everybody always has a tendency to run
the other way. And when they learn that I am a specialist in English, they have looks of horror for fear
they are going to slip up and say "ain't." I often wish
I sold shoes or insurance or fixed automobiles or
plumbed pipes. I would have more friends.

My story is not a great deal different from others—
except in a few specific details. All the roads of alcoholism lead to the same place and condition. I suppose
I have always been shy, sensitive, fearful, envious, and
resentful, which in turn leads one to be arrogantly independent, a defiant personality. I believe I got a Ph.D.
degree principally because I wanted to either outdo or
defy everybody else. I have published a great deal of
scholarly research—I think for the same reason. Such
determination, such striving for perfection, is undoubtedly an admirable and practical quality to have,
for a while; but when a person mixes such a quality
with alcohol, that quality can eventually cut him almost to pieces. At least it did so to me.

I began drinking as a social drinker, in my early
twenties. Drinking constituted no problem for me

until well after I finished graduate school at the age of thirty. But as the tensions and anxieties of my life began to mount, and the set-backs from perfection began to increase, I finally slipped over the line between moderate drinking and alcoholism. No longer would I drink a few beers or a cocktail or two and let it go at that. No longer did I let months or even weeks go by without liquor. And when drinking, I entered what I now know was the dream-world of alcoholic fantasy. Then for about five years of progressively worse alcoholic drinking, of filling my life and home with more and more wreckage, it looked as if I were going to ride this toboggan of destruction to the bitter end.

Maybe I didn't get as bad as some of the others. I must confess that I never went to teach one of my classes drunk or drinking—but I've been awfully hungover. My pattern was to be drunk at night, boil myself out to creep to work in the morning, drunk the next night, boil myself out in the morning, drunk again the next night, boil myself out the next morning. I may not have drunk as much whiskey as some, but there isn't anybody who's drunk any more Sal Hepatica than I have!

Now there are all kinds of drunks: melancholy drunks, weeping drunks, traveling drunks, slap-happy and stupid drunks, and a number of other varieties. I was a self-aggrandizing and occasionally violent drunk. You wouldn't think a little fellow like me could do much damage, but when I'm drunk I'm pure dynamite. I'm not going into any of the details—the University can fire me yet!

I came to believe actually that life was not worth living unless I could drink. I was utterly miserable and sometimes desperate, living always with a feeling of impending calamity (I knew something was bound to "break loose"). And to do away with such a fear, I would try a little more drinking, with the inevitable result—for by this time one drink would set up in me that irresistible urge to take another and another until I was down or hungover and in trouble. In the hungover stage I would vow never to touch another drop, and then be drunk the next night.

I knew at least that there had to be some changes made. I tried to change the time and place and amount of my drinking. I tried to change my environment, my place of living—like most of us who at one time or another think that our trouble is geography rather than whiskey. I even entertained the idea of changing wives. I tried to change everything and everybody, *except myself*—the only thing I *could* change.

I did not know that it was physically impossible for me to drink moderately. I did not know that my body's drinking machinery had worn out, and that the parts could not be replaced. I did not know that just one drink made it impossible for me to control my behavior and conduct and my future drinking. I did not know, in short, that I was powerless over alcohol. My family and my friends sensed or knew these things about me long before I did.

Finally, as with most of us in A.A., the crisis came. I realized I had a drinking problem which had to be solved. My wife and a close friend tried to persuade me to contact the only member of Alcoholics Anonymous we knew of in town. This I refused to do. But I agreed that I would stop drinking altogether, maintaining stoutly and sincerely that I could and would solve this problem "on my own." I would feel much better doing it that way, I insisted. I stayed sober for two entire weeks! Then I pitched a "lulu"—a terrific drunken affair in which I became violently insane. I also landed in the City Jail.

I don't know exactly what happened on this bender, but here are some things that did happen which I was told about subsequently. First, the officers who had come out to my house did not want to take me in—but I insisted! Also, I insisted that they wait in the living room while I went back to the bedroom and changed into my best and newest suit (with socks and tie to match), so that I would look nice in jail! I don't remember the ride downtown, but when I "came to" in the jail corridor, I didn't like the looks of the little cage they were shoving me into, so I took issue about that with three officers and indulged in some fisticuffs with all three of them at once—each one of them twice my size and armed with a gun and a blackjack. Now what kind of thinking and acting is that? If that isn't insanity, or absurd grandiosity, or some sort of mental illness, what is it? Because I yelled so loud and made so much noise, I ended up downstairs under the concrete in a place they call "solitary." (That's a fine place—now isn't it?—for a college professor to spend the night!) Two days later I was willing to try A.A., which I had only vaguely heard of a few months before. I called at the home of the man who started the A.A. group in my town, and I went humbly with him to an A.A. meeting the following night.

As I look back, something must have happened to me during those two days. Some forces must have been at work which I do not understand. But on those two days—between jail and A.A.—something happened to me that had never happened before. I repeat, I don't know what it was. Maybe I had made a "decision"—just a part of Step Three (I had made lots of promises but never a decision)—though it seems to me that I was at the time too confused and fogged up to make much of one. Maybe it was the guiding hand of God, or (as we Baptists say) the Holy Spirit. I like to think that it was just that, followed by my own attempt to take the Twelve Steps to recovery. Whatever it was, I have been in A.A. and I have been dry ever since. That was more than six years ago.

A.A. does not function in a way which people normally expect it to. For example, instead of using our "will power," as everyone outside A.A. seems to think we do, we give up our wills to a Higher Power, place our lives in hands—invisible hands—stronger than ours. Another example: If twenty or thirty of us real drunks get away from home and meet in a clubroom downtown on Saturday night, the normal expectation is that all thirty of us will surely get roaring drunk, but it doesn't work out that way, does it? Or talking about whiskey and old drinking days (one would normally think) is sure to raise a thirst, but it doesn't work that way either, does it? Our program and procedures seem to be in many ways contrary to normal opinion. And so, in connection with this idea, let me pass on what I consider the four paradoxes of how A.A. works. (A paradox, you probably already know, is a statement which appears to be false, but which, upon careful examination, in certain instances proves to be true.)

1. We SURRENDER TO WIN. On the face of it, *surrendering* certainly does not seem like *winning*. But it is in A.A. Only after we have come to the end of our rope, hit a stone wall in some aspect of our lives be-

yond which we can go no further; only when we hit "bottom" in despair and surrender, can we accomplish sobriety, which we could never accomplish before. We must, and we do, surrender in order to win.

2. We GIVE AWAY TO KEEP. That seems absurd and untrue. How can you keep anything if you give it away? But in order to keep whatever it is we get in A.A., we must go about giving it away to others, for no fees or rewards of any kind. When we cannot afford to give away what we have received so freely in A.A., we had better get ready for our next "drunk." It will happen every time. We've got to continue to give it away in order to keep it.

3. We SUFFER TO GET WELL. There is no way to escape the terrible *suffering* of remorse and regret and shame and embarrassment which starts us on the road to getting well from our affliction. There is no new way to shake out a hangover. It's painful. And for us, necessarily so. I told this to a friend of mine as he sat weaving to and fro on the side of the bed, in terrible shape, about to die for some paraldehyde. I said, "Lost John"—that's his nickname—"Lost John, you know you're going to have to do a certain amount of shaking sooner or later." "Well," he said, "for God's sake let's make it later!" We suffer to get well.

4. We DIE TO LIVE. That is a beautiful paradox straight out of the Biblical idea of being "born again" or "in losing one's life to find it." When we work at our Twelve Steps, the old life of guzzling and fuzzy thinking, and all that goes with it, gradually dies, and we acquire a different and a better way of life. As our shortcomings are removed, one life of us dies, and another life of us lives. We in A.A. die to live.

HIS CONSCIENCE

*It was the only part of him that was
soluble in alcohol.*

*H*ow was I to know that I was an alcoholic? No
one ever told me that I was or even hinted that I
had passed the point of no return.

Some years ago my thinking was that alcoholics
just did not live in my world. Yes, I had seen them on
my infrequent visits to the seamy side of town. I had
been panhandled by them in almost every city in
Canada. In my estimation an alcoholic was a down-
and-out, a badly dressed bum who much preferred
drinking to working.

If I had been asked I would have said that I did not
even know an alcoholic. As for being one, it was the
very farthest thing from my mind. I would have bitterly resented any such suggestion. Besides, I thought
that any alcoholic was a misfit with a mental quirk of
some kind. It was my opinion that they were all intro-
verts and on tests I had twice been classified as an ex-
trovert.

Certainly I did not know that alcoholism was an
illness. Furthermore, I had no idea that it was a progressive illness.

I come from a family of five children and I had a
very happy childhood in a small Canadian town. Both
my mother and father were religious, without over-
emphasizing it. In due time, I went through grade and

high school and entered college as a little better than average student.

The First War had broken out before I got around to taking my first drink. I joined the Army fairly early in that war.

Oddly enough, I drank very little while in the service for the very good reason that every time I took a drink something disagreeable happened to me. My first drink was scotch undiluted. It put me temporarily out of business through strangulation. The second drink made me sick at my stomach. After the third trial I went to sleep in the summer sun and was painfully sunburned. In France I gave away my rum ration far more often than I drank it.

With the War half over I was sent back to Canada for my discharge from wounds and shock. During the period of waiting for my final papers, along with friends, I spent a good deal of time in a neighboring speakeasy enjoying a few social drinks.

Out of the Army, my drinking dropped away to a drink or two on very special occasions, two or three times a year. So it went for the next ten years, no pattern, no problem.

Toward the end of the twenties the company by which I was employed went through a merger. I was given a more responsible position which entailed a great deal of traveling from Coast to Coast. I found that a few drinks with agreeable companions, in sleeping cars or hotels, helped while away the time. Frankly, I preferred the company of those who took a drink or two to those who did not.

For the next few years I had a lot of fun with alcohol. I liked the taste of it; I liked the effect of it. I conducted myself properly and no harm came of it.

Without realizing it, I came to look forward to several drinks before dinner and then to some during the evening. I gradually developed into a heavy drinker with the result that I didn't feel so well in the mornings.

I would like to make it clear at this point that neither business pressure nor added responsibility had anything to do with my drinking. I had the capacity for handling business without any fear of criticism. I enjoyed the companionship of drinking friends, but I began to notice that there was this difference between us; they were still satisfied with one or two drinks, but alcohol was having a different effect on me. My system seemed to need more alcohol than theirs. In retrospect, my only conclusion is that at that time I was becoming more physically sensitive to and losing my tolerance for alcohol.

But obviously my illness was progressing because it wasn't very long until I started experiencing blackouts. There were times when I would lose my car. At this distance it seems funny, but in those days it was a serious business. With some serious drinking in mind, I would take great care to park my car in some inconspicuous place, some distance from where I intended to do this drinking. After several hours, I would return only to find that it wasn't there. At least it wasn't where I thought I had left it. Then I would start walking up blocks one way and down blocks the other way until I would finally locate it, usually in an entirely different direction than where I was sure I had parked it. On these occasions, I would always end up with a feeling of remorse not far removed from a loathing of myself and the condition I was in. And, of course, I was always terribly afraid of being seen by someone who knew me.

It wasn't long until traveling even by train became a hazard. I could somehow manage to catch a train, but all too often it was not the train which I intended to catch. Sometimes it would be going in the wrong direction, and I would end up in a town or city where I had no intention of being and, therefore, had no business to transact.

Having blackouts also meant that I couldn't clearly remember all of what had transpired the night before, and then it was only a short step to not being able to remember any of it. This became very embarrassing to me. I began to avoid discussing the happenings of the night before. In fact, I no longer wanted to talk about my drinking. I took to drinking alone.

Up to this point, my rise in the business world had been steady. I had become vice-president of the Canadian end of a large company known the world over. Now I found myself delaying making decisions, putting off appointments because my eyes were bloodshot and I didn't feel so well. It was difficult for me to concentrate and even to follow closely a business conversation.

Time and time again I went on the wagon; I said I was through with drink, and at the time actually meant what I said. The end result was always the same. Sooner or later, I started in all over again and binges came closer and closer together.

From time to time friends and relatives spoke to me about my drinking. My wife and family asked me to control it, to pull myself together, to use my will power, to drink like a gentleman. I made dozens of promises and at the time of making them, I sincerely meant to keep every one. I became two different people, one person when I was sober and an entirely different one when I was drinking.

I discovered the morning drink and soon it took two, three or four to straighten me out. I had the shakes so badly that shaving became a task that I feared and dreaded because my hand was so unsteady. I discovered that the shakes came only when I allowed the alcoholic content of my system to drop too low. All too often when I brought it up with some stiff jolts, I went into a blackout. Striking an even balance seemed beyond my power.

I will never forget the first time I became conscious of that over-powering compulsion. No matter what happened—I simply had to have a drink. This compulsion soon became part of my make-up.

One Monday morning when the compulsion was on me, I met an old drinking friend. Our meeting was generally the signal for a bender of some proportions. I always thought that he was the one who should watch his drinking habits—not me. On this particular morning, he was clear-eyed and sober, truly a minor miracle for Monday. He looked well and he looked happy. He said he felt fine and that he had stopped drinking. I asked him whether he had got religion. He said no, but that he had joined A.A. That was the first time I had ever heard of such an organization. Since he couldn't produce a drink, I went on my way and forgot about it.

From this time on, my drinking progressed rapidly. My family life deteriorated. My friends no longer wanted to drink with me. Business trips always became benders. One bender ended by starting another. I discovered that the conscience was the only part of a human being that was soluble in alcohol. I lied about my drinking. I lied about everything else—even things that didn't matter. I thought that everyone was watching me.

The company for which I worked told me politely but firmly that, unless I controlled my drinking, we would have to part. I promised to do better and mend my ways. I was drunk within the hour. Two months later I appeared drunk at a meeting and the next day I was on my own.

I promptly went on the wagon, got another good position and stayed sober for a year. Although this new position offered many opportunities, I did not take advantage of them. I'm sure that this was because I found out that being on the wagon was the most miserable of all existences. I was moody and irritable. My mind was never at rest. I imagined all sorts of things. I worried about the past and I could see no hope for the future. On occasions, I attended parties where there was some drinking and good-natured fun. I hated every minute of it because I just could not join in with this fun. I sat morosely by myself, wondering how soon the endless evening would be over. In short, I was just plain sorry for myself. After several evenings like this, I did everything I could to avoid social engagements and felt more lonely than ever before. I had lost the art of being friendly. The people I had liked best irritated me most.

At the end of the year I fell off the wagon, promising myself that I would stop after just a drink or two. Within two weeks I was drinking harder than I ever had before. The only way I knew to drive away remorse was to drink more and more.

After nine months of mental suffering and physical torture, I sat at home one night alone with a bottle beside me. I had been drinking hard all day, but no matter how much I drank the shakes did not even diminish. My mind was clear, but the bottle on which I depended did not do anything for me. My way of life passed before me as on a screen. I saw how I had slipped and how rapidly I was deteriorating. The cure of the bottle, on which I had grown to depend, no longer worked. I broke out in a cold sweat. I was without hope. I could not stop drinking. The ceiling came down. The walls pressed in. The floor came up. I could think of no answer. There seemed no way out. Was it too late?

There just wasn't any use of taking another drink; even that didn't help. Then across my mind came the picture of my drinking friend whom I had met three years before—clear-eyed and sober. Then and there I decided to try A.A. I put the bottle away.

Next morning, I made my first contact with A.A. I was asked some questions, one of which was, "Do you turn to lower companionship and inferior environment while drinking?" Ashamed, I felt as if they had been reading my mail. This, and other questions, convinced me that here were people who understood my problem.

One thing my A.A. friend said to me that morning was, "Today could be the most important day in your life." It was and still is, for nothing but good has come to me through A.A.

After admitting and accepting the fact that I was powerless over alcohol, my first great feeling of relief was that I was no longer alone. I was in a fellowship of people who had the same problem that I had; indeed, most of them had been very much worse off than I.

Having enjoyed good companionship for many years, my loneliness near the end of my drinking had become a real hell to me, but this new fellowship of understanding people gave me new life and new strength. I now realize that an alcoholic cannot get along alone, any more than anyone else can. I, like all men, was a social being who desperately needed fellowship and acceptance. These I found in A.A., where hands were reached out to me. I was not condemned. On the contrary, I was greatly encouraged by these people who spoke my language and, what was so important, offered me hope.

When I became a member of A.A., I immediately went to the president of the company for which I worked and told him about it. His hearty handshake and unmistakable look of approval were all that passed between us. That was enough. I knew I was on my way up again—as long as I remembered to stay away from the first drink.

As sober days passed into sober weeks, I was soon back in the confidence of men who once again respected my judgment in business. I no longer had any fear of interviews with fellow executives because my eyes were clear and my hand was steady. My home life improved and today it is happier than ever before.

Certainly, I still have my ups and downs in my new life without alcohol, but during my years in A.A., I have been and am continually learning to accept the things I cannot change, being given courage to change the things I can, and the wisdom to know the difference.

How has all this happened to me? I have already mentioned how important was this newfound fellowship, but I am sure there is more to it than that alone.

Right from the start of my attending A.A. meetings, I heard various speakers give all credit to a Power greater than themselves. One morning as I was walking to work, from seemingly nowhere at all, there came a thought that there was a possibility that I might never drink again. I have had no desire to drink since that time. It was certainly nothing that I myself could have done that brought this newfound peace. There was only one answer. This Power greater than myself had, as to so many others, restored me to sanity.

Finally, let me say that I am sure that I could not have in the past seven years, nor can I in the future enjoy my happy and contented sobriety unless I try to share it with others. Therefore, my earnest hope in relating my experience here is that it will help someone, anyone with a drinking problem, but particularly that person who may still be hanging on to his job or business, or may still be holding his home together.

It has often occurred to me that, if I had been a baseball player and had lost an arm, I would soon have reconciled myself to the fact that I could no longer play baseball. Similarly, with the great help of the fellowship, I have reconciled myself to the fact that I can no longer handle alcohol, even to the extent of taking a single drink.

A.A. has given me a happy and contented way of living, and I am very deeply grateful to the founders and early members of A.A. who plotted the course and who kept the faith.

NEW VISION
FOR A SCULPTOR

His conscience hurt him as much as his drinking.
But that was years ago.

I think that life, when I was growing up, was the most wonderful life that any kid ever had. My parents were very successful and every new luxury and every new beauty that came into the house was keenly appreciated by all of us. We didn't have things thrown at us. They came little by little.

My parents were both Jews and, in my family life, we were always keenly alive to the beauty of religion, although we were not orthodox. I always saw God as a wonderful force that was a great deal like my father, only magnified to the Nth degree. I once asked my grandfather, when I was a little boy, what God was like. He asked me what my dad was like. I went into superlatives about dad because I really loved him so much. He was such a friendly, wonderful father, and so my grandfather said, "Well, your father is the head of your family. God is the head of the entire human family and of the whole universe. But what makes him 'Dear God' is that you can speak to him just as you would talk to your own dad. He's not only a universal father, but an individual father too." So I'd always had that wonderful comparison of my own father with God.

When they found out that I could create sculpture at a very early age, it made both my parents very happy; my two older brothers were not artists, but they were good students. I was a very bad student and very much of an artist. Instead of resenting that, they encouraged my art. So my childhood was really art and music, and I got along at school, usually, by leaving the day before examinations or getting measles or something else like that and being put in the next grade for trial. The teacher of the grade that I left would never take me back under any circumstances.

I was ecstatically happy. My brothers and their friends lived on horses as I did from six years old on. We did everything, all of our playing and wild games, on horseback. This was up to World War I. I was about nineteen years old then. I don't think I had any fears at all up to that time.

We were a very close family. Everything was very vital, anything that happened to one happened to another. When war broke out all I could hear in my heart was the echoes of what father and mother had told me so often; how grateful I should be to the United States. Both my grandfathers had come over from the other side, one from Bohemia and one from Prussia, because at that time there was persecution in those countries, and they wanted to live and be a part of the "land of the free." They both had magnificent lives and were able to pull themselves up and live happily and die in luxury. I was very grateful to the United States for that.

I loved my grandparents very dearly and I had watched my father's great financial success. So I felt that I didn't want either of my two brothers to go to war. They were both married, but certainly one of the family should show what we thought and felt about the United States. So I told my folks that I was going to join the Army and that scared them to death, but after a while they heard that a nearby hospital was forming a unit and I think my mother had a picture of my going to war with my personal family doctor. Nothing could be more luxurious! So, they gave their consent that I should join the unit, never realizing that you could transfer when you got to the other side.

I was a terrible soldier as far as drilling was concerned, but I had been studying anatomy and dissecting for my art work, so a hospital was sort of second nature to me. I got along very well in that part of the Army, very well indeed.

I went through World War I without actually getting drunk. I did learn to drink heavily in France, but it didn't do anything for me or to me. I mean to say I didn't drink for relief or escape, and I was always flattered that I could out-drink almost anybody and take them home. Many of the patients insisted that when they got well they were going to take me down and get me drunk in appreciation. It was usually a hike of two and one-half kilometers to get the patient back to the hospital! These were walking wounded.

I had one bad experience in which a truck that I was in was blown up, and I woke up in Vichy a couple of days later in a bathtub. I thought I was in heaven. The whole room was full of steam. An enormous sergeant came through the steam and said, "Don't move, young fellow." I said, "Where am I?" He told me. I started to upbraid him, "Why shouldn't I move?" He said, "Don't move. That's all." I did, and found it was very painful. I had an injury to my spine. When it was time to get me out of the bathtub that enormous guy just picked me up as though I were a baby and put me on a stretcher. That was about three days before the Armistice.

On Armistice Day everyone pushed all the hospital beds onto the street and had a grand parade of them. Everybody hugged and kissed us and gave us candy and drinks, and the sergeant came along with a glass and said, "The doctor says you're to finish this right away." I turned it upside down and believe me the bed swam from then on. It didn't last very long because as soon as I got something to eat I got over that. But I think that was my very first feeling of being dizzy or drunk.

When I got back from World War I, there didn't seem to be any alcoholic problem at all. I could drink or not drink, but when I did I liked to out-drink other people. This stupid desire to out-drink people, and then drinking more and more myself, was the first sign of my alcoholism.

I married in 1920. In 1928, my wife and I returned to Paris with two children, and I'd get insomnia and get up and go to the dining room and take a glass of brandy and that would put me back to sleep. I thought people took brandy to go to sleep.

Meanwhile, back in this country, I began to notice the family got worried when I was drinking and I didn't like to see them worried. I thought, if it worries them so much, well, I'd drink over at the studio and take my friends over there. Because, by that time, I'd worked up a good, artistic reputation and the critics were particularly kind to me. I had loads and loads of work, all that I could take care of, and I liked work. I always had a long day. To me, sunrise is the most gorgeous time of the day and the most spiritual, and I love to say my prayers and watch the sunrise at the same time. I am grateful for the new day and for the beauty of it.

This drinking over at the studio and then finally at barrooms—anything so as not to drink at the house—became progressively worse. This was when my "guilt complex" started, with this secret drinking. I went to Europe several times and the cycle seemed to be broken each time because I was never drunk over there, except when we lived in Paris after I was actively alcoholic. I was only actually drunk there twice that I know of.

The drinking got heavier and heavier and the compulsion got heavier and heavier. I could still come home without staggering and I was very proud of that. But I was very unhappy too because I was making the folks at home unhappy, and then my legs began to get unsteady and they could see by my bloodshot eyes that I'd been drinking on the sly, and then guilt really started in. And with the guilt there started fears and I was very unhappy, so I decided that I would quit—and then I found that I couldn't quit. This one didn't count. This one was medicine. By that time I was in my thirties. That's just about the time I did such crazy things. I'd sneak away from the house on my motorcycle because I thought I could be wilder and have a grander time on a motorcycle than I could in a car because a car had four wheels and, incidentally, a motorcycle could go faster. But I found that was very lonely, so I got a sidecar and took a chauffeur. Very often when I'd go out with the chauffeur, he would drive out and I would have to drive him home because he didn't have my capacity.

My wife always had faith that this was only a sickness, but she did worry. She knew nothing about A.A.

and I knew nothing of it. But, she always realized that this was not her husband, that something had distressed him and that something had to be understood, although I was arrogant and rotten.

After father died in 1934, I drank for oblivion. That was a terrible shock. In my insecurity I thought that all the security in the world had gone with him.

The next few years were really terrible. So many things happened and the net was closing in. One of the most terrible things was that in my guilt I lost God. That was the big thing. I had no right to pray to God. I had no right to go into the temple or church. When we lived in Rome I used to go into one of the cathedrals every night on my way home from work and, to me, a house of God was a house of God and was beautiful and dedicated to His worship. Now I was robbed of God, because I was so ashamed, and so I had no help and I didn't know how to quit. It was very terrible.

We had a dear friend up near us in Westchester by the name of Gabrielle. She had a wash-woman whose son was a cripple. He had created some really beautiful works of art. She asked me if I would go and see his work and help him. I couldn't refuse Gabrielle anything, and I promised her that I would go, and that was really the beginning of the end of my alcoholic experience. I gathered together the most beautiful books of pictures from the Vatican. Like a big shot alcoholic I did everything in style! I got gorgeous new art materials and fine new paper. I couldn't get the train at my own station—that was impossible! I had to go down the line and beat the train by twenty minutes and spend those twenty minutes in a barroom. That held me till I got to 125th Street and the bars were open.

(Prohibition had been repealed while I was drinking and getting up the steam to go and visit this poor cripple.) So I went to a bar on 7th Avenue and when I got there the welcome was warmer than any welcome I ever received in my life; there were a lot of bar-flies around, and everybody was treating everybody, and I was gulping them down as fast I could. Finally, when I found myself with sixteen drinks in front of me, still to be taken, and this big package of pictures, I hurried up and finished the sixteen drinks and told the men that I would be back later, that I had to deliver this bundle. Then I began a most peculiar trek down 7th Avenue until I reached where I was going. I stumbled and staggered and fell in area-ways and I became absolutely filthy. I can see to this day the colored people grabbing their children so that I didn't throw them into the gutter or area-way or knock a baby carriage under a truck. It was almost like a musical comedy when the hero comes downstage and everybody gives way before him.

I finally reached my destination and, to my horror, found that it was on the fifth floor of a walk-up tenement house. How I made the five flights I really don't know. I was just about to put my hand on the door knob when I realized what a drunken, awful mess of humanity I was. I became thoroughly frightened and instinctively I asked God, "Please help me not to bring further suffering to this family. It's bad enough what they have to go through, but if anything happens to me there, or if I misbehave, think how terrible it would be! Please, please, help me get through these few minutes." Having said the prayer, I straightened myself up and licked my handkerchief and washed my face with it, and slicked back my hair. Then I took off my overcoat and shook it and tried to make myself presentable as best I could, and rang the doorbell. The boy's mother was a sweet, little colored lady in stiff, starched white, absolutely immaculate. The place too was immaculate and the sun was streaming in. I could see the crippled boy in the chair, looking up and watching for me as though I were some great person. I don't know how I did it, but I stayed there two and a half hours. I looked at all of his portfolios and work and showed him how to use the new art material. I told him about the originals of all the pictures in the book and left him, thank God, very happy. When I got out the reaction set in and I took a taxi down to what used to be a speakeasy and was then wide open, and what happened from then on for the next ten days I don't know very much about.

I was in the country and in bed, and the bottle was under the pillow and my hand was firmly around the neck of it. Every time I came to I took another swig and got drunk all over again. During this drunk I had many flashbacks, and I remembered strange things. For instance, I'd seen a play years before called "The Dybbuk," down at the Neighborhood Playhouse. It opened with two rabbis in a sub-sub cellar, talking about another rabbi and they said, "His words have always been so great. From the highest heights to the deepest depths the soul may plunge, but, in itself, the plunge contains the resurrection." Those words just came to me. I thought, how much further and how much lower can I go? I'm at the bottom; I've taken the plunge. Suddenly I remembered that on the day I had visited my young colored friend I had prayed before I rang the doorbell, and that God had answered my prayer. I knew that the barrier to prayer was broken, and I turned around in bed and prayed as I had never prayed before. I prayed for instruction and knowledge, not to do something *for* me, because I didn't deserve it, but to do something *to* me, and to show me the right way so that I could do something for myself. I realized at that moment that alcohol was the basis of all my trouble, that all the rest was fantasy; nothing had happened, yet everything was happening all the time. Nothing was real. I bawled like a baby, as all drunks do, and I cried myself to sleep.

I awakened at dawn, before sunrise even, but it was dawn and very beautiful, and for the first time in years I awakened without a hangover. I didn't have the dry heaves. The bed wasn't full of sweat and all the other horrible things that went with the usual early morning awakening. I had a feeling that I had had a bath in a clean stream, mental, moral, physical and spiritual. All of a sudden I was clean. And, as I lay there in bed trying to understand this feeling, a thought came to me that was foreign to any thoughts I had ever had because of its simplicity, and that thought kept flashing on and off like a neon sign repeating itself, "You're not going to have your last drink. You have had it!" Then, as the sun actually began to rise, the thing dawned on me. The rat race was over and I was ecstatically happy. I went in the next room because I didn't want to disturb my wife. I said so many prayers of thanksgiving that they were all jumbled up. It was the most wonderful feeling because I had read the handwriting on the wall. In my alcoholic fantasy, I had wanted to have a tremendous party, a drunk to end all drunks. I was going to out-Hollywood Hollywood, and I could see myself in the end, up on the model's stand finishing it all up with a

Royal Canadian quart and falling back in the arms of some other drunk. That would have been it! But this was simple, beautiful and real, "I've had my last drink." The release was there.

I was not quite forty at the time, 1937, three years after father died. It was in the late spring around Decoration Day, because I had my last drink on Decoration Day.

My doctor put me in the hospital because he wanted me to get over my nervous period. He was very happy that I had stopped drinking, and he put me there in order to help me help myself. He started giving me certain drugs to stop me from shaking, among which was one that was jam full of bromides. I left the hospital very happily after just a couple of days, but about a week later I began staggering and began driving my car so far up on the right-hand side that I was practically in the gutter and sometimes on the sidewalk. When I tried walking around the room I'd bump into everything on the right-hand side, and then I couldn't walk at all. They finally got a male nurse and put me to bed and a doctor came up from New York, and said, "Oh, yes, I know all about Fred. I've seen them go like that before. There's nothing you can do about it." That didn't satisfy my wife, thank God. That was the doctor that I had recommended, a very nice doctor. Every time I'd tell him about my drinking problem, he helped me drink some cocktails with him and told me to drink as he did. My wife got a really good doctor from New York, just in the nick of time. He suggested my going to a neurological institute that night with him. The minute I got into the hospital the horrors started. They took blood tests at once. By that time I was clear of alcohol, but I was jammed full of bromides. Bromide poisoning had started, and caused a swelling of the brain. I went from bad to worse there, but they started the therapy at once with tons and tons of salt injections, salt water baths and drinking salt. I had to drink seven and a half pitchers of salt water ever day. I went into the horrors, which lasted for a whole month. I was in a strait-jacket all the time, in the bathtub and even in the padded cell. I came out of it finally within a month, with the loss of some thirty-five or forty pounds. I was a skeleton when I came out. The horrors were awful, but that never seemed to matter much because I blamed them on the bromides. I felt it was none of my doing. But alcohol was.

I stayed sober for the next ten years. I think I use that word inadvisably. I should say I stayed dry for the next ten years. I wasn't a nice person. There were certain dividends which were tremendous. My family was very happy believing I was sober. They took almost anything from me, though I was just as emotionally high at times as when I was drinking. But they were so glad I wasn't drinking that they stood for anything. They were terrible years.

It was during World War II, and we had lost two of our nephews. There was death, death in the family, one after the other as the youngsters went. Too, it always seemed to take a toll of two or three of the older members of the family at the same time. They were pretty horrible years, and yet I didn't drink. I didn't drink because I never wanted to break the wonderful covenant that I felt I had made, having gotten a release when I prayed to God for it.

After things were adjusted after World War II, mother died. She died after seeing me sober, or dry, for eight years. She died very happy on account of that. Then old John Barleycorn started to talk to me and say, "Well, you've been dry for ten years now. Isn't that enough?" The severe temptation came when my thinking started telling me that after ten years of not drinking I could certainly drink like a normal human being.

So I planned that on Decoration Day my wife and I would try a bottle of champagne, and that if I stayed sober I could drink with her normally like anybody else, and that would have made her happy too.

A week or ten days before Decoration Day, I was having gasoline put into my car, and a very dear friend who had gone to school with me and who had a severe alcoholic problem of his own—he was an A.A., whatever that was—came up to me and instead of just putting the gasoline in and saying, "Good Morning, how many gallons of gasoline?," which was his usual daily greeting, he said, "Hello, Fred, how's your alcoholic problem?" I laughed. I said, "I haven't any alcoholic problem. In fact, on Decoration Day my wife and I are going to try a bottle of champagne." He got as white as a sheet, and put his hand on my arm and said, "Look, before you take that first drink will you please come to an A.A. meeting? There's one in town tonight and I'll call for you." I just had to say "Yes," and that was ten days before I was going to drink. That man had been wanting to talk to me for ten years about my drinking and never had the courage to mention it. That was about May 20, 1947.

I went to that meeting with my tongue in my cheek. I told my wife I was a joiner again. I said I had to do it, but it was no place for a lady. I'd tell her about it later. I went up there and found so many wonderful people who wouldn't normally associate with me and, altogether, such a smiling, happy, delightful group of people that I couldn't believe my eyes and still had to be convinced. The leader was a splendid man, a college man, very quiet, who started the meeting by saying, "Alcoholism is an incurable, progressive disease. Whether you are dry one year, ten years or fifty years, you're still one drink away from a drunk." Then he pulled out his pipe. The floor seemed to give way under me, but immediately it steadied because my reaction was, "Thank God I didn't take that first drink! Thank God I came here!" And I realized at last that, after all these years, before I took that drink, I was going to be told the truth and then make the right choice for myself. The whole experience was so beautiful that I was thrilled by it, and a thing mother had said years before when I had come home drunk and she had seen me, came to my mind. The only time that she ever broke down and wept was that night. She said, "This must be somehow good. This cannot be all negative. Some good must come out of it." Mother had been dead two years.

Toward the end of my first A.A. evening, I heard about the Twelfth Step where, as an alcoholic and having gone through the experience, I might be able to reach some other poor alcoholic where doctors, medicine, science and religion by themselves, had failed. Immediately, "That's somehow good," came to my ear. Thank God I have been able to turn it into "Somehow good."

That's my story.

JOE'S WOES

These were only beginning when he hit Bellevue for the thirty-fifth time. He still had the State Hospital ahead of him; and even after A.A., a heartbreaking test of his new-found faith.

I never drank in high school or college, because I never *went* to high school or college. I've never been to Knickerbocker Hospital, I've never been to Grasslands, I've never been to Towns, that swanky place on Central Park West. But I've been to Bellevue's alcoholic ward thirty-five times. That should qualify me, because they don't take you in the Bellevue alcoholic ward for sinus trouble.

I made a few jails, maybe sixty-five or seventy-five times in my drinking. I made my first trip to Bellevue at the age of seventeen. I was called an alcoholic when I was eighteen or nineteen, but I just couldn't believe it. I didn't know what an alcoholic meant. I had trouble with alcohol, but at that age I wasn't bothering anybody. I was single. I just went on about my business, and I made up my mind. "Well, I'll lick this thing my way. Someday I'll be able to stop."

I made up my mind I was going to stop drinking when I got married. In 1926 I met the right girl, and we got married. I thought it would be as easy as the snap of a finger to stop drinking. Well, I didn't stop because I couldn't stop. I couldn't leave it alone. I just went on, but now it went into tragedy drinking, because I had brought three children into the world and it went from bad to worse. It was a matter of hospitals and jails and that merry-go-round we all go through.

My wife stood this for about eleven years. Then she got a resentment—she was going to leave me! She had tried to leave me before many times, but it was only to try to get me to sober up. But this time I got home one night in the early evening, and everything was crated ready to go to storage. She was going her way with the three children. I was left to go my way with the bottle.

My sister heard about this, and she came running over to the house and says to my wife, "Now wait a minute, before you do a tragic thing like this and leave my brother! Do you realize he is a sick man?" Boy, I thought that this was out of this world—such kind words as "a sick man"! You ought to hear what my family called me before that! My sister says, "Let me stand the expense of taking my brother to the Medical Center to interview one of the best psychiatrists."

I thought I was real ripe for a psychiatrist, because I was beginning to do a lot of things I didn't want to do. I thought I was really going out of my mind. I had gotten to the stage where I'd get up in the morning, and I'd look in the mirror, and then I'd start talking to myself, and I'd say, "For cripe's sake, will you stand still long enough till I shave?"

And then I got to the stage where I'm walking the streets of New York, and my eyes go up to an ad on a great big billboard. The ad read, "Old Dutch Cleanser." Now that's an everyday ad, but on this can of Old Dutch Cleanser there happened to be an old woman with a club. Next thing you know, she got off the sign and chased me into the 51st Street police station. I ran in there for help. She was right behind me. I went up to the lieutenant's desk and said, "Help me, she's out there!" He said, "*Who's* out there?" I start raving, "There she is with the club! She's followed me from 54th Street!" He looked me over and says, "Oh, *I* see what you mean, Mac." He hollers for Patrolman Murphy, and Murphy comes out, and this lieutenant says, "Take that bum to Bellevue!" So away I go.

So later on when my sister mentioned the Medical Center and a psychiatrist I thought I had no choice. Next day we walk into the Medical Center and I'm perfectly sober, and we see a certain doctor there. I had made my mind up I would do anything in the world that this man says. So we get appointed to Dr. So-and-so, office so-and-so. We walk in, and there's a little psychiatrist sitting down at his desk. He gets up, and he turns out to be a little squirt about that high. Right away my mind changes! I says to myself, "I'm bigger than this guy." I kept staring at him. I didn't think he knew more than I did. I was bigger than he was. I came to the conclusion in the end, "One good drink would kill that guy!"

He started asking me a lot of questions. He says, "Why do you drink?" My sister is paying fifty dollars for that question! "Why do you drink!" Well, I had interviewed psychiatrists before, and I started asking *him* a lot of questions. He couldn't get to first base with me because I wasn't cooperating. Finally he threw me out of the office and called my wife and sister in and talked to them about an hour. The conclusion was that he suggested that I go to Bellevue! What did Bellevue have for me after being there over twenty-five times?

But I made up my mind to do anything that man

suggested. So the next day we walk into Bellevue, and I shocked the doctor that was sitting at the admittance office. He had seen me come in on a stretcher; he had seen me come in on crutches; he had seen me come in with a cop under each arm; and when he saw me walk in with two ladies, he was shocked.

He says, "I don't get this. What is this?" He thought I was really nuts, I guess. "Doctor," I says, "I am having a little trouble with alcohol." I told him about this bird up in the Medical Center that sent me down here to commit myself to a State institution. He says, "You really want to go through with this?" I says, "Yes. I really want to get straight and I think this is going to help me." He says, "Well, all right, I'll draw out a voluntary commitment. You sign it and you're in!"

He didn't tell me *where* I was in! Ten days later I get on the bus and the first thing I know I'm up in the booby-hatch. Well, I resented that because I thought I was going to one of these drying-out places. I didn't know I was going up there with a lot of nuts.

A few days later another bus came up from Bellevue, and on this bus there happened to be two boys that had made several trips to Bellevue. One of those boys had been in here and knew the ropes. He says, "Don't worry about this place; this ain't the worst place in the world." Well, he was right, because ten days later the three of us were drunk right up there in the booby-hatch!

I left three children and a wife on the outside, absolutely penniless. One of the children, a boy ten years old, wrote me a letter to try and encourage me. He thought I was up there getting shots in the arm and different medicines and that when I came out I would never take another drink. Well, he wrote me a letter, and he says, "Don't worry, dad. Do anything the doctors tell you, no matter how long they keep you there. I hope you come out a dad like my friends have." He could bring boys, his friends, up to the house now, and he couldn't do that while I was drinking because I didn't want anybody around me. I was one of those nasty drunks. He went on in this letter. "Don't worry about the house, because I went into business." His business was that he made himself a shoe-shine box and went out and shined shoes—while I'm up in this hospital drinking!

On one of her visits my wife left me a dollar. I thought it was five dollars. I stuck it in my pocket, and when she left I took it out and saw it was a dollar, and I says, "Why, that cheap so-and-so! What am I going to do here with one dollar for the next two weeks?" Two days later one of the head doctors called me into his office and says, "Do you know your wife had to borrow money to get back to New York, that she left you her last dollar in the world?" He pointed out that my children didn't have the price of a glass of milk the next morning. That made me feel pretty cheap. I says to myself, "*I'm* the cheap so-and-so." I told this doctor, "I'm going to do something about this." He says, "Why don't you sign yourself out—you're able to do that—and go out and get yourself a job, and cut out all this monkey business? Take care of your family. You got a fine little family there. Go out and take care of them." And I swore to God in front of that man that day that I would do that. I swore, "I'll never take another drink as long as I live!"

At the time, I meant it. I did sign myself out, and I did get a job, and for two weeks I did not take a drink.

Two weeks is a pretty long period with me. I happened to get paid that first two weeks' pay with a check. I didn't know where to go and cash that check except in a saloon. Nobody knew me, nobody would trust me, only these bartenders. But I knew I couldn't get away with going in there and buying one drink. I says to myself, "So help me God, I won't have any more than three drinks. I'll cash this check and I'll bring this money home." I had my three drinks, cashed the check, picked up the change, and then the bartender says, "Will you have one on the house?" So I did. Well, after that I don't have to tell you what happened. I never got home with a nickel of that money.

I lost my job, but it was easy at the time and I got another one. Then another. And then it was one job after another, until I couldn't beg, borrow or steal any more. Then I think I went as low as a man will ever go. When I couldn't get a job anymore, and that kid was still out shining shoes, I used to go around to where he was shining shoes and tell that kid that his mother had sent me over to get the money that he'd made. That kid knew all the time that I wasn't going to bring that money home, but he never refused me. He always gave me all the change he had. And I went out and drank it.

The day came when I finally wound up in Bellevue again. I was in the alcoholic ward and I was pretty sick going in there. One of the doctors ordered a big dose of paraldehyde for me to knock me out. An hour and a half later, three men were trying to wake me up. One of them was the night attendant of the hospital, one was a policeman in uniform, and one was a plain clothes man. The law had been looking for me for four or five days, but they finally caught up with me in

Bellevue. It was for something I had done in the black-out that I didn't know anything about. They took me out of the alcoholic ward and took me to the Bellevue prison ward, where I spent quite a few months.

I was up against a very serious charge. I was supposed to go to Sing Sing for between seven and a half and fifteen years for it. But somehow or other, I don't know how it happened—maybe it was through the prayers of my wife, or maybe help by my family, or somehow or other—when I was brought up on trial I was sentenced to the State Hospital again instead of Sing Sing. This was in late 1938 when I got back up there. This time I wasn't on my own. I was there with the sentence of three judges.

Early in 1939, when the A.A. book was fresh off the press, I was called into the doctor's office, the chief doctor of the State Hospital. One of the founders of A.A. was there with five other men from A.A., trying to get A.A. into the hospital. The way A.A. was put to me, this doctor says to me, "The medical profession has nothing for you. The clergy has nothing for you. There's nobody in God's world can help you. You're a chronic alcoholic, period!" Then he says, "Maybe these men and this book can help you."

I read the book. In the meantime they had meetings in South Orange, New Jersey. There used to be a group from South Orange that would come up to the hospital and take some of the boys down to a meeting and bring them back. I wanted to know what was going on at these meetings. I got one of the boys that was there and I says, "What are these meetings all about?" He says, "It's a bunch of people that get up there and swap stories. They talk to each other and you talk to them. They're all a bunch of ex-drunks. And they're all happy looking. They all have a lot of fun, they're all dressed up, they have a collar and tie. Some are working and some are not, but they're all happy." He says, "Why don't you ask the doctor to let you come down there sometime? You ought to see the spread these people put out after the meeting—chicken sandwiches and . . ." Oh, he laid out a beautiful picture for me! "Home-made cakes" . . . something you weren't getting at the hospital! I says, "Gee, that looks pretty good."

I never been to a meeting before in all my life where there was a bunch of alcoholics where nobody didn't have a bottle! So I asked the doctor, and he let me go down to the meeting. I figured, "Well, I'll go down there, I'll get a coupla drinks and I'll beat it, and phooey to A.A. and everything else!" I went down there this first time, and I was introduced to this happy looking bunch of people. They put me in my class with real two-fisted drinkers. They sat me in a corner talking to these guys. I couldn't get away from them. In the meantime, I'm looking for live wires. Anybody going down towards the water section. I look him over. Well, out of a clear sky there's four rough looking guys over there, and all at once they decide to go down to the water section. Right away I says, "Oops, well, excuse me—I gotta go." And I walked in there figuring as soon as these guys get in there, one of the four is going to pull out a bottle. But I was stunned—I was surprised—no bottle! I says, "What is the matter with these guys?"

I went to A.A. meetings for about seven months and I lost the idea of drink. I didn't think of it any more. I was amazed when I was called into the doctor's office and told that I was going out on parole. I got a year's parole, and on my parole card was "In the custody of your wife and A.A."

My wife used to come to every A.A. meeting with me, but one particular night we got company, and my wife says, "What are we going to do?" I says, "Look, you tend to the company. I wouldn't miss that meeting for the world. It means too much to me."

I went to the meeting that night, and it was a swell meeting until the last speaker got up. This fella says, "As long as you are an alcoholic, you'll never be able to take another drink as long as you live!" Oooh, that was rough! A little later on in the same talk, he says, "And don't forget—not even a glass of beer!" and he pointed his finger right at me sitting in the back. That was it! I says, "Why that bunch of Bible-backed-bums, where do they get that stuff?"

That's one meeting I didn't stay for the Lord's Prayer. The speaker got through and sat down and everybody applauded and I said, "Phooey!" and went out of the place. I got over to Lexington Avenue and found a saloon. I went in there and I says, "Gimme a glass of beer." I drank it and walked right out of the place. I stood under a lamp post on the corner there at 59th and Lexington. I stood there maybe fifteen or twenty minutes. I was waiting for something to happen because I had a glass of beer. I thought maybe twenty minutes after you have this beer you get some chemical change in you. Maybe you explode. I didn't know what would happen.

Well, I didn't explode. I didn't do anything. So I jump on the subway up to the Bronx, and when I get off at the subway station instead of going home I automatically walk into a saloon and I have another beer and another beer and another. When the man came up with that seventh beer, I says, "Wait a minute, make that a double whiskey." Well, he did. And to make a long story short, what do you think happened to me? I landed back in the State Hospital—that's what!

Don't get me wrong. I didn't wind up in there that night or the next week or the next month. It took me three months, but it was that one glass of beer that started the merry-go-round going.

I asked myself, "Now what am I doing up here again?" In my heart and soul I knew that A.A. had something. I wanted to see where I had made my mistake, and I asked the doctor to please give me that book again to read. My number one mistake was I wasn't honest with myself or with anybody in the world. And I knew A.A. didn't fail me. I failed A.A.

So how do I get honest? I cleaned up. I saw a priest there at the hospital, and I really came clean for the first time in my life. I really worked with A.A. up there in the hospital.

Well, I got out and tried to get a job, but I couldn't. They had opened an A.A. clubhouse on 24th Street, so I used to go out in the morning and look for a job. Then I went down to the Club and helped scrub floors. I helped to do everything. I stayed nights for the meeting and I went home when the place closed. That's the way I spent my time.

This went on for about eleven months, and then my wife had got into the family way again for her fourth childbirth. She was told after her third child that she wouldn't be able to have a fourth. But she saw that it meant the world to the children. They were happy, I was happy, she was happy, and I was in A.A. in full swing and getting along fine. So she just ignored the doctor's orders and went through with it. I took my wife to the hospital one night, and the following afternoon I go to visit her. And before I could see her I had to go see the doctor. He says, "Joe, how do you feel?" I says, "I feel pretty good, doctor." He says, "Sit down," and then he says, "How do you feel now?" I says, "I *still* feel pretty good. What are you driving at?" He was trying to tell me my wife was almost ready for delivery, and that they had done everything they could, but that she was in danger. "I'm sure you're doing all you can. What can I do?" I ask the doctor. He says, "Well, your record shows you're a Catholic, so you know how to pray."

I went home, and there was my mother and my mother-in-law, two old ladies waiting for news from the hospital. I never let on what they had told me at the hospital, but my mother-in-law started digging, if you know what I mean. Well, I blew my top. I said, "Nuts to it." The next thing I know I'm down in the corner saloon. I got a dollar bill on the bar and I'm ready to order a drink. But A.A. stepped right into this picture, and I says, "Now what am I doing here at a time like this?" I heard in A.A. when you're in trouble, try a little prayer. Well, I was in a lot of trouble and I tried a prayer. When the bartender got tired of waiting for me to order, he hollered at me. "Hey, Mac!" he says, "Didja make up your mind? What're you havin'?" I ordered a ginger-ale and a lot of ice. That's how my prayer was answered.

I went down to the Clubhouse at 24th Street. Some of the boys there talked me out of the idea of a drink. I stayed for the meeting that night and went home and went to sleep.

About one o'clock in the morning I got a telegram from the hospital. I was afraid to open it. I thought it was the last telegram I would ever get about my wife. I paced the living room floor for about half an hour, like a prisoner in his cell, with that telegram in my hand. I was still afraid to open it. I finally got down on my knees and asked God Almighty, I says, "Gimme the courage to open this thing." Then I opened the telegram. My wife had given birth to a girl and everything was all right. Where would I have been, or where would she have been, if I had blown my top and taken a drink at a point like that? I thank God Almighty that I didn't.

It took me seventeen months before I got a job. I kept sober, using what I learned in A.A. Then I got a job that I didn't like very much, and it was keeping me away from A.A. I made up my mind, "If nothing happens within this week, nuts to A.A.!" I planned it out—another drunk for myself. I gave myself a week, see? I just didn't take that drink; I allowed myself a week.

Before that week was up, I go home one night and out of a clear sky there's two old bosses of mine sitting down on the sofa waiting for me. They were two brothers I had worked for a long time before, fellas who swore they'd never have anything to do with me any more. I'm bringing this out because I want you to know that good news travels in A.A. They heard I was in A.A. and doing all right, back with my family and everything, and they came and asked me to go to work for them. Well, I did go to work for them, and I'm on that job till this very day.

Now then, I'm going back about six years. Something happened again. That boy of mine that was shining shoes at the age of ten, in the meantime he had grown up to be a six-foot-one inch fella. And almost to the day of his birthday, the sixteenth birthday, I lost that boy in a trolley car accident only two blocks away from my house. I was in Philadelphia when it happened, and they called me up and drove me in from Philadelphia to see my boy. He regained consciousness once in the thirteen hours I was there. He looked up at me and says, "Dad, what happened to me?" I says, "Well, son, you just keep your chin up. You'll be all right." The doctors had told me the boy was going to pull through. He was strong and he was fighting.

Well, the kid didn't make it. He was trying to tell me in that last handshake that he'd lost his battle. He was trying to tell me, "I'm losing this battle, dad, but don't let this throw you." That's what he was trying to put across to me. I realize that now. But in spite of all that, when they took that kid away from me, I made up my mind I was going on a suicide drunk. I figured I would go home first and take care of the funeral arrangements. Then I would lock myself in some hotel and drink myself to death. If liquor didn't kill me, I was going to jump out the window.

Before I could do this I get a telephone call. It's an A.A. member in Ohio. How that news traveled to Ohio in thirty-five minutes I don't know till this day. This fella says, "I just heard what happened to you. The reason I'm calling you is I know what's running through your mind. But I hope you don't. I hope you don't take that drink. Nobody in the world or nobody in A.A. can condemn you for it. But don't forget, there's a couple hundred members here, and we all got our fingers crossed; we're all praying for you."

When he got off the wire, somebody else was calling me, somebody from Connecticut. I was so busy answering calls that I just couldn't get out. While I was still answering calls, one of my A.A. friends walked in. He stayed with me that night, so I didn't have a chance to get out. This fella and I sat in the kitchen all night, smoking cigarettes and drinking coffee.

The next morning the undertaker came up to take me to the hospital morgue to identify my son. This A.A. fella came with me. The undertaker was an A.A. too. Well, when that slab was pulled out for me to identify my son's body, if I didn't have A.A. on my right and A.A. on my left I wouldn't be alive today. I'd be in the same grave with that kid.

So you can see that my length of sobriety wasn't handed to me on a silver platter. If things are going to happen, they're going to happen. But I'm in A.A. and sober for eleven years now. I had my last drink of alcohol eleven years and seven months ago. Thanks to the good people of A.A., and last but not least, by the Grace of God.

And if I can do it, so can you!

THERE'S NOTHING THE MATTER WITH ME!

That's what the man said as he hocked his shoes for the price of two bottles of Sneaky Pete. He drank bayzo, canned heat, and shoe polish. He did a phony routine in A.A. for a while. And then he got hold of the real thing.

I never drank because I liked the flavor, but I did like the effect it produced. And one or two little drinks on a Saturday night soon blossomed into three or four. A little bit at a time, I discovered that I enjoyed the stuff. It did things for me that nothing else could do.

I happen to be in the furniture business, and a more miserable business was never invented. In the furniture business you must have a little drink to celebrate an excellent sale. Also you must have a little drink to drown your sorrows when there are no sales. Hah!

First I drank in celebration and in depression, and then I drank all the time. The little three-quarters of an ounce developed into a big fifth. That was during Prohibition, and we had flasks that were about *that* long, and I didn't carry a little bit at a time, I carried it all at once, and it hit me right in the shoulder blades. You could always tell who had the flask by the way he walked around. I liked that! I liked it because they had to come to me to get a drink.

From the little bit of drinking that we'd do on Saturdays and weekends, it went into a long, steady grind of drinking all the time. And little by little I developed a persecution complex. It seemed that everyone was after me. My business associates said I drank too much. I was married to a very charming girl, and she expected me to bring home money on payday. All that silly stuff. I belonged to a golf club over in Jersey in those days, and I didn't play much golf, but I spent a lot of time drinking the liquor. It got so bad that whenever I went into the nineteenth hole for a drink, everybody would move down the other way. Finally they asked me to resign. It seemed I didn't pay my tabs on the first of the month. A miserable bunch of people!

So, a little bit at a time, it began to filter through that I was no longer wanted. I felt very sorry for myself. I knew I was a wonderful fellow. While shaving in the morning, I would look in the mirror and say, "Aaaa, Bill, you're a doll!" Now that's a poor way to go through life, whether you're an alcoholic or not!

So then I decided that I would try will power. All you have to do to stop drinking is precisely that— stop! Well, I didn't drink Tuesday, and I didn't drink Wednesday, and I didn't drink Thursday, and I said to myself, "There's nothing to this!" So I went out Friday and got drunk.

About this time a bartender friend of mine told me about that little drink in the morning. He was a lovely fellow! He gave me this prescription: You take a jigger of gin, the white of an egg, and a dash of orange bitters. Can you picture this trembling drunk pouring out the white of an egg? For a few mornings I would go down to the bar and he'd make this concoction for me and it was wonderful. But pretty soon I dispensed with the egg. I didn't have the bitters handy and there were no small glasses, so I drank the gin right out of the bottle.

My years of flight started from that point. I sold my business, loaded my car with whiskey, and away I went. I didn't stop at five hundred miles. I went out to Seattle. I couldn't go any further because that's the end of the line. I went into business out there, and in twenty months I was bankrupt. I felt awful sorry for myself, because now I'd entered into the "sick" stage. I would get so sick that when I had to get a room in a hotel I'd always get twin beds, one to sleep in and one to be sick in.

It took me nine months to get from Seattle back to New Jersey. I went the long way, by way of San Diego. When I got back I had fifty dollars, a beat-up Oldsmobile, and no whiskey. I felt very sorry for myself. I'd been robbed, lied to and cheated. And, I told myself, it was all their fault!

I wake up one morning and the Oldsmobile is gone and so is the fifty dollars, and I'm standing in the middle of my wardrobe. I have a pair of dungarees with the fanny out of them, a blue shirt, a pair of shoes and no socks. I'm sitting on the end of this bench down in Lincoln Park, and another bum comes along and he says, "Hello, Slim! Hey, that's a fine pair of shoes you have there!" Well, right away I could tell that this fellow knew class when he saw it. I liked this boy. And I started to tell him of my former exploits. Well, he seemed to want to concentrate on the shoes. At that time, shoes were bringing seventy-five cents in pawn. So I went down and pawned the shoes and got two bottles of Sneaky Pete and a pair of canvas relievers. This was November. There's nothing the matter with me! I'm all right!"

I'd gone down to the bottom of the barrel. Not all at once; it took twenty-five years, a lot of money and a lot of heartaches. There we sat on this bench, this bum and I, telling each other of the wondrous things we'd done, and he loved me and I loved him. There's no love like one drunken bum for another. As I looked off into the sky, and the snow started to fall, I said, "You know, it's getting cold on this bench . . ." and I turned around, and the bum was gone. The dirty dog took the other bottle with him!

Pretty soon another guy comes along, and he says, "If you don't get off that bench you'll freeze to it, and you'll get pneumonia, and you'll die." I always hated to think about dying, because I was such a lovely fellow I knew they'd miss me on earth. He says, "What do you say we go down to Sally?" Well, I didn't know who Sally was, but I knew in my condition she wouldn't care for me. "No," he says, "we'll go down to the Salvation Army." I hope none of you have to resort to the Salvation Army as a means of food and shelter, but they're wonderful people, understanding people. They have a deep love of God that many of us who walk around in our daily business world never will understand. They give just for the glory of giving. They took us in and gave us a bed, and next morning they put us out in the bailing room. For that labor we received ninety-five cents a week and our room and board, a magnificent sum for one as dirty as I was. But like all drunks, when they start to sober up for real, I looked around me and I saw all these other bums, and gee! I knew I was head and shoulders over these other guys. I worked hard for two weeks, and finally I got promoted to be the helper on the truck at three dollars a week. A little bit at a time I progressed, until I became a driver. Utopia! I didn't have to sleep in a dormitory where there were two hundred any more. I slept in a room with absolute privacy—there were only six! And now I was getting five dollars a week.

Well, I don't have to tell you what happened. No drunk can stand prosperity. So I ended up back out in the street, only this time I had a pair of shoes, and a fellow had given me a size forty-six gabardine suit. I have since developed into a forty-long, but a forty-six has always been just a little roomy for me. I wondered what to do then. I didn't believe in God because I knew God was something that had been cooked up for public consumption, mass appeal; you got to have something to keep the dummies in check.

I was going places, and I did. I went from store to store, and from door to door, and I slept under the bridge. I drank bayzo, canned heat, Sneaky Pete, shoe polish, anything that had an alcoholic content. Why I didn't die, God only knows. I didn't wash for weeks on end. I was just a dirty, filthy, slimy thing that came out from under a flat rock. How God in His wisdom let such a thing live only He knows. I don't. No sense of responsibility, no moral code, no sense of ethics—nothing.

One day, on Broad and Market Streets, I ran into my wife. She said, "Well, what happened to you?" I said, "Why—uh—hello, Ma—I—I don't *feel* well. I been a bad boy!"

My wife was raised very tenderly and gently in a parochial school. She never had to work as a young woman. She ended up slinging hash in a dime hash-house to support my daughter and herself.

She took me to the hospital. The doctor said, "Let him try A.A." I stayed in the hospital ten days. I promised her I'd go to an A.A. meeting. She took me home, bought me a fifteen dollar suit, and I went out and got a job working for a guy who used to work for me. And every Wednesday night I'd go down to the A.A. meeting. I'd look in—some guys talking about the grace of God. I'd go home. On the way home I'd stop and have one, two, three, four. When I got home, my wife would ask, "How was the meeting?" And I'd say, "Oh, the meeting's all right; it's just not for women. You know they have a lot of old bums there. And next to the speakers' table they have another little table, and they got a bowl of cracked ice on the table, and a bottle of rye and a bottle of scotch." She said, "What is all that stuff for?" "Well," I said, "they just put that there to test you." So when I'd come home and she'd smell liquor on my breath, I'd tell her I'd just been testing. And I did test, a little bit at a time, until I came home one night about two o'clock in the morning, drunk as a goat, and twice as stinking. I'm pounding on the door and I fell in. She said, "What happened to you?" And I drew myself up to my full height and I looked down at her—my wife is only about five foot two—and I said, "Madam, they put me to the test, and I have failed!"

So ends the sordid part of my story. It's not a pretty thing. But I don't want to ever forget, because three quarters of an ounce of whiskey can put me right back there. Now for the story of how I finally got the A.A. program.

It seems that this particular Sunday I'm lying flat on our parlor rug. I know I'm dying. I know this is it. "Oh, God, if I could only try that A.A. again!" So we call up the Alanon Club. A guy answers the phone and says, "Alanon Club, Louie speaking." Right away I knew it was a phony deal. He told me who he was! "Hi!" I said. "This is Mr. G." "Oh, is that so?" "Yes," I said, "this is B.G." "Well," he said, "would you like to come up to the Club?" "Yeh!" "You got a car?" "No." "Well, get on the bus and come on up." And up we go.

The Alanon Club, in 1945, was a big mausoleum with thirteen steps leading up into it and bare as a barn. We walked up, and here was this great big guy about six foot two, broad as a house, smoking a pipe. "Hiya, boy! My name is Charlie!" This guy I don't want to talk to. I want to see Louie. "Well, that's all right. Meet Joe." Joe's a boy about so broad, bronzed from the sun to the color of a mahogany table. Seems he was keeper of the greens at a golf club somewhere. "How are you?" he says, "What is your name?" "I'm not gonna tell you!" "Well," he says, "my name's Joe, this is Charlie, and this is Frank." "All right, mine is Bill. But fellows, you don't know how sick I am. . . ." Everybody laughed.

In to see Louie, and then we go into the coffee bar. "Give him some coffee." A meeting upstairs. Joe's on one side, Charlie's on the other. The girls have swept up my wife and taken her off into another room to tell her the facts of life. Their version, not mine. I looked over at my wife and waved, and she looked at me and waved back. They'd been talking to her, you see. And the meeting started.

The first speaker got up and he started way back at the Boer War and brought us all the way up to the White Cliffs of Dover. Then he took us back into the African campaign, and I said to Charlie, "What does this have to do with being . . ." and he says, "Shaddup!" The second speaker told a most poignant story. He had a lovely wife and three beautiful children. It seemed that he just purchased a new electric stove a week before Thanksgiving. She had Thanksgiving dinner cooking on this new electric stove. He had one of his cronies ring the front doorbell, and when she went to answer the bell, he and two other fellows took stove, dinner, and all right out the back door. Oh, did that make me feel good! I looked over at my wife and grinned. I never did *that*!

Finally the meeting is over, and we go home. My wife says, "Sit in the chair and read that A.A. book." "I can't *see,* Ma!" "You sit there and read it!" "What are you gonna do?" "I'm gonna make a nice pot of coffee!" So the night passes. I read a little, drink a little coffee. Very sad.

Somehow ten days pass in rapid succession. I recognize food for what it is. I begin to feel alive again. I was sober for the first time in my life because I had a desire for sobriety greater than any other desire. Meetings and more meetings. Three months went by, and they said, "Bill, get up and say a few words." We had about eight people in the group then, and I looked at these eight people and I stuttered and stammered, and finally I said, "I'm glad to be here!" And I sat down. The applause was tremendous.

At six months I had begun to speak at different meetings. Pretty soon my halo was killing me. My ermine cloak was smothering me. I used to look down and wonder what the other little people did for a living. I didn't walk in, I swept in. All that I'd accomplished in six months was sobriety. I was as dry as dust, and just about as useless. One night we went into the Club and Jack said, "Bill, we're short a speaker, will you say a few words tonight?" "Of course!" The meeting started, and I didn't see Jack any more. They called on the first speaker—and it wasn't me, and they called on the second speaker, and the third speaker—and the meeting was over! I had brought my harp to the party, but I didn't get to play!

That taught me the most important lesson I have ever learned in my entire life. That is that A.A. doesn't need me, but I need A.A. Very desperately, very sincerely, very humbly. Not all at once, because you can't get it all at once, just a little bit at a time. They told me, "You've got to get out and work a little; you've got to give." They told me that giving was living, and living was loving, and loving was God. And you don't have to worry about God, because He's sitting right in front of your eyes.

You get just a little sobriety, and you get just a little humility. Not much, just a little. Not the humility of sackcloth and ashes, but the humility of a man who's glad he's alive and can serve. You get just a little tolerance, not too much, but just enough to sit and listen to the other guy.

Somewhere along the line, if you've forgotten how to pray, you learn a little about that too. I divorced myself from the Church when I was twenty-one. I got to thinking about that, and I spoke to Father McNulty about it. "Don't worry, Bill," he said, "you'll develop an awareness of God."

We had a basement apartment, and it faced right on the sidewalk, and outside our bedroom window there was a little bush about so high. One morning I awoke, and there was a little city sparrow taking a bath on this little bush. The weight of this tiny creature's body caused the branch to rise and fall. Isn't that a wonderful thing to see? An awareness of God, yes!

You're aware of the sunset, you're aware of the blades of grass, you're aware of food cooking on the stove.

You delight in walking down the street, and you see someone you know, and the first thing that enters your mind is, "What is there good about that guy that I know?" You find that big people discuss ideals, average people discuss things, and little people—they just talk about other people. And you realize that if you put all this together, you get a little humility, a little tolerance, a little honesty, a little sincerity, a little prayer—and a lot of A.A.

ANNIE THE COP FIGHTER

For thirty-five years she fought God, man, and the
police force to keep on being what she wanted to
be—a drunk. But a telephone call from a gin mill
where she was celebrating Mother's Day brought
in the nosey A.A.'s to change her life.

I started to drink in 1913, when the women sat in
the back rooms. We had a good time in those
back rooms. I had two little boys at the time, but my
family didn't worry me, because one drunk always led
to another. Of course there were days in between when
I was sober because I was broke. But mostly I was
drunk. So my husband left me and took the two boys;
one was six and one was nine. They were going off to
school in those days and it didn't worry me a bit. I
loved the liquor and I loved the crowd that I hung out
with. As far as my family was concerned, I lost everything of love and respect and everything else.

Believe me, this is no made up story. This is a true
story from my own life. When my husband left me, I
had to be on my own. I never worked before, but I had
to get out and get a job if I wanted to drink. So I got a
pretty tough job. I wasn't any chicken. I was a woman
of thirty-one when I had my first drink. I got a job as
cleaner after mechanics in buildings. I would have
done anything to get the money for drink. Any place I
threw my hat was home-sweet-home to me. It could be
a basement or a cellar or a backyard. I fell plenty low,

but if I tell it maybe it will help some gal or some guy so they don't have to get down that low.

Finally, one day as usual, drunk, I was standing on a corner waiting for a streetcar, and a guy comes over to me and he says, "Lady you're on the wrong side." And I says, "Mind your own business!" And as I looked up, it was a feller in uniform! So we had a few words, and he pushed me, and I wasn't going to let anybody get the best of me, and I shoved him back, and we had a little tussle there, and finally I had two buttons off his overcoat, and he says, "I'm takin' you in!" And I says, "Do as you damn please!" I was a tough piece of furniture in those days; if the Almighty God had come down I'd have done the same thing to Him. So I landed in the 67th Street station house on the east side, and I stayed there all night long. The next day I had to appear, and I was fingerprinted for molesting a policeman's uniform. So I got five days in the House of Detention. It didn't bother me whatsoever. The only thing I was worrying about was how was the gang making out without me. I thought I was missed all over! But they made out all right.

So I got out, and then I had to grab myself another job again, so what did I get into but hotel work! That was during the Prohibition days, and the bottles were flying all over the place. When I went to work on the floor, my first idea was to look in the guests' closets where the bottles were. I was all right going in, but I was cockeyed drunk coming out. And I'd have the help drunk with me. One time I got so drunk I blacked out and fell asleep in the guest's bed. I had the nerve to go back on the job the next morning—I didn't know what happened the day before—and the housekeeper was right there with her little note and my check.

"Your service is no longer required." And I had the nerve to ask, "Why?" I was told, all right. Well, in those days you could get jobs anytime. It wasn't like today. If they had ever looked for references from me I think I'd never have got a job, because I never stayed in one.

I never hit hospitals, and I don't know why, because I was fit for hospitals many a time. All the time I saw queer things crawling up the wall in my bedroom. In 1918, I got pinched again for the same thing. I turned out to be a cop fighter; I thought I could beat the whole force. I landed in the same court, had the same judge, and he asked me was I ever arrested before. I says, "No, your Honor!" Just as brazen as can be. And all he done was give me that sneering look, and he says, "For lying in court," he says, "you're not getting away with five days this trip!" I had gone under an assumed name, and I had forgot that I was fingerprinted, and I thought, being away for two years, he wouldn't know who I was! Playing so innocent! But I got thirty days then, five days off for good behavior, over on the Island.

Another time I was in court on the same old charge of Drunk and Disorderly. "Thirty days," says the Judge. And I was that mad and disgusting that I reared right up and spit clean in the judge's eye. It was a distance of at least five feet, too! You should have seen him leap. "Another thirty days," he says, "for spittin' in the eye of the Court." "Nuts to you," says I, but I had to serve the whole sixty days just the same.

I was worrying about my liquor and I was worrying about the crowd I hung out with. As far as my family was concerned, they never entered my mind. So I did my twenty-five days on the Island, and all I could do was look through the bars across the East River and see First Avenue and the joints that I hung out in.

When I got out of the workhouse that time I got a domestic job, and it was right up my alley because I got paid every day, and paid by the hour. In my day, the women only got twenty-five cents an hour, but the liquor was cheap, and that would be all there was to it—maybe. I had blackouts, and many a night I don't know how I ever got home. I always did say, well, thank God I'm in one piece. But where I had been I would never know.

I had been away from home for fifteen years, and one day I was walking up First Avenue and I met my beloved husband. He called to me and he said, "Where are you going?" I was running like blue blazes to a speakeasy to get a drink, and I didn't know what to say, so I said, "I'm goin' up to the Five and Ten to get hairnets." I wanted to beat it, but he says, "Wait a minute." So I did, and we had a few words, and he looked me over, and he says, "You smoke too, don't you?" He didn't know what all I was into; he should have known the rest! I said, "Listen here, you! This is my body and soul, and I can do as I please about it! I have been on my own for all these years, and I can still do as I please!" He didn't get angry over it, and then finally he popped the question to me: "Would you like a drink?" Whooh! There's what I was running for! And I says, "Sure, I would." So we went into a speakeasy up along the line and we had quite a few drinks, and we talked things over and I went back home with him.

But believe me, when I went back home it was too much of a decent life for me to lead. I didn't want that decent, clean life. I wanted to be what I was, a drunk.

So I spent more time over on First Avenue than I did at home. Of course when I went back home, my two boys were raised, which I will give my husband the credit for. He raised them as gentlemen. The oldest boy was married, and the youngest boy was going to Delehanty's—to become a policeman! Brother! Well, it was all right. I had to take it and accept it. But every time I thought of that uniform, it killed me! After he had been in the force one year he got married. I was invited to that wedding with his father. But I invited myself to the old gin mill over on First Avenue again, and celebrated his wedding with my crowd that I hung out with. That's the kind of a mother I was.

I went back home again anyway. I was always forgiven, somehow or other. But I wasn't back home very long before it was the same old round-about—back again to the friends and the blazes with the family. When the doors opened up for the women to sit at the bars, I thought that was the terriblest thing—for a woman to sit at the bar! Well, it didn't take me a long while until I got myself initiated to the bar. I was thrown off those stools so often that, believe me, it wasn't funny.

I had everybody's answers. I butted in to everybody's conversation. If a guy would fall asleep and leave his change on the bar, I was handy to help myself. He couldn't sleep and spend his money, so what was I waiting for? And I'd hang around like an old jackass until I got loaded. Brother, was I black and blue! I was kicked and I was banged and pulled by the hair. I'm surprised today that I'm not lame or something like that, the way I was knocked and kicked.

Then I got so low that I hung out with the guys and gals that were on the Bowery. I was loused up too.

My whole clothes on my body were full of lice. How low can a woman get!

I got in tow with a gal named Irene, and we used to drink. When we had good money, we'd drink the best, but when we had only a little bit, beer was good enough. So one day in 1946, I happened to go into our hangout again as usual, and I asked Irene what she was drinking. She says, "Anna, to tell you the truth, I can't take the first drink. I'm havin' coke." (She nearly knocked me dead!) I says, "Saints above! What happened to you?" She says, "I can't take the first drink." "Well," I says, "nuts to you. I'm havin' mine!" "But," she says, "I'm gonna get you yet!" I says, "Over my dead body!"

She got into A.A. in March of 1946, and in May of that year, Mother's Day was on the 12th. The day before that I was having a good time in a gin mill again, and I don't know whatever come over me, but I asked some of the younger folks that could dial the phone to call Irene. I don't remember doing it. This was all told to me after. The next day was Mother's Day, and like everyone else I wanted to be such a wonderful mother that I had to buy a gardenia for my coat. I went up to this same gin mill to celebrate Mother's Day. I sat on the stool drinking, and pretty soon in comes my friend.

"Oh!" I says, "Hello, Irene!" She says, "Hello, my eye! You got me lookin' all over the town for you! You made a date with me yesterday!" I says, *"I?"* She says, "Not you, but the crowd in here had the ears rung off me with the telephone. They said that you wanted to meet me tonight and you wanted me to take you where I go on Sunday nights." "Hmmmm," I says, "That's news to me. Have a drink?" "No," she says, "I can't take the first drink. There's a cab there waitin' for me to take you down to A.A."

So down to the old 41st Street Club House I landed. In those days they used to have three meetings a week—Sunday, Tuesday, and Thursday. So I went down to that A.A. meeting that night. They took me to the beginners' meeting. I don't know what was said, but I do remember that when the meeting was over, when the door of the 41st Street Club House opened, I sobered up that very night after thirty-two years of knocking liquor around. I drank coke there that night and I went back and forth to the meetings for eight months.

I was sober for eight months, physically, but not mentally. I never mingled with a soul in the meetings. I never shook hands or said hello to my neighbor sitting alongside of me. I never stopped for coffee. I just ran in and out. In the meanwhile I got married the second time. I picked a swell partner, another drunk like myself. I would come home from the meetings and tell him all about these stories, about these women hitting all the jails so often and all the hospitals so often, and he says, "You old so-and-so, you should've been there yourself!" That's what I got for an answer. But it didn't bother me.

Then one night a little argument started. I think I was waiting to start something. It was a foolish thing, over pig's knuckles, believe it or not. I was waiting for that pig's knuckles argument. He told me he was gonna have the gang up to eat up my sauerkraut and pig's knuckles for Saturday night, and I said, "You will in a pig's eye!" And I went out and got a fine load on. I only drank for two days, but I carried enough for a year in those two days.

I got off that two-day drunk through the A.A.'s. The nosey A.A.'s caught up with me somehow or other. They went to the place where I worked. The woman there was very interested in alcoholics. She said to me, "You're drinking." I says, "How do you know?" She said, "Come on in—sit down awhile and rest yourself." She says, "Charlie called up." I says, "That son-of-a-gun! He's got me so advertised that this damn organization knows my whole business! Nobody stepped over my territory before in my life! Now I gotta get in to a thing like this and they know it all!" "Don't get excited," she says. "They're comin' up to see you tonight." I nearly dropped dead.

They came up all right. And I humbled myself. I felt so guilty. I don't know what A.A. does to you, but you never can drink the same again. So they suggested to me to go up to a farm in Connecticut, nothing but wide open spaces in the Berkshire Hills. It was a beautiful place. I stayed up there two days, and I came back a new woman.

Today I have a lot to be thankful for. A.A. has taught me the way of life. It has given me back my respect. It has given back the love of everybody I know. It has taught me to show gratitude, which I never did before. It has taught me to be humble when I have to be humble.

I am what you call a lucky woman. I live alone now. I have a television which my boys have treated me to, and now I have a telephone too! I do love to go to A.A. meetings, and I meet with everybody, the old and the new. I'm a twenty-four hour person. I live on that twenty-four hour plan. I am five years and seven months without a drink, but I could go out tonight, but for the grace of God, and get drunk. There's another thing I must remember, that once an alcoholic always an alcoholic. I don't mind the name of alcoholic, because I was called son-of-a-this and son-of-a-that, and alcoholic is a good enough name for me. So I'm very, very happy. To newcomers I say, go to meetings, and God take care of each and every one of you!

THE INDEPENDENT BLONDE

The lady was blonde, self-supporting, and self-sufficient. Then she began slamming doors, kicking shins, and waking up in psychopathic wards. At last the day came when all this changed.

I have to tell you a little of the way I lived before I got into A.A. so you can see why I made the choice that I did. I started drinking at the age of seventeen, but I was in trouble with myself long before that. I never got along at home, and at the age of thirteen I stepped off and decided I'd go out for myself. I decided that no one loved me and I didn't love them, and I was going off and making myself independent.

My father brought us up to give no quarter and seek no quarter, and that was just the way I lived. I gave nothing, and I took nothing. I suppose I lived mostly for pleasure, or what I know for pleasure, which to me was just going out at night. I worked all day, and went out and stayed out at night. That was about as much as I knew about life. I rebelled against everything I'd ever heard as a child, and I lived to suit myself.

I never thought much about settling down. I thought anyone who got under the dominance of another human being was pretty foolish, but when I was twenty-nine I did get married. I was never trained to live with anyone else, and I took on a pretty big job I wasn't capable of handling. After I was married I was in much more trouble with myself and I drank a great deal more, but now I had someone to blame it on. All my life I had blamed everything that ever happened to me on someone else, and I usually could find someone. Now I had a husband. If I was drinking worse now, it must be his fault.

One night I was out drinking by myself, which I didn't do as a rule. I sat in a bar drinking martinis for a long time, and somewhere on the way home I fell down in the street, and a cop came along and picked me up and took me to St. Vincent's Hospital. They pronounced me Drunk and Disorderly and took me over to Bellevue.

When I came to the next morning, I was in the psychopathic ward. The doctor who tested me and asked me a few personal questions was a psychiatrist. I asked him to call up where I worked and tell them I wouldn't be in. I thought they'd just give me my clothes and let me leave quietly. They told me that I was not able to go out on the street alone, that I was not a responsible citizen. They said someone would have to call for me. To someone as arrogant as I was, who had taken care of herself, that was kind of rough.

I thought I would never get in such a situation again, and I thought the way to get over it would be not to drink. I was so naïve that I thought that would be possible—by just wishing not to drink! I didn't take a drink for three months, but on New Year's Eve everybody was drinking, and about two-thirty in the morning I started. In about one hour I was drunker than anyone there. I kicked someone in the shins and slammed the door on his fingers. I knew I shouldn't be drinking, and I was scared to death. I was in real trouble. I didn't know why I was drinking, and I didn't know why my behavior had changed so. I thought if I left my husband things would be different. I thought I would be different if I could live by myself again. Which I did—and proceeded to drink worse than ever before.

Then I decided that I was in trouble because I was living in New York and everyone knew me, and I used to drink too much with people, and maybe I didn't know the *right* people. So I moved away. I never thought about changing myself, I always thought about changing people, or changing places.

I went down to Virginia, of all places, to stop drinking. I was down there one month when I bumped into a fellow I knew from Greenwich Village who was on the same army post. We were glad to see each other, and he invited me out, and I said, "Oh, I can't go out. I don't drink anymore." I really thought if you didn't drink, you couldn't go out! And he said, "Oh, that's all right. Come on over to the Club and have a few beers." And I said, "Well, that I can do." About midnight that night, when they wanted to close up the Club, they announced that if anybody was missing his companion, she was in the ladies' room, passed out. That was me, in my brand new environment, with the right people!

So I left there and went to another army post, where some Red Cross workers took me out on a date with some British officers. I got drunk with the British officers, and I don't need to tell you what I told the British officers, I being Irish. I left the next day, telling my boss that I needed a very serious operation, and he agreed with me. I never had the courage to wait to be fired. I left every place I'd ever been. I ran away from life. I never knew myself until I got into A.A.

I had heard about A.A. about a year before I came

in, but I thought it was some organization that helped you out financially, and I was always too independent for that. But on June 1, 1945, I had lost all of that kind of independence. I had been drunk for nine days, sick and alone and desperate. They didn't have to tell me that alcoholism was a sickness. When you take a bottle and lock the door and go in by yourself, that is death.

This day I decided to give up. I don't know why you give up one day and not another—I have never been able to understand that. I had suffered on drunks before, but as they explained it to me in A.A., that particular day I hit bottom. I decided to call up A.A., but I didn't know that the Clubhouse didn't open until noon. So I kept drinking and calling up, and drinking and calling up. Finally, I got someone on the telephone, and I told her I was in trouble and asked what I should do. The girl asked me if I could walk. And I said to myself, "My God, how understanding! Somebody who knows that you couldn't walk and why you couldn't walk!" I said to her, "I don't know, I haven't tried." She said, "Well, the only reason I ask is, if you can't we'll come over to you." And I reared up in all my arrogance and I said, "You'll never come to me, but I'll go to you!" It took me until four o'clock that day to get there.

I never shall forget how comforted I felt that there was a building, there was a place, there were people who were interested in what was wrong with me. I walked in that door and the girl asked me my name, and I said, "I'd rather not give you my name." She said, "We don't care if you haven't *got* a name, just so you have an alcoholic problem!" Well, I was put to shame, and I told her my name. She assigned me to another girl who took me upstairs. I looked into this girl's eyes, and I thought, "If only my eyes would ever be that clear again, then I'd be grateful for that alone." Little did I ever think that many more things would happen to me than clear eyes.

The first thing I learned that day was that if I never took another drink I would never have another problem with alcohol. That went over in my mind like a Victrola record. I had never thought about the first drink. I had schemed and stolen drinks, but it was never the first one. And here I had a very simple problem—one drink, and that's all I was able to understand.

About seven o'clock someone came over to this girl and asked her to speak at a meeting in Brooklyn. I was scared this girl would leave me. It was the first time in my life I ever had *needed* someone, and I knew it. I looked at her to see what she would say. She looked at me and said, "Would you like to go to Brooklyn?" I don't like to go to Brooklyn when I'm cold sober! But I wanted to stay sober, and I went to Brooklyn. I don't know who spoke first, last, or what, but someone got up and said he had been in Bellevue thirty-five times. I thought, "Oh, my God! I'll look like St. Cecilia here!" I was so glad to be able to tell this dark secret that I had had for eight years that I nudged a man alongside of me and said, "Mister, do you know I was in Bellevue once?" He said, "Okay, girlie, you'll get the program." I guess he figured I was just another psycho!

The next day I started back for the Clubhouse. On my way over, that thick head of mine started saying to me, "I don't know that you're such a drunk. I think you're far too dramatic about this whole thing. Why do you have to go over there with that bunch of people?" I was walking along a Bowery sort of street with music playing and those awful neon lights all around, and suddenly a little man started to follow me. Not the kind of man that follows nice girls. And suddenly I said to myself, "Listen, Toots, there's something the matter with you when a guy like that follows you, and you better get over to the Clubhouse and find out what it is!" I always like to say that on my second day I was "wolfed" into A.A.

I heard that I had to make amends, and do something good for someone—that I was too self-centered. I thought of a girl friend who had a brand new baby, and she used to like to get drunk on Saturday night. And I thought, "That'll be it. That'll be good." I called her up and told her I'd mind the baby while she went out and got drunk. That's how much I knew about doing good! The next day I called my boss and told her what had happened to me and asked her if she would take me back to work. It was the first time in my life that I ever showed any sort of humility, that I ever asked anybody for anything. And I went back there to work. I learned that going back and facing something unpleasant, regardless of how tough it is at the time, is a lot easier than running away. I went to meetings every night in the week, because I'm that kind of person. I either do a thing or I don't do it. I didn't have to give up very much, because my life before A.A. was very empty, very lonely, and very superficial. Then I was always afraid of being a sucker, for some unknown reason—I always thought people were taking advantage of me.

One day a call came in to the Clubhouse for someone to go out and do a Twelfth Step job. And they looked at me and said, "How long are you in?" And I said, "A week or so." And they said, "Oh, you can't go. You have to be sober three months." And then I realized that here I had spent all my life afraid that people were trying to get something out of me, and I had nothing to give! Now I was in an organization where they needed someone that had something I didn't have; someone who was sober three months, who had some sort of stability; someone that had kindness is their hearts for other human beings, and compassion for their suffering. I had to wait until these people gave it to me so that I could go out and give it away.

Then I began to have trouble with myself, and I went to see Dr. Silkworth and he explained to me what honesty was. I always thought honesty had something to do with telling other people the truth. He explained that it had to do first with telling myself the truth. I spent most of my life worrying about myself, thinking that I was unwanted, that I was unloved. I've learned since being in A.A. that the more I worry about me loving you, and the less I worry about you loving me, the happier I'll be.

I discovered a fellowship of human beings that I'd never seen before. I learned how to have self-respect through work that A.A. gave me to do. I learned how to be a friend. I learned how to go out and help other people—there was nowhere else I could have done that. I have learned that the more I give, the more I will have; the more I learn to give, the more I learn to live.

Part Three

The stories in this section were deleted from the third edition when the fourth was published in 2001, but 15 of the 25 were published in the second edition and reflect A.A. in the 1950s.

In the quarter of a century between publication of the third and fourth editions, A.A. and the surrounding society experienced phenomenal changes. A.A.'s estimated membership had doubled, to two million or more, and there were more than 100,000 groups meeting in approximately 150 countries. But numbers were only part of the story, as alcoholics of every walk of life and nuance of lifestyle or belief heard the message and achieved sobriety. The influx of women and young people continued, and more than half of new members were reaching A.A. with the help of professionals. The Fellowship was carrying the message to physically challenged alcoholics, and welcoming people who might earlier have been too afraid of a negative stigma to seek the help they needed. And as the computer age took hold, alcoholics were able to communicate in new ways, with online meetings available not only for homebound members but also for those who wanted to share their experience with A.A. friends they might never meet face to face.

In view of such complexity within the Fellowship, the process of developing a fourth edition was destined to be the most comprehensive of all. The basic criteria for story selection repeated Bill W.'s insistence on A.A. experince, strength and hope. A subcommittee of the trustees' Literature Committee received more than 1,200 manuscripts in response to their initial request, and through a painstaking process of review, narrowed these down to the 25 new stories in the final product. With 17 "keepers" from the third edition, their final selection reflected the full range of racial, ethnic, gender, religious, age, occupational, and lifestyle experiences that are woven into the rich tapestry of A.A. life.

At the same time, the committee had the difficult responsibility of eliminating old material to make room for the new. The October-November 2001 issue of *Box 4-5-9* asked: "How is it possible to select the 'best' when dealing with A.A. sharing?" The subcommittee of the trustees' Literature Committee charged with the responsibility of developing the fourth edition would answer that question quite simply: "It is not. There is no such thing as 'best.' Yet choices had to be made—not only in selecting new material, but also in deciding which stories to retain from the third edition and which to leave out. . . . In developing guidelines, the subcommittee was mindful of Bill W.'s observation that 'the audience for the book is people who are coming to Alcoholics Anonymous now. Those who are here have already heard our stories.' . . ."

After lengthy consideration, the committee eliminated the stories you are about to read. As a historical record they are invaluable. But their primary value is that of simple A.A. sharing—one alcoholic talking to another in the language of the heart.

HE HAD TO BE SHOWN*

"Who is convinced against his will is of the same opinion still." But not this man.

I was the oldest of three children, and my father was an alcoholic. One of the earliest memories that I have is of a bottle sitting on his desk with a skull and crossbones and marked "Poison." At that time, as I remember, he had promised never to take another drink. Of course he did. I can also remember that he was a salesman and a very good one. When he was up-town—we were living in the little town of Moscow—I went up to try to get some money from him to buy groceries. He wouldn't give me any money for the gro-ceries, but he did take me across the street and buy me a bag of candy, which I later took back and traded for a loaf of bread. I was not more than six at that time.

My father died in 1901 when I was eight years old and I was in the second or third grade at school. I im-mediately quit school and went to work, and from that time until I was high school age there was never a return to school. I always built up in my own mind the great things that I was going to do, and in fact I ac-complished about 50 percent of them and then lost in-terest. That continued through my entire life. When I was sixteen years old, my mother remarried and I was given the opportunity of going back to school. I went

*This story appeared in the first edition as "The Car Smasher." It was completely rewritten for the second edition under the title "He Had to Be Shown."

into the high school grades, but having missed all the intermediate grades, I didn't get along too well, so I developed the habit of going back to school just long enough for the football season and then quitting.

There was always a tremendous drive and ambition to become a great guy, because I think I recognized inwardly that I didn't have any special talents. At a comparatively early age, I can remember being jealous of my brother. He did things much better than I did because he applied himself and learned how to do them, and I never applied myself. Whether I could have done as well as he, I don't know.

I was married at the age of nineteen to a grand girl and had good business prospects. I had bought a piece of ground in Cuyahoga Falls and cut it into lots and had a profit of approximately $40,000 and that was a lot of money in those days. With that profit, I built a number of houses, but then I neglected them. I wouldn't put sufficient time on them. Consequently, my labor bills ran up. I lost money, and then just fooled away a large part of that profit.

When I was eighteen, at the end of high school, the high school team had a banquet at a well-known roadhouse outside of Akron. We boys drove out in somebody's car and went to the bar on the way to the dining room and I, in an effort to impress the other boys that I was city-bred, having lived in Scranton and Cleveland, asked them if they didn't want a drink. They looked at one another queerly and, finally, one of them allowed he'd have a beer and they all followed him, each of them saying he'd have a beer too. I ordered a martini, extra dry. I didn't even know what a martini looked like, but I had heard a man down the bar order one. That was my first drink. I kept watching the man down the bar to see what he did with a contraption like that, and he just smelled of his drink and set it down again, so I did the same. He took a couple of puffs of a cigarette and I took a couple of puffs of my cigarette. He tossed off half of his martini; I tossed off half of mine and it nearly blew the top of my head off. It irritated my nostrils; I choked; I didn't like it. There was nothing about that drink that I liked. But I watched him, and he tossed off the rest of his, so I tossed off the rest of mine. He ate his olive and I ate mine. I didn't even like the olive. It was repulsive to me from every standpoint. I drank nine martinis in less than an hour.

Twenty-two years later, Doctor Bob told me that what I had done was like turning a switch and setting up a demand for more alcohol in my system. I didn't know that then. I had no more reason to drink those martinis than a jackrabbit. At that particular time, the boys put me on a shutter and took me out to the shed, and I lay in the car while they enjoyed their banquet. That was the first time I ever drank hard liquor. Blackout drinking at once. I had no pleasure out of the drinking at all. All of a sudden I found myself guzzling. Right then I determined that never so long as I lived would I have anything more to do with martinis. They acted on me like the beating of a club.

I think it was probably more than a year before I had anything more to do with liquor. I was opening up these lots that I spoke of. I had a crew of men working there and I wanted them to work Sunday afternoons so that I could sell lots on Sunday. I went over and bought a jug of hard cider and a gallon of wine that I gave these fellows to drink. When they got through the day's work, part was left which I proceeded to drink.

During the day, looking over the contracts and money in my pocket, I found that I had sold six lots that I couldn't even remember, and didn't even know the people I had sold them to. I had to look in the telephone book later to find out who these people were. Another blackout. Wine and hard cider.

I early discovered that if I drank anything, I was not accountable for what happened. I decided that I couldn't drink. Anyhow, I recognized the fact that I couldn't drink like normal people, but I tried hard and kept on trying for twenty-two years.

I sold three lots to an elderly lady in Cleveland. I came to Cleveland with the deeds to these lots and to pick up my money. She paid me in cash. The next morning I woke up in jail in Cleveland and the jailor had $1,175 of my money in an envelope. I didn't remember anything that had happened. This was six or eight months after the last drinking episode.

Then I got married. (As I've said, I was nineteen.) I felt having gotten married, I was an adult and one of the first things I did was to buy two cases of whiskey with no idea of drinking it. (I might say right here that never in my life did I ever *intend* to get drunk. I never had any desire to get drunk. So I consciously thought.) I was a very young married man, having his whiskey in the cupboard over the sink, and when I helped my wife with the dishes at night I would take a cup of tea and spike it with whiskey. I could get through an evening with just a couple of snorts.

This was a regular occurrence for a little while. Eventually, there would be a ball game, or a show, or some sort of special occasion to celebrate and I would turn up drunk. About that period, too, came increasing procrastination and the avoidance of responsibilities. I would put off doing anything that I could until the next day, and consequently, everything would pile up and then there would be the blackout.

At the end of this selling of lots, just prior to World War I, I got into the crude rubber business, and six months later there was only one broker and myself left in Akron. So in spite of anything that I might do, I prospered, being one of only two brokers in the rubber center of the world.

I found, however, that when I would leave Akron to go to Chicago, I would get drunk. As long as there was everyday business, I could drink occasionally and didn't always get drunk. I was a periodic. A big event of any kind precipitated heavy drinking. It had long since become a serious problem. I was prone to do everything on a big scale. I can well remember sitting with seven dollars in my pocket, planning on giving my family a hundred or two hundred dollars, when I made it next year. But I didn't do a thing about giving them any part of the seven bucks I had in my pocket.

The rubber prosperity went on for about six years—1916 to 1922. It fell apart in the twenties. Every company in the country, except Firestone, was reorganized at that time. I was always able to skate along the fringe of big money. I made a point of knowing important people. I could work a deal up to where all I had to do was to go ahead with it; all the planning had been done, all the financing had been done, but then I'd say, "Nuts to it!" and walk away. Near success, only near. I figured the only difference between me and a millionaire was that I hadn't the strength, or that he got the breaks and I didn't.

Akron was really on the boom in those days, 1919–1920; expansion was terrific. I optioned a piece of land just off East Market Street to put up a three-hundred suite apartment. One hundred for unmarried women at one end, one hundred for men at the other, and one hundred for married couples in the middle. In the basement were to be dry-cleaning facilities, a barbershop, a pool room, a grocery shop and everything. I had contracted for half of it, at least verbally, and the contactors were taking half of the second mortgage bond. At that particular stage, I lost interest in it, sold the option for $5,000 and forgot the whole deal. Another time, I had a rubber pool project. My idea was to have all the companies pool their funds and buy rubber when rubber was cheap and then put it in a pool. When rubber reached a certain low point, they would draw on the rubber out of the pool and buy. With the big companies, and with the amount of money we could have gotten and the promises I had, it could have been done. I worked along until I had really big names in rubber on a tentative contract, and then I neglected to go through with it.

To my mind, drinking didn't have anything to do with not going through with things. I don't know whether I drank to cover up being a failure, or whether I drank and then missed the deals. I was able to rationalize it anyway. I can well remember over a long period of years when I thought I was the only person in the world who knew that sooner or later I was going to get drunk. I can remember occasions when friends recommended me for positions or business opportunities that I wouldn't take because I felt that at some future date I'd get drunk and they would be hurt.

In the meantime, the domestic situation was not getting along too well. We had two children, a boy and a girl, and when the boy was about twelve, we broke up the marriage. That was at my suggestion. I can remember telling the poor little soul that I could probably quit drinking if I wasn't married to her, and told her that, after all, I didn't like restraint! I didn't like having to come home at a certain time; I didn't like this, I didn't like that, and I think the poor girl actually divorced me to help me stop drinking! Naturally, what little restraint I had exercised before was gone now, and my drinking became worse.

Long since I had come to believe I was insane because I did so many things I didn't want to do. I didn't want to neglect my children. I loved them, I think, as much as any parent. But I did neglect them. I didn't want to get into fights, but I did get into fights. I didn't want to get arrested, but I did get arrested. I didn't want to jeopardize the lives of innocent people by driving an automobile while intoxicated, but I did. I quite naturally came to the conclusion that I must be insane. My big job was to keep other people from finding it out. I can remember well thinking that I would quit drinking, really go to work hard, apply myself eight hours a day, five days a week, make a lot of money, and then I could start drinking again. That was the reverse of my former pattern of fearing to go to work because I might drink! Always at the end of these dreams was drinking. Now I attempted to quit. I think this was about 1927. I was divorced in 1925 or 1926. I determined that I wouldn't drink. I remember one occasion when I did not drink for three hundred and sixty-four days, but I didn't quite make the year.

Another time, I had gone around to Max R. trying to get a job driving one of his trucks. He had known something of my drinking pattern, and he asked me what I was doing about it. I told him that I had not had a drink for ninety days and that I had come to the conclusion that I was one of those individuals who couldn't drink. So, knowing that, I had determined that so long as I lived I would never take another drink. On that statement and the fact that I had been sober for ninety days, he gave me a job selling lots in an allotment he had. I was moved in as Sales Manager and had four men working under me. At the end of about four months, I not only had good looking clothes—and I might say that at the time I first talked to Max I didn't have a suit of clothes I could bend over in real sudden; now I had six suits of clothes. I had an automobile. Everything in the world a man could possibly want, and I was driving from Akron to Cleveland, having just been to the bank and discovered that I had approximately $5,000. I drove towards Cleveland wondering why I found myself in such a changed set of conditions as compared with those of six months before. I came to the conclusion it was because I hadn't been drunk. And I hadn't been drunk because I hadn't taken a drink. And I then and there said a prayer, if you please. An offer of appreciation for not having had a drink for those few months and then and there, without anybody promising me anything or threatening me, I made a solemn vow that never so long as I lived would I take another drink.

(My mother and father were Catholics and I had been baptized, but at the end of my instructions for Confirmation I had not gone to church, and then when my mother remarried, she married a Protestant and the whole religious angle was forgotten. So I had never had any lasting contact with any kind of religion.)

So I was driving to Cleveland when I made this

solemn promise never to drink again. That was at
three-thirty in the afternoon. At three-thirty the next
morning, I was in Champlain Street Station, in jail for
driving while intoxicated and insulting an officer; and
the suit of which I was so proud was in such shape
that the turnkey had to get me a pair of trousers to go
into court in the next morning. I had run into a man I
always drank with. Whenever this man and I met—I
didn't know his name then nor do I know it now—we
would always get drunk. I had run into him, and he
looked real prosperous; his face and eyes looked clear
and he started to compliment me on my good front
and how well I looked, and I said, "I haven't had a
drink for nine months." He said, "Well, I haven't had
a drink for three months." And we stood there for
twenty minutes, telling each other how much better
we were, how much better we looked, how much
better off we were financially, mentally, physically,
morally, and in every way, shape and manner. And
then we both realized we should go. We shook hands,
and he hung onto my hand for a moment and said,
"Tell you what I'll do for old times sake. I'll buy you
one drink, and if you suggest a second one, I'll poke
you right in the nose." And I think we calculated, or I
did, that there wasn't anybody who knew that I wasn't
drinking. I could take one drink and get right back on
the wagon. Nobody would know it, so I agreed to
have the one drink. We went into a bootleg joint and I
don't remember leaving that place. I was picked up at
two-thirty that morning with my car smashed up by a
street-car because I had run into a big concrete safety
zone, and the street-car had run into me, and they
took me out through the roof—there's where I lost the
suit. I had lost a hundred dollars I had in my pocket,

and lost a wristwatch too. I lost the car, of course. But more important, I lost my sobriety. And I continued to drink, on and off then, until every dollar I had in the world was gone again and I was right back living at my sister's, getting my cigarettes by calling her grocer and telling him to put in a couple of cartons with her order, exactly as I had before I started to work at Max's.

In 1932, some friends of mine advised me that I might try Christian Science, which had done a lot for some of their friends. So I started to investigate Science through some friends of mine who were Readers in the church. I accepted their help, and it was helpful. I quit drinking immediately. The circumstances under which I reached these people were very odd because I was led there through things that I said when I couldn't even remember speaking. I told somebody that I was going down to get Christian Science and they took me down, but I don't remember saying that. Yet I wound up at this place. I attended their meetings every Sunday and Wednesday for about nine months. If there was a lecture on the subject within a hundred miles of Akron, I attended. Then, I started to miss meetings because it was raining or snowing or something else. Pretty soon, I wasn't going at all, and was avoiding those people who had been so kind to me. I avoided them rather than explain why they weren't seeing me. My sobriety continued for another six months.

At the end of fifteen months, I tried the beer experiment. After drinking one glass of beer at the end of my work period for about five days, I thought I'd better find out whether I really had the stuff licked. So I didn't have a beer one night, and as I drove home I was breaking my arm patting myself on the back because I had proved I could lick liquor. I had proved that liquor was not my master. I had avoided a drink this time. So having licked it, there was no reason why I shouldn't have a drink, and I stopped in before I got home and had one. Then I got into the habit of having beers, and decided that a drink of whiskey was not any worse; so I would get the one drink of whiskey but, on second thought, I decided that as long as I was only going to have one, I might as well make it a double-header. So I had one double-header every night for about two or three weeks. I didn't drink very long at a time. I think the longest drunk I was ever on was eleven days, but usually only two days with a complete blackout for a day, and then backing off by drinking as long as I could get anything.

This Christian Science experience with a sobriety of fifteen months was in 1932. Then I started drinking again, with possibly a little more restraint, periods a little bit longer than they had been before, but substantially the same pattern. During the latter part of the Christian Science experience I had gotten a job and was working at Firestone. I was bouncing along and not doing too badly. There were times when I got to drinking, and I had been warned by Firestone that they wouldn't stand for this much longer, so, clearly, they were conscious of the fact that I drank too much and too often.

To show you the point to which this obsession went, there came an occasion when I had spent a most delightful weekend, and at nine o'clock on Sunday night I was on my way home, and I thought I would get a drink. I went into a bar, and there I got into a fight. I was arrested and taken to jail where I was beaten up by two or three fellows who were already in there and whom I tried to boss. I was badly beaten. I tried to conduct a kangaroo court and hit them with a broomstick. I had a broken nose, a fractured cheek-bone, and was black from the lower part of my face up into my hair. I was black and blue, with my lips all swollen, when they roused us to go into court in the morning. I looked so terrible in the court that the judge suggested that I get a continuance and let me sign all the papers to go to a hospital and to a doctor. I went downstairs and there was the grizzly old veteran police officer in charge of the property desk, and as he gave me the stuff, he asked, "Are you going out in the street that way?" I said, "I'm certainly not going to stay in here!" I had white trousers on, white shoes and a white shirt that was streaked with blood. He said, "Well, why don't you take a cab?" I said, "All right, call me a cab," as though I was talking to a bellboy. He did call me a cab and when I got into the cab, I said, "Drive me to a liquor store." We drove to a store in North Hill and I sent him in with what money I had to get a quart. He brought the quart out and I took a good swig. When I got home I had to give him a check for the taxi fare. I drank some more and slept through the day. At night, I woke up and the folks with whom I roomed were home by then. I offered them a drink, and they came to the bottom of the stairs and I stuck my face around the top of the stairs and the good woman fainted, just looking at me. So they decided that I should have a doctor. They called a doctor and it happened that they called one I knew. He came in and took a look at me and sent me to the hospital.

When I had been in the hospital ten days, Sister Ignatia, who has played such a part in the development of A.A. in this area, stuck her head in the door one morning and announced, looking at me quizzically, that they might be able to make something human out of my face after all. And at the end of fourteen days, they let me out. Three days later I went to work. The next day, they called me in for an examination, and the doctor wouldn't let me continue working and pardoned me from the plant for ten days because he said my eye had been injured. So I was barred from the plant for ten days, and during that ten-day period I was drunk twice, showing how little control these restraints had on me.

Shortly after that, my brother, who had then become associated with a group of people and had stopped drinking, urged me to attend meetings with him. Naturally, I wanted no part of any meetings. I explained to my sister that some of the people he was meeting with had been in hospitals. I couldn't afford to be found with those people, but I said I would certainly pay his dues if it would keep him from drinking. But me, I wanted no part of it! I didn't have any need of such an association!

One morning, after I had been on a binge for a couple of days, I awoke to find my brother and Doctor Bob in my room talking to me about not drinking. My only thought that day was getting a drink, and how to get rid of those clowns was my big problem. They asked me if I would take some medicine, and I promised that I would if they got me a drink. So Paul was dispatched and brought back a pint. I got two drinks, each of them a quarter of that pint, in me, and was talking along with these people, but I felt that sooner or later they were going to have me cornered because they were smarter than I was and the drink was beginning to take effect; but as I reached for the third drink

Bob said, "Listen, Buster, you promised to take some medicine if we got you a drink. Now we got you the drink, but you haven't taken the medicine." I agreed with him and told him in no uncertain terms that I never broke my word in my life. I told him I'd take the medicine and I would take it, but I hadn't told him when, and thereupon I got away with the third drink. I then began asking a lot of questions of both my brother and Dr. Bob about how this thing worked, and I suppose I was becoming more glassy-eyed all the while, for eventually I said to Bob, "You're all dried up. You're never going to want another drink, are you?"; and this answer of his is very important to those of us who are victims of alcoholism. He said, "So long as I'm thinking as I'm thinking now, and so long as I'm doing the things I'm doing now, I don't believe I'll ever take another drink." And I said, "Well, what about Paul, have you got him all dried up?" He said Paul would have to answer for himself. So Paul repeated substantially what Dr. Bob had said. And I said, "Now you want to dry me up. I'm not going to want another drink?" "Well," the doctor said, "we have hopes in that direction." I said, "In that case, there's no use of wasting this," and I got the last of the pint. A few minutes later, Dr. Bob left, leaving with my brother some medicine I should get. Paul measured the medicine out, but he figured that with my track record that little bit wouldn't be enough, so he doubled it and added a few drops more and then gave it to me. I immediately became unconscious. This was on Thursday. I regained consciousness on Sunday. I had taken five and a half ounces of paraldehyde. Because if affected me so strenuously, they felt that hospitalization was indicated and I awoke in a hospital.

On Sunday when I came to, it was a bad, wet, snowy day in February 1937, and Paul and Doc and a lot of the other fellows were in Cleveland on business. The people in the group hadn't been around that day; part of my family was in Florida and the rest of them weren't speaking to me, so I spent a very lonesome day and by evening I was feeling very sorry for myself. It was getting pretty dark and I hadn't turned on any lights, when some big fellow stepped inside the door and flipped on the light switch. I said, "Look, Bub, if I want those lights on, I'll turn them on." I'll never forget, he never even hesitated and I had never seen him before in my life. He took off his hat and his overcoat, and he said, "You don't look very good. How are you feeling?" I said, "How do you suppose? I'm feeling terrible." He said, "Maybe you need a little drink." That was the smartest man I'd met in months. I thought he had it in his pocket, so I said, "You got some?" He said, "No, call the nurse." And he got me a drink. Then he started to talk to me about his drinking experiences, what his drinking had cost him, how much he had drunk and where, things like that, and I remember I was quite bored because I had never seen the guy before and had no interest at all in what, where and when he drank. The man turned out to be Bill D., a very early member of A.A., and I couldn't tell you a word of what he said. Not one experience registered with me. When he left, I realized from his story that as a drinker I was just a panty-waist. I knew I could quit because he had quit; he hadn't had a drink for over a year. The important thing was that he was happy. He was released, relieved from his alcoholism and was happy and contented because of it. That I shall never forget.

The next day, others from the group came in to see me. I remember well one fellow, Joe, walking nearly three miles through slush, wet and snow to come to the hospital to see a man that he had never seen before in his life, and that impressed me very much. He walked to the hospital to save bus fare and did it gladly in order to be helpful to an individual he had never even seen. There were only seven or eight people in the group before me and they all visited me during my period in the hospital. The very simple program they advised me to follow was that I should ask to know God's will for me for that one day, and then, to the best of my ability, to follow that, and at night to express my gratefulness to God for the things that had happened to me during the day. When I left the hospital I tried this for a day and it worked, for a week and it worked, and for a month, and it worked—and then for a year and it still worked. It has continued to work now for nearly eighteen years.

HE THOUGHT HE COULD
DRINK LIKE A GENTLEMAN

But he discovered that there are some
gentlemen who can't drink.

I was born in Cleveland, Ohio, in 1889, the last
child of a family of eight children. My parents
were hard working people. My father was a railroad
man and a Civil War veteran. I can remember that in
my childhood, he was ill at ease with the children because he attempted to assert an army discipline that
had been ground into him during his three and a half
years of army service. The differences between my
father and my sisters, who were school teachers, made
an excellent environment for the type of child I was —
that is, slick and cute enough to take advantage of any
adult quarrel. In other words, I was always safe from
the discipline of my father, and, having developed
along that line, I had considerable difficulty in school.
Rules were made for others, but not for me. Of course,
it was always my aim to have my own way without
being caught.

My mother was eighty-nine years old when she
died, and I was a full-blown alcoholic at the time of
her death. She was a woman devoted to her family and
loyal to her husband, but quarrels did not make a
happy environment for her. I had four brothers and
three sisters. As I look back, all the brothers developed
personality problems. The sisters seemed to remain
unaffected. I seemed to react by developing a streak of

varying meanness, which would cause me to do things to create excitement and to get attention. I very early sampled the effects of alcohol. In fact, on one occasion, I was picked up by the police and brought home. I was then about sixteen years old. I didn't go to high school. I went to five grade schools, primarily because I was expelled for my conduct, but I eventually graduated from the eighth grade.

I was always interested in mechanics and after having about twenty miscellaneous jobs, lasting from one day to two weeks, I obtained a job as a toolmaker apprentice. Being intensely interested in the work, I changed my conduct sufficiently to master the job. I finished my apprenticeship and was moved into the drafting department. That was in Cleveland. As a draftsman, I worked for several large companies and gained a variety of experience. Not far from where I lived they built a new technical high school and one of the teachers sold me on the idea that I needed a little mechanical drawing if I were going to be a good toolmaker. I proceeded to take up the drawing and advanced rapidly in it. The school then obtained a job for me in the drafting department of another company. After I was on the drafting board about two years I decided I wanted a technical education. I was then about eighteen. I did not have a high school education, so I went to night school to take the full high school course, which I finished in two years and nine months. I apparently was willing to subdue these personality disturbances in a tremendous drive to succeed. I had an objective. I could discipline myself but along the way there would be festivities and occasions when I got drunk. Although, during this period I was not addicted to any pattern of alcohol consumption, when I did drink the drinking was pretty wild.

I then entered Case School and worked while I went to school and finished there. This was an engineering college. Following graduation, I was offered a pretty good job which I took. In the fall of the graduating year, I became involved in some litigation over the ownership of inventions and patents. This experience sent me to law school where I went at night and which course I completed in less than three years, taking the highest state bar examinations and passing them. The law school experience was not inspired by a desire to follow patent law, which has been my profession since: I went to law school primarily to learn the law of contracts following my own experience with litigation. A year later, after I completed the course in contracts, I quit the law school, and undertook some engineering work for a patent law firm on behalf of clients who were in difficulties and who desired to keep their troubles from their own engineering department. This work consumed a period of about two-thirds of a year, and worked out successfully so I decided to follow patent law. I went back to law school, and doubled up on the courses because I was then approaching thirty years of age and I wanted to get through as quickly as possible. I was supporting myself through all this education by being a toolmaker and a draftsman.

I married when I was twenty-eight years old, and started in law school after I was married. As a matter of fact, I had two children at the time I was admitted to the bar.

I kept myself so busy that, outside of some school and group parties, I didn't go overboard on drinking very much between the ages of twenty-five and thirty. My life was fairly well crowded and I didn't seem to need any stimulants to keep me going. By the time I had completed law school I had picked up some experience in patent law, for I remained with the patent law firm and worked too in Washington where they found that I was a capable infringement investigator. In 1924, I had acquired enough clients of my own so that the firm made me a junior partner. My drinking career began about four years after I had moved up into partnership and had joined certain clubs, societies and so forth, and during which period we had Prohibition. I was then about thirty-seven or thirty-eight.

All during Prohibition, every alcoholic felt that he made the best hooch, regardless of how bad it was. I became a specialist in making elderberry blossom wine.

There had been some occasions—there was an automobile wreck, for instance—when I had police escort home but not to jail, all of which, instead of doing me a favor, did me harm because I was then full of self-esteem as to the progress I had made both professionally and financially. The first definite indications of an alcoholic pattern began to arise when I would go to New York on business and disappear, and wind up in Philadelphia or Boston for two- or three-day periods. I would have to return to New York and pick up my bills and bags. These periods became more frequent and I resolved that when I became forty, which was very shortly, I was going on the wagon. Forty came and went and then the resolution was advanced to forty-one, forty-two, and so on in the usual pattern. I realized that I had a problem, although my realization was not very deep because my own conceit wouldn't admit that I had any personality problems. I could not see why I couldn't drink like a gentleman, and that was my primary ambition—until I landed in A.A. This pattern deepened and became worse. I became a constant drinker with a terrific fight to control the amount of my consumption each day.

My practice had advanced to the point where it could stand a lot of abuse and it got it. Whenever a situation arose that fast talk wouldn't explain away, I simply withdrew. In other words, I fired the client before the client fired me. I was willful, full of will to do things I wanted to do and to get the things that I wanted to have.

Insofar as religion was concerned, I had a Catholic training in my youth. I went to both Catholic and public schools. I never left the church, but I was a fringe member, and the thought simply never occurred to me that through the exercise of what I had I might find the answer to my problem, simply because I wouldn't admit that I had a problem. The successful demonstration I had made of my life problems in other respects convinced me that some day I was gong to be able to drink like a gentleman.

When I was about forty-seven, after indulging in all kinds of self-deception to control my drinking, I arrived at a period when I felt convinced I had to have so much alcohol every day and that the real problem was to control how much. After two or three years of effort along this line, I reached the point of actual despair that I ever would be able to drink only a harmless amount each day. And then my thinking became calculation as to how much longer I had to live, how long the assets would last. By that time, I had one boy in college, another a senior in high school, and a daughter about twelve years old. My efficiency as a professional man was probably reduced to twenty-five percent of what it should have been.

I had two partners. They suffered from my conduct without saying anything, but the reason for this was that I still managed to hang onto a very substantial practice. They probably felt that it was useless, that surely I had enough intelligence to know what I was doing. They were wrong. They never raised the issue. In fact, as I look back, I have often thought that they probably concluded that they would put up with me for a couple of years, that I couldn't live much longer, and that they would inherit whatever was left of the practice. That is not unusual.

As far as my home was concerned, I did not see then, though of course I can see now, that it was anything but a happy situation for my wife. My children had lost respect for me and, in fact, it was only after three or four years of sobriety that any of them ever said anything to me to indicate that I had recouped even a little of their respect.

I was forty-nine and a half years old when I was first approached about the Akron Group. It was not known to me as a group, but I later learned that my wife had known about it for nine months and had prayed constantly that I would stumble into Akron some way or another. She knew that at that time any suggestion she made about my drinking would only build up a barrier, a consideration for which I am ever grateful. Had anyone undertaken to explain to me what the A.A. movement was, what its real function was, I probably would have been set back several years and I doubt if I would have survived at all.

So the story of my introduction into A.A. begins

with the activities of my wife. She had a hairdresser who used to tell her about a brother-in-law who had been quite a drinker and about some doctor in Akron who had straightened him out. My wife didn't tell me this, but one Sunday afternoon when Mary was trying to get the cobwebs out of my mind, Clarence and his sister-in-law, the hairdresser, called at the house. I was introduced to them and Clarence proceeded to put on his Twelve Step work. I was kind of shocked about anybody talking about themselves the way he did, and my impression was that the guy was a little "touched." However, on a couple of other occasions, Clarence seemed to bob up at the last saloon that I would stop at on the way home every day. I resented it of course, and I offered Clarence his commission, whatever it might be, if he would please not bother me because I had arrived at the conclusion that he was a solicitor for some alcoholic institute. One evening I had gone out after dinner to take on a couple of double-headers and stayed a little later than usual, and when I came home Clarence was sitting on the davenport with Bill W. I do not recollect the specific conversation that went on but I believe I did challenge Bill to tell me something about A.A. and I do recall one other thing: I wanted to know what this was that worked so many wonders, and hanging over the mantel was a picture of Gethsemane and Bill pointed to it and said, "There it is," which didn't make much sense to me. There was also some conversation about Dr. Bob and I must have said that I would go down to Akron with Bill in the morning.

The next morning, my wife came into my room and wakened me and said, "That man is downstairs and he said you said you'd go to Akron." I said, "Did

I say that?" She said, "Well, he wouldn't be here if you didn't say so." And being a big-shot man of my word, I said, "Well, if I said so, then I'll go." That's about the spirit in which I went to Akron. Bill bought me a drink or two on the way, and Dorothy S. came with us, and the three of us went over to the City Hospital. We drove my car and I left it down in the yard. Bill left me at the elevator and said, "Your room is so and so," and I didn't see him again for six months. The intern came along with a glassful of bleached lightning that put me away for about fifteen hours. I went into the hospital in April 1939.

My experience in the hospital I considered to be terrific because Dr. Bob told me very quickly that medicine would have very little to do with it, outside of trying to restore my appetite for food. I had had no hospitalization up to this time because I would not call doctors when I was getting over a bad one. I would use barbiturates. In fact, the last three years of my drinking was a routine of barbiturates in the morning, so that I could stop shaking enough to shave, and then alcohol beginning about four-thirty or five o'clock, with a struggle not to take a drink at noon or during the day, because I had the idea that if I took one drink, I would smell as though I had had a pint.

Dr. Bob did not lay out the whole program. He startled me by informing me that he was an alcoholic, that he had found a way which so far enabled him to live without taking a drink, and the main idea was to find a way how not to take that first drink. He told me that there were some other fellows that had tried this with success, and if I cared to see any of them he'd have them come in to see me. I believe every member of the Akron Group did come to see me, which impressed me terrifically, not so much because of the stories they told, but because they would take the time to come and talk to me without even knowing who I was. I did not know there was such a thing as group activity until I left the hospital. I left on a Wednesday afternoon, had dinner in Akron and then went to a house where I encountered my first meeting. I had attended several of these meetings before I discovered that all those who were there were not alcoholics. That is, it was sort of a mixed bunch of Oxford Groupers, who were interested in the alcoholic problem, and of alcoholics themselves. My reaction to those meetings was good. In fact, I never lost my faith, since I had been prepared by some conversations toward the end of my sojourn in the hospital with Dr. Bob, conversations pretty much along spiritual lines. There was one experience with Doc which made a terrific impression upon me. The afternoon that I was to leave the hospital, he came in to see me and asked me if I were willing to attempt to follow the program. I told him that I had no other intention. That was at the end of eight days in which I had had no liquor. He then pulled up his chair with one of his knees touching mine and said, "Will you pray with me for your success?" And he then said a beautiful prayer. That was an experience that I have never forgotten, and many times in my own work with A.A. newcomers I feel kind of guilty because I haven't done the same thing.

One of the things that came up repeatedly in the stories they told me was that once they had accepted the program, they never had a desire to take a drink. That was skeptically received by me when I first heard it, but after some twenty-eight or thirty fellows had come to see me, and pretty nearly all of them had said the same thing, I began to believe it. In my own experience I was so jubilant at finding myself sober, and I had so many things to catch up on, that a month went by before the thought even occurred to me. I had a genuine release right from the start. I've never had a desire to take a drink.

Doc dwelt on the idea that this was an illness, but Doc was pretty frank with me. He found that I had enough faith in the Almighty to be fairly frank. He pointed out to me that probably it was more of a moral or spiritual illness than it was a physical one.

We went to Akron for about six weeks and we did a lot of visiting among the people in Akron. There were, at that time, in the neighborhood of twelve or thirteen Cleveland members who had been sober anywhere from a year and a half to a couple of months. They had all been to Akron. It was finally decided to undertake the organization of a Cleveland group and toward the end of May 1939, the first meeting was held in Cleveland in my home. At that meeting, there were a number of Akron people and all the Cleveland people.

Professionally, after I was sober for a month or so I realized that I should school myself to dissolve the partnership I was in because I felt that I would never regain the respect of my partners no matter how long I was sober, and that I would be at a disadvantage. I still had enough practice to earn a good living if I would only work, so I resolved that in January of 1940 I would launch a patent law firm of my own.

Shortly after I came to this conclusion, I was importuned by another well-known patent law firm to help them out on some trial work because their trial man had had a heart attack and had been forbidden to go into the courtroom. Somewhere in one of the conversations, I mentioned that I was contemplating forming a new firm. On hearing that, these people induced me to make the move immediately and join them as a senior partner, which I did. I found in the fall of 1939, that I was not mentally impaired, so far as trial work was concerned, and thereafter took up where I had left off when I was about forty-five years old. My physical health was badly shaken, but I began to pick up. In fact, after six months of living on food instead of on whiskey, I gained about thirty pounds.

I realized that there wasn't anything I could say to place myself in a more favorable light with my children, that it was going to be a matter of time; for I also understood the intolerance of young people towards deficiencies in their elders. I believe though that it helped my family tremendously to have the A.A. meetings every week in my own home. My oldest child sometimes sat in on the meetings.

I had accepted Catholicism somewhat as an inheritance. My education had been pretty much pagan— science. I resolved that if I were going to continue with the Catholic Church, I was going to know the roots of the doctrine, since those roots had caused me some confusion. So I enrolled at the university for night courses in religion, and I pursued those courses for a year. In summing up, I can say the A.A. has made me, I hope, a real Catholic.

THE EUROPEAN DRINKER

Beer and wine were not the answer.

I was born in Europe, in Alsace to be exact, shortly after it had become German, and practically grew up with the "good Rhine wine" of song and story. My parents had some vague idea of making a priest out of me and for some years I attended the Franciscan school at Basle, Switzerland, just across the border, about six miles from my home. But, although I was a good Catholic, the monastic life had little appeal for me.

Very early I became apprenticed to harness-making and acquired considerable knowledge of upholstering. My daily consumption of wine was about a quart, but that was common where I lived. Everybody drank wine. And it is true that there was no great amount of drunkenness. But I can remember, in my teens, that there were a few characters who caused the village heads to nod pityingly and sometimes in anger as they paused to say, "That sot, Henri" and "Ce pauvre Jules," who drank too much. They were undoubtedly the alcoholics of our village.

Military service was compulsory and I did my stretch with the class of my age, goose-stepping in German barracks and taking part in the Boxer Rebellion in China, my first time at any great distance from home. In foreign parts many a soldier who has been abstemious at home learns to use new and potent drinks. So I indulged with my comrades in everything the Far East had to offer. I cannot say, however, that I acquired any craving for hard liquor as a result. When I got back to Germany I settled down to finish my apprenticeship, drinking the wine of the country as usual.

Many friends of my family had emigrated to America, so at twenty-four I decided that the United States offered me the opportunity I was never likely to find in my native land. I came directly to a growing industrial city in the middle west, where I have lived practically ever since. I was warmly welcomed by friends of my youth who had preceded me. For weeks after my arrival I was fêted and entertained in the already large colony of Alsatians in the city, and among the Germans in their saloons and clubs. I early decided that the wine of America was very inferior stuff and took up beer instead.

Fond of singing, I joined a German singing society which had good club headquarters. There I sat in the evenings, enjoying with my friends our memories of the "old country," singing the old songs we all knew, playing simple card games for drinks and consuming great quantities of beer.

At that time I could go into any saloon, have one or two beers, walk out and forget about it. I had no desire whatever to sit down at a table and stay a whole morning or afternoon drinking. Certainly, at that time I was one of those who "can take it or leave it alone." There had never been any drunkards in my family. I came of good stock, of men and women who drank wine all their lives as a beverage, and while they occasionally got drunk at special celebrations, they were up and about their business the next day.

Prohibition came. Having regard for the law of the

land, I resigned myself to the will of the national legis-
lators and quit drinking altogether, not because I had
found it harmful, but because I couldn't get what I was
accustomed to drink. You can all remember that in the
first few months after the change, a great many men,
who had formerly been used to a few beers every day
or an occasional drink of whiskey, simply quit all alcoholic drinks. For the great majority of us, however,
that condition didn't last. We saw very early that Prohibition wasn't going to work. It wasn't very long before home brewing was an institution and men began
to search feverishly for old recipe books on wine-
making.

But I hardly tasted anything for two years and
started in business for myself, founding a mattress
factory which is today an important industrial enterprise in our city. I was doing very well with that and
general upholstering work, and there was every indication that I would be financially independent by the
time I reached middle age. By this time I was married
and was paying for a home. Like most immigrants I
wanted to be somebody and have something and I was
very happy and contented as I felt success crown my
efforts. I missed the old social times, of course, but
had no definite craving even for beer.

Successful home-brewers among my friends began
to invite me to their homes. I decided that if these fellows could make it I would try it myself, and so I did.
It wasn't very long until I had developed a pretty good
brew with uniformity and plenty of authority. I knew
the stuff I was making was a lot stronger than I had
been used to, but I never suspected that steady drinking of it might develop a taste for something even
stronger still.

It wasn't long before the bootlegger was an established institution in this, as in other towns. I was doing well in business, and in going around town I was frequently invited to have a drink in a speakeasy. I condoned my domestic brewing along with the bootleggers and their business. More and more I formed the habit of doing some of my business in the speakeasy, and after a time I did not need that as an excuse. The "speaks" usually sold whiskey. Beer was too bulky and it couldn't be kept in a jug under the counter ready to be dumped when John Law came around. I was now forming an entirely new drinking technique. Before long I had a definite taste for hard liquor, knew nausea and headaches I had never known before, but as in the old days, I suffered them out. Gradually, however, I'd suffer so much that I simply had to have the morning-after drink.

I became a periodic drinker. I was eased out of the business I had founded and was reduced to doing general upholstery in a small shop at the back of my house. My wife upbraided me often and plenty when she saw that my "periodics" were gradually losing me what business I could get. I began to bring bottles in. I had them hidden away in the house and all over my shop in careful concealment. I had all the usual experiences of the alcoholic, for I was certainly one by this time. Sometimes, after sobering up after a bout of several weeks, I would righteously resolve to quit. With a great deal of determination, I would throw out full pints—pour them out and smash the bottles—firmly resolved never to take another drink of the stuff. I was going to straighten up.

In four or five days I would be hunting all over the place, at home and in my workshop, for the bottles I had destroyed, cursing myself for being a fool. My "periodics" became more frequent until I reached the point where I wanted to devote all my time to drinking, working as little as possible, and then only when the necessity of my family demanded it. As soon as I had satisfied that, what I earned as an upholsterer went for liquor. I would promise to have jobs done and never do them. My customers lost confidence in me to the point where I retained what business I had only because I was a well-trained and reputedly fine craftsman. "Best in the business, when he's sober," my customers would say, and I still had a following who would give me work though they deplored my habits, because they knew the job would be well done when they eventually got it.

I had always been a good Catholic, possibly not so devoted as I should have been, but fairly regular in my attendance at services. I had never doubted the existence of the Supreme Being, but now I began to absent myself from my church where I had formerly been a member of the choir. Unfortunately, I had no desire to consult my priest about my drinking. In fact I was scared to talk to him about it, for I feared the kind of talk he would give me. Unlike many other Catholics who frequently take pledges for definite periods—a year, two years or for good, I never had any desire to "take a pledge" before the priest. And yet, realizing at last that liquor really had me, I wanted to quit. My wife wrote away for advertised cures for the liquor habit and gave them to me in coffee. I even got them myself and tried them. None of the various cures of this kind were any good.

Then occurred the event that saved me. An alcoholic who was a doctor came to see me. He didn't talk like a preacher at all. In fact his language was perfectly suited to my understanding. He had no desire to know anything, except whether I was definite about my desire to quit drinking. I told him with all the sincerity at my command that I did. Even then he went into no great detail about how he and a crowd of alcoholics, with whom he associated, had mastered their difficulty. Instead he told me that some of them wanted to talk to me and would be over to see me.

This doctor had imparted his knowledge to just a few other men at that time—not more than four or five—they now number more than seventy persons. And, because as I have discovered since, it is part of the "treatment" that these men be sent to see and talk with alcoholics who want to quit, he kept them busy. He had already imbued them with his own spirit until they were ready and willing at all times to go where sent, and as a doctor he well knew that this mission and duty would strengthen them as it later helped me. The visits from these men impressed me at once. Where preaching and prayers had touched me very little, I immediately desired further knowledge of these men.

I could see they were sober. The third man who came to see me had been one of the greatest business-getters his company had ever employed. From the top of the heap in a few years he had skidded to becoming a shuffling customer, still entering the better barrooms but welcomed by neither mine host nor his patrons. His own business was practically gone, he told me, when he discovered the answer.

"You've been trying man's ways and they always fail," he told me. "You can't win unless you try God's way."

I had never heard of the remedy expressed in just this language. In a few sentences he made God seem personal to me, explained Him as a being who was interested in me, the alcoholic, and that all I needed to do was to be willing to follow His way; that as long as I followed it I would be able to overcome my desire for liquor.

Well, there I was, willing to try it, but I didn't know how, except in a vague way. I knew somehow that it meant more than just going to church and living a moral life. If that was all, then I was a little doubtful that it was the answer I was looking for.

He went on talking and told me that he had found the plan has a basis of love, and the practice of Christ's injunction, "Love thy neighbor as thyself." Taking that as a foundation, he reasoned that if a man followed that rule he could not be selfish. I could see that. And he further said that God could not accept me as a sincere follower of His Divine Law unless I was ready to be thoroughly honest about it.

That was perfectly logical. My church taught that. I had always known that, in theory. We talked, too, about personal morals. Every man has his problem of this kind, but we didn't discuss it very much. My visitor well knew, that as I tried to follow God I would get to studying these things out for myself.

That day I gave my will to God and asked to be directed. But I have never thought of that as something to do and then forget about. I very early came to see that there had to be a continual renewal of that simple deal with God; that I had perpetually to keep the bargain. So I began to pray; to place my problems in God's hands.

For a long time I kept on trying, in a pretty dumb

way at first, I know, but very earnestly. I didn't want to be a fake. And I began putting into practice what I was learning every day. It wasn't very long until my doctor friend sent me to tell another alcoholic what my experience had been. This duty together with my weekly meetings with my fellow alcoholics, and my daily renewal of the contract I originally made with God, have kept me sober when nothing else ever did.

I have been sober for many years now. The first few months were hard. Many things happened; business trials, little worries, and feelings of general despondency came near driving me to the bottle, but I made progress. As I go along I seem to get strength daily to be able to resist more easily. And when I get upset, cross-grained and out of tune with my fellow man I know that I am out of tune with God. Searching where I have been at fault, it is not hard to discover and get right again, for I have proven to myself and to many others who know me that God can keep a man sober if he will let Him.

THE VICIOUS CYCLE

*How it finally broke a Southerner's obstinacy and
destined this salesman to start A.A. at Philadelphia.*

*J*anuary 8, 1938—that was my D-Day; the place,
Washington, D.C. This last real merry-go-round
had started the day before Christmas and I had really
accomplished a lot in those fourteen days. First, my
new wife had walked out, bag, baggage and furniture;
then the apartment landlord had thrown me out of the
empty apartment and the finish was the loss of another
job. After a couple of days in dollar hotels and one
night in the pokey, I finally landed on my mother's
doorstep—shaking apart, with several days' beard and,
of course, broke as usual. Many of these same things
had happened to me many times before, but this time
they had all descended together. For me, this was It.

Here I was, thirty-nine years old and a complete
washout. Nothing had worked. Mother would take
me in only if I would stay locked in a small storeroom
and give her my clothes and shoes. We had played this
game before. That is the way Jackie found me, lying
on a cot in my skivvies, with hot and cold sweats,
pounding heart and that awful itchy scratchiness all
over. Somehow I had always managed to avoid D.T.'s.

I had not asked for help and seriously doubt that I
would have, but Fitz, an old school friend of mine,
had persuaded Jackie to call on me. Had he come two
or three days later I think I would have thrown him
out, but he hit when I was open for anything.

Jackie arrived about seven in the evening and talked until three a.m. I don't remember much of what he said, but I did realize that here was another guy exactly like me; he had been in the same laughing academies and the same jails, known the same loss of jobs, same frustrations, same boredom and the same loneliness. If anything, he had known all of them even better and more often than I. Yet he was happy, relaxed, confident and laughing. That night for the first time in my life I really let down my hair and admitted my general loneliness. Jackie told me about a group of fellows in New York, of whom my old friend Fitz was one, who had the same problem I had, and who by working together to help each other were not now drinking and were happy like himself. He said something about God or a Higher Power, but I brushed that off—that was for the birds, not for me. Little more of our talk stayed in my memory, but I do know I slept the rest of that night, while before I had never known what a real night's sleep was.

This was my introduction to this "understanding fellowship" although it was to be more than a year later before our Society was to bear the name Alcoholics Anonymous. All of us in A.A. know the tremendous happiness that is in our sobriety, but there are also tragedies. My sponsor, Jackie, was one of these. He brought in many of our original members, yet he himself could not make it and died of alcoholism. The lesson of his death still remains with me, yet I often wonder what would have happened if somebody else had made that first call on me. So I always say that as long as I remember January 8th that is how long I will remain sober.

The age-old question in A.A. is which came first,

the neurosis or the alcoholism. I like to think I was fairly normal before alcohol took over. My early life was spent in Baltimore where my father was a physician and a grain merchant. My family lived in very prosperous circumstances, and while both my parents drank, sometimes too much, neither was an alcoholic. Father was a very well-integrated person, and while mother was highstrung and a bit selfish and demanding, our home life was reasonably harmonious. There were four of us children, and although both of my brothers later became alcoholic—one died of alcoholism—my sister has never taken a drink in her life.

Until I was thirteen I attended public schools, with regular promotions and average grades. I have never shown any particular talents nor have I had any really frustrating ambitions. At thirteen I was packed off to a very fine Protestant boarding school in Virginia, where I stayed four years, graduating without any special achievements. In sports I made the track and tennis teams; I got along well with the other boys and had a fairly large circle of acquaintances but no intimate friends. I was never homesick and was always pretty self-sufficient.

However, here I probably took my first step towards my coming alcoholism by developing a terrific aversion to all churches and established religions. At this school we had Bible readings before each meal, and church services four times on Sunday, and I became so rebellious at this that I swore I would never join or go to any church except for weddings and funerals.

At seventeen I entered the University, really to satisfy my father who wanted me to study medicine there as he had. That is where I had my first drink and I still remember it, for every "first" drink afterwards did exactly the same trick—I could feel it go right through every bit of my body and down to my very toes. But each drink after the "first" seemed to become less effective and after three or four they all seemed like water. I was never a hilarious drunk; the more I drank the quieter I got, and the drunker I got the harder I fought to stay sober. So it is clear that I never had any fun out of drinking—I would be the soberest-seeming one in the crowd and all of a sudden I was the drunkest. Even that first night I blacked out, which leads me to believe that I was an alcoholic from my very first drink. The first year in college I just got by in my studies, and that year I majored in poker and drinking. I refused to join any fraternity, as I wanted to be a free lance, and that year my drinking was confined to one-night stands, once or twice a week. The second year my drinking was more or less restricted to weekends, but I was nearly kicked out for scholastic failure.

In the spring of 1917, in order to beat being fired from school, I became "patriotic" and joined the Army. I am one of the lads who came out of the service with a lower rank than when I went in. I had been to OTC the previous summer, so I went into the Army as a sergeant, but I came out a private, and you really have to be unusual to do that. In the next two years I washed more pans and peeled more potatoes than any other doughboy. In the Army, I became a periodic alcoholic—the periods always coming whenever I could make the opportunity. However, I did manage to keep out of the guardhouse. My last bout in the Army lasted from November 5th to 11th, 1918. We heard by wireless on the 5th that the Armistice would be signed the next day (this was a premature report) so I had a couple of cognacs to celebrate; then I hopped a truck and went AWOL. My next conscious memory was in Bar le Duc, many miles from base. It was November 11th and bells were ringing and whistles blowing for the real Armistice. There I was, unshaven, clothes torn and dirty with no recollection of wandering all over France but, of course, a hero to the local French. Back at camp, all was forgiven because it was the End, but in the light of what I have since learned I know I was a confirmed alcoholic at nineteen.

With the war over, and back in Baltimore with the folks, there were several small jobs for three years and then I went to work soliciting as one of the first ten employees of a new national finance company. What an opportunity I shot to pieces there! This company now does a volume of over three billion dollars annually. Three years later, at twenty-five, I opened and operated their Philadelphia office and was earning more than I ever have since. I was the fair-haired boy all right, but two years later I was blacklisted as an irresponsible drunk. It doesn't take long.

My next job was in sales promotion for an oil company in Mississippi where I promptly became high man and got lots of pats on the back. Then I turned two company cars over in a short time and Bingo— fired again. Oddly enough, the big shot who fired me from this company was one of the first men I met when I later joined the New York A.A. Group. He had also gone all the way through the wringer and had been dry two years when I saw him again.

After the oil job blew up, I went back to Baltimore and mother, my first wife having said a permanent "Goodbye." Then came a sales job with a national tire company. I re-organized their city sales policy and eighteen months later, when I was thirty, they offered me the branch managership. As part of this promotion, they sent me to their national convention in Atlantic City to tell the big wheels how I'd done it. At this time I was holding what drinking I did down to weekends, but I hadn't had a drink at all in a month. I checked into my hotel room and then noticed a placard tucked under the glass on the bureau stating "There will be positively NO drinking at this convention" signed by the president of the company. That did it! Who, me? The Big Shot? The only salesman invited to talk at the convention? The man who was going to take over one of the biggest branches come Monday? I'd show 'em who was boss! No one in that company saw me again—ten days later I wired my resignation.

As long as things were tough and the job a challenge I could always manage to hold on pretty well, but as soon as I learned the combination, got the puzzle under control and the boss to pat me on the back, I was gone again. Routine jobs bored me, but I would take on the toughest one I could find, work day and night until I had it under control; then it would become tedious and I'd lose all interest in it. I could never be bothered with the follow-through and would invariably reward myself for my efforts with that "first" drink.

After the tire job came the thirties, the Depression and the down hill road. In the eight years before A.A. found me, I had over forty jobs—selling and traveling—one thing after another, and the same old routine. I'd work like mad for three or four weeks without a single drink, save my money, pay a few bills and then "reward" myself with alcohol. Then broke again, hiding out in cheap hotels all over the country, one night jail stands here and there, and always that horrible feeling "What's the use—nothing is worth while." Every time I blacked out, and that was every time I drank, there was always that gnawing fear, "What did I do this time?" Once I found out. Many alcoholics have learned they can bring their bottle to a cheap movie theater and drink, sleep, wake up and drink again in the darkness. I had repaired to one of these one morning with my jug and when I left late in the afternoon, I picked up a newspaper on the way home. Imagine my surprise when I read in a page one "box" that I had been taken from the theater unconscious around noon that day, removed by ambulance to a hospital and stomach-pumped and then released. Evidently I had gone right back to the movie with a bottle, stayed there several hours and started home with no recollection of what had happened.

The mental state of the sick alcoholic is beyond description. I had no resentments against individuals—the whole world was all wrong. My thoughts went round with "What's it all about anyhow? People have wars and kill each other; they struggle and cut each other's throats for success and what does anyone get out of it? Haven't I been successful, haven't I accomplished extraordinary things in business? What do I get out of it? Everything's all wrong and the hell with it." For the last two years of my drinking I prayed on every drunk that I wouldn't wake up again. Three months before I met Jackie I had made my second feeble try at suicide.

This was the background that made me willing to listen on January 8th. After being dry two weeks and sticking close to Jackie, all of a sudden I found I had become the sponsor of my sponsor, for he was sud-

denly taken drunk. I was startled to learn he had only
been off the booze a month or so himself when he
brought me the message! However, I made an SOS call
to the New York Group, whom I hadn't met yet, and
they suggested we both come there. This we did the
next day, and what a trip! I really had a chance to see
myself from a non-drinking point of view. We checked
into the home of Hank, the man who had fired me
eleven years before in Mississippi, and there I met Bill,
our founder. Bill had been dry three years and Hank,
two. At the time, I thought them just a swell pair of
screwballs, for they were not only going to save all the
drunks in the world but also all the so-called normal
people! All they talked of that first weekend was God,
and how they were going to straighten out Jackie's and
my life. In those days we really took each other's in-
ventories firmly and often. Despite all this, I *did* like
these new friends because, again, they were like me.
They has also been periodic big shots who had goofed
out repeatedly at the wrong time, and they also knew
how to split one paper match into three separate
matches. (This is very useful knowledge in places
where matches are prohibited.) They, too, had taken a
train to one town and had wakened hundreds of miles
in the opposite direction, never knowing how they got
there. The same old routines seemed to be common to
us all. During that first weekend I decided to stay in
New York and take all they gave out with, except the
"God stuff." I knew they needed to straighten out
their thinking and habits, but *I* was all right, *I* just
drank too much. Just give me a good front and a couple of bucks and I'd be right back in the big time. I'd
been dry three weeks, had the wrinkles out and had
sobered up my sponsor all by myself!

Bill and Hank had just taken over a small automobile polish company and they offered me a job—ten dollars a week and keep at Hank's house. We were all set to put DuPont out of business.

At that time the group in New York was composed of about twelve men who were working on the principle of every drunk for himself; we had no real formula and no name. We would follow one man's ideas for a while, decided he was wrong and switch to another's method. But we *were* staying sober as long as we kept and talked together. There was one meeting a week at Bill's home in Brooklyn, and we all took turns there spouting off about how we had changed our lives overnight, how many drunks we had saved and straightened out, and last, but not least, how God had touched each of us personally on the shoulder. Boy, what a circle of confused idealists! Yet we all had one really sincere purpose in our hearts and that was not to drink. At our weekly meeting I was a menace to serenity those first few months, for I took every opportunity to lambaste that "spiritual angle" as we called it, or anything else that had any tinge of theology. Much later I discovered the elders held many prayer meetings hoping to find a way to give me the heave-ho, but at the same time stay tolerant and spiritual. They did not seem to be getting an answer, for here I was staying sober and selling lots of auto polish, on which they were making one thousand percent profit. So I rocked along my merry independent way until June, when I went out selling auto polish in New England. After a very good week, two of my customers took me to lunch on Saturday. We ordered sandwiches and one man said, "Three beers." I let mine sit. After a bit, the other man said, "Three beers." I let that sit too. Then it was my turn—I ordered "Three beers," but this time it was different, I had a cash investment of thirty cents and, on a ten dollar a week salary, that's a big thing. So I drank all three beers, one after the other, said, "I'll be seeing you, boys," and went around the corner for a bottle. I never saw either of them again.

I had completely forgotten the January 8th when I found the fellowship, and I spent the next four days wandering around New England half drunk, by which I mean I couldn't get drunk and I couldn't get sober. I tried to contact the boys in New York, but telegrams bounced right back and when I finally got Hank on the telephone he fired me right then. This was when I really took my first good look at myself. My loneliness was worse than it had ever been before, for now even my own kind had turned against me. This time it really hurt, more than any hangover ever had. My brilliant agnosticism vanished, and I saw for the first time that those who really believed, or at least honestly tried to find a Power greater than themselves, were much more composed and contented than I had ever been, and they seemed to have a degree of happiness which I had never known.

Peddling off my polish samples for expenses, I crawled back to New York a few days later in a very chastened frame of mind. When the others saw my altered attitude they took me back in, but for me they *had* to make it tough; if they hadn't I don't think I ever would have stuck it out. Once again, there was the challenge of a tough job, but this time I was determined to follow through. For a long time the only Higher Power I could concede was the power of the group, but this was far more than I had ever recognized before, and it was at least a beginning. It was also an ending, for never since June 16th, 1938, have I had to walk alone.

Around this time our big A.A. book was being written and it all became much simpler; we had a definite formula which some sixty of us agreed was the middle course for all alcoholics who wanted sobriety, and that formula has not been changed one iota down through the years. I don't think the boys were completely convinced of my personality change, for they fought shy of including my story in the book, so my only contribution to their literary efforts was my firm conviction, being still a theological rebel, that the word God should be qualified with the phrase "as we understand him"—for that was the only way I could accept spirituality.

After the book appeared we all became very busy in our efforts to save all and sundry, but I was still actually on the fringes of A.A. While I went along with all that was done and attended the meetings, I never took an active job of leadership until February 1940. Then I got a very good position in Philadelphia and quickly found I would need a few fellow alcoholics around me if I was to stay sober. Thus I found myself in the middle of a brand new group. When I started to tell the boys how we did it in New York and all about the spiritual part of the program, I found they would not believe me unless I was practicing what I preached. Then I found that as I gave in to this spiritual or personality change I was getting a little more serenity. In telling newcomers how to change their lives and attitudes, all of a sudden I found I was doing a little changing myself. I had been too self-sufficient to write a moral inventory, but I discovered in pointing out to the new man his wrong attitudes and actions that I was really taking my own inventory, and that if I expected him to change I would have to work on myself too. This change has been a long, slow process for me, but through these latter years the dividends have been tremendous.

In June 1945, with another member, I made my first—and only—Twelfth Step call on a female alcoholic and a year later I married her. She has been sober all the way through and for me that has been good. We can share in the laughter and tears of our many friends, and most important, we can share our A.A. way of life and are given a daily opportunity to help others.

In conclusion, I can only say that whatever growth or understanding has come to me, I have no wish to graduate. Very rarely do I miss the meetings of my neighborhood A.A. group, and my average has never been less than two meetings a week. I have served on only one committee in the past nine years, for I feel that I had my chance the first few years and that newer members should fill the jobs. They are far more alert and progressive than we floundering fathers were, and the future of our fellowship is in their hands. We now live in the West and are very fortunate in our area A.A.; it is good, simple and friendly, and our one desire is to stay *in* A.A. and not *on* it. Our pet slogan is "Easy Does It."

And I still say that as long as I remember that January 8th in Washington, that is how long, by the grace of God as I understand Him, I will retain a happy sobriety.

THE NEWS HAWK[*]

*This newsman covered life from top to bottom; but
he ended up, safely enough, in the middle.*

With nothing but a liberal arts education, very
definitely estranged from my family and already
married, soon after graduation from college I became
a bookmaker's clerk on the British racing circuits, far
better off financially than the average professional
man. I moved in a gay crowd in the various "pubs"
and sporting clubs. My wife traveled with me, but
with a baby coming I decided to settle in a large city
where I got a job with a commission agent which is a
polite term for a hand-book operator. My job was to
collect bets and betting-slips in the business section, a
lucrative spot. My boss, in his way, was "big business." Drinking was all in the day's work.

One evening, the book, after checking up, was very
definitely in the red for plenty through a piece of studied carelessness on my part, and my boss, very shrewd
and able, fired me with a parting statement to the effect that once was enough. With a good stake I sailed
for New York. I knew I was through among the English "bookies."

Tom Sharkey's brawling bar on 14th Street and the
famous wine-room at the back were headquarters for
me. I soon ran through my stake. Some college friends

---

[*]Originally published under the title "Traveler, Editor, Scholar" in the
first edition. The title was changed to "The News Hawk" and the
story was edited for the second edition.

got me jobs when I finally had to go to work, but I didn't stick to them. I wanted to travel. Making my way to Pittsburgh, I met other former friends and got a job in a large factory where piecemakers were making good money. My fellow-workers were mostly good Saturday night drinkers and I was right with them. Young and able to travel with the best of them, I managed to hold my job and keep my end up in the barrooms.

I quit the factory and got a job on a small newspaper, going from that to a Pittsburgh daily, long ago defunct. Following a big drunk on that sheet, where I was doing leg-work and rewrite, a feeling of nostalgia made me buy a ticket for Liverpool and I returned to Britain.

During my visit there, renewing acquaintance with former friends, I soon spent most of my money. I wanted to roam again and through relatives got a supercargo job on an Australian packet which allowed me to visit my people in Australia where I was born. But I didn't stay long. I was soon back in Liverpool. Coming out of a pub near the Cunard pier I saw the Lusitania standing out in the middle of the Mersey. She had just come in and was scheduled to sail in two days.

In my mind's eye I saw Broadway again and Tom Sharkey's bar; the roar of the subway was in my ears. Saying goodbye to my wife and baby, I was treading Manhattan's streets in a little more than a week. Again I spent my bankroll, by no means as thick as the one I had when I first saw the skyline of Gotham. I was soon broke, this time without trainfare to go anywhere. I got my first introduction to "riding the rods and making a blind."

In my early twenties the hardships of hobo life did not discourage me, but I had no wish to become just a tramp. Forced to detrain from an empty gondola on the other side of Chicago by a terrific rainstorm which drenched me to the skin, I hit the first factory building I saw for a job. That job began a series of brief working spells, each one ending in a "drunk" and the urge to travel. My migrations extended for over a year as far west as Omaha. Drifting back to Ohio, I landed on a small newspaper and later was impressed into the direction of boy-welfare work at the local "Y." I stayed sober for four years except for a one-night carousal in Chicago. I stayed so sober that I used to keep a quart of medicinal whiskey in my bureau which I used to taper off the occasional newspaper alcoholics who were sent to see me.

Lots of times, vain-gloriously, I used to take the bottle out, look at it and say, "I've got you licked."

The war was getting along. Curious about it, feeling I was missing something, absolutely without any illusions about the aftermath, with no pronounced feeling of patriotism, I joined up with a Canadian regiment, serving a little over two years. Slight casualties, complicated however by a long and serious illness, were my only mishaps. Remarkably enough, I was a very abstemious soldier. My four years of abstinence had something to do with it, but soldiering is a tough enough game for a sober man, and I had no yen for full-pack slogging through mud with a cognac or vin rouge hangover.

Discharged in 1919, I really made up for my dry spell. Quebec, Toronto, Buffalo, and finally Pittsburgh, were the scenes of man-sized drunks until I had gone through my readjusted discharge pay, a fair sum.

I again became a reporter on a Pittsburgh daily. I applied for a publicity job and got it. My wife came over from Scotland and we started housekeeping in a large Ohio city.

The new job lasted five years. Every encouragement was given me with frequent salary increases, but the sober times between "periods" became shorter. I myself could see deterioration in my work from being physically and mentally affected by liquor, although I had not yet reached the point where all I wanted was more to drink. Successive Monday morning hangovers, which despite mid-week resolutions to do better, came with unfailing regularity, eventually caused me to quit my job. Washington, D.C. and newsgathering agency work followed, along with many parties. I couldn't stand the pace. My drinking was never the spaced doses of the careful tippler; it was always gluttonous.

Returning to the town I had left three months before, I became editor of a monthly magazine, soon had additional publicity and advertising accounts and the money rolled in. The strain of overwork led me to the bottle again. My wife made several attempts to get me to stop and I had the usual visits from persons who would always ask me "Why?"—as if I knew! Offered the job of advertising manager for an eastern automotive company, I moved to Philadelphia to begin life anew. In three months John Barleycorn had me kicked out.

I did six years of newspaper advertising, and trade journal work with many, many drunks of drab and dreary hue woven into the pattern of my life. I visited my family just once in that time. An old avocation, the collecting of first editions, rare books and Americana,

fascinated me between times. I had some financial success through no ability of my own and, when jobless
and almost wiped out in 1930, I began to trade and
sell my collection; much of the proceeds went to keep
my apartment stocked with liquor and almost every
night saw me helpless to bed.

I tried to help myself. I even began to go the rounds
of the churches. I listened to famous ministers—found
nothing. I began to know the inside of jails and work-
houses. My family would have nothing to do with me,
in fact couldn't because I couldn't spare any of my
money, which I needed for drink, to support them. My
last venture, a book shop, was hastened to closed doors
by my steady intoxication. Then I had an idea.

Loading a car with good old books to sell to col-
lectors, librarians, universities and historical societies,
I started out to travel the country. I stayed sober during the trip except for an occasional bottle of beer because funds barely met expenses. When I hit Houston,
Texas, I found employment in a large bookstore. Need
I say that in a very short time I was walking along
a prairie highway with arm extended and thumb
pointed? In the two succeeding years I held ten different jobs ranging from newspaper copy-desk and
rewrite, to traffic director for an oil field equipment
company. Always, in between, there were intervals of
being broke, riding freights and hitch-hiking inter-
minable distances from one big town to another in
three states. Now on a new job I was always thinking
about payday and how much liquor I could buy and
the pleasure I could have.

I knew I was a drunkard. Enduring all the hangover hells that every alcoholic experiences, I made the
usual resolutions. My thoughts sometimes turned to

the idea that there must be a remedy. I have stood listening to street-corner preachers tell how they beat the game. They seemed to be happy in their fashion, they and their little groups of supporters, but always pride of intellect stopped me from seeking what they evidently had. Sniffing at emotional religion, I walked away. I was an honest agnostic, but definitely not a hater of the church or its adherents. What philosophy I had was thoroughly paganistic—all my life was devoted to a search for pleasure. I wanted to do nothing except what it pleased me to do when I wanted to do it.

Federal Theatre in Texas gave me an administrative job which I held for a year, only because I worked hard and productively when I worked, and because my very tolerant chief ascribed my frequent lapses to a bohemian temperament. When it was closed through Washington edict I began with Federal Writers in San Antonio. In those days my system was always to drink up my last paycheck and believe that necessity would bring the next job. A friend who knew I would soon be broke mounted guard over me when I left my job of writing the histories of Texas cities and put me aboard a bus for the town I had left almost five years before.

In five years a good many persons had forgotten that I had been somewhat notorious. I arrived drunk, but I promised my wife I would keep sober, and I knew I could get work if I did. Of course I didn't keep sober. My wife and family stood by me for ten weeks and then, quite justifiably, ejected me. I managed to maintain myself with odd jobs, did ten weeks in a social rescue institution, and at length wound up in a second-hand bookstore in an adjacent town as manager. While there I was called to the hospital in my home town to see a former partner who had insisted that I visit him. I found my friend was there for alcoholism and now he was insisting that he had found the only cure. I listened to him, rather tolerantly. I noticed a Bible on his table and it amazed me. I had never known him to be anything but a good healthy pagan with a propensity for getting into liquor jams and scrapes. As he talked I gathered vaguely, (because he was a faltering beginner then, just as I am now) that to be relieved of alcoholism I would have to be different.

Some days later, after he had been discharged, a stranger came into my shop in the nearby town. He introduced himself and began to tell me about a bunch of some sixty former drinkers and drunkards who met once a week, and he invited me to go with him to the next meeting. I thanked him, pleaded business engagements and promised I'd go with him at some future date.

"Anyhow, I'm on the wagon now," I said. "I'm doing a job I like and it's quiet where I live, practically no temptations. I don't feel bothered about liquor."

He looked at me quizzically. He knew too well that didn't mean a thing, just as I knew in my heart that it would be only a question of time—a few days, a week, or even a month, it was inevitable—till I would be off on another bender. The time came just a week later. As I look back on the events of two months, I can clearly see that I had been circling around, half-afraid of encountering the remedy for my situation, half wanting it, deferring fulfillment of my promise to get in touch with the doctor I had heard about. An accident while drunk laid me low for about three weeks. As soon as I could get up and walk I started to drink again and kept it up until my friend of the hospital, who, in his first try at the new way of life had stubbed his toe in Chicago but had come back to the town to take counsel and make a new start, picked me up and got me into a hospital.

I had been drinking heavily from one state of semi-coma to another and it was several days before I got "defogged," but subconsciously I was in earnest about wanting to quit liquor forever. It was no momentary emotionalism born of self-pity in a maudlin condition. I was seeking something and I was ready to learn. I did not need to be told that my efforts were and would be unavailing if I did not get help. The doctor who came to see me almost at once did not assail me with any new doctrines; he made sure that I had a need and that I wanted to have that need filled, and little by little I learned how my need could be met. The story of Alcoholics Anonymous fascinated me. Singly and in groups of two or three, they came to visit me. Some of them I had known for years, good two-fisted drinkers who had disappeared from their former haunts. I had missed them myself from the barrooms of the town.

There were business men, professional men, and factory workers. All sorts were represented and their relation of experiences and how they found the only remedy, added to their human existence as sober men, laid the foundation of a very necessary faith. Indeed, I was beginning to see that I would require implicit faith, like a small child, if I was going to get anywhere. The big thing was that these men were all sober and evidently had something I didn't have. Whatever it was, I wanted it.

I left the hospital on a meeting night. I was greeted warmly, honestly, and with a true ring of sincerity by everyone present. That night I was taken home by a former alcoholic and his wife. They did not show me to my room and wish me a good night's rest. Instead, over coffee cups, this man and his wife told me what had been done for them. They were earnest and obviously trying to help me on the road I had chosen. They will never know how much their talk with me helped. The hospitality of their home and their fine fellowship were freely mine.

I had never, since the believing days of childhood, been able to conceive an authority directing the universe. But I had never been a flippant, wise-cracking sneerer at the few persons I had met who had impressed me as Christian men and women, or at any institution whose sincerity of purpose I could see. No conviction was necessary to establish my status as a miserable failure at managing my own life. I began to read the Bible daily and to go over a simple devotional exercise as a way to begin each day. Gradually I began to understand.

I cannot say that my taste for liquor has entirely disappeared. It has been that way with some, but it has not been with me and may never be. Neither can I honestly say that I have forgotten the "fleshpots of Egypt." I haven't. But I can remember the urge of the Prodigal Son to return to his Father.

Formerly, in the acute mental and physical pain during the remorseful periods succeeding each drunk, I found my recollection of the misery I had gone through a bolsterer of resolution and afterward, perhaps, a deterrent for a time. But in those days I had no one to whom I might take my troubles. Today I have. Today I have Someone who will always hear me; I have a warm fellowship among men who understand my problems; I have tasks to do and am glad to do them, to see others who are alcoholics and to help them in any way I can to become sober men. I took my last drink in 1937.

FROM FARM TO CITY

She tells how A.A. works when the going is rough.
A pioneer woman member of A.A.'s first Group.

I come from a very poor family in material things, with a fine Christian mother, but with no religious background. I was the oldest in a family of seven, and my father was an alcoholic. I was deprived of many of the things that we feel are important in life, such as education particularly, because of my father's drinking. Mine was far from a happy childhood. I had none of those things that children should have to make them happy.

We moved in from the country at the age when girls want all sorts of nice things. I remember starting to city school, coming from a country school, and wanting so very, very much to be like the other girls and trying flour on my face for powder because I wasn't able to have any real powder. I remember feeling that they were all making fun of me. I feared that I wasn't dressed like the rest. I know that one of the outfits I had was a skirt and a very funny looking blouse that my mother had picked up at a rummage sale. I look back and remember these things because they made me very unhappy, and added to my feeling of inferiority at never being the same as other people.

At the age of sixteen, I was invited to spend the summer with an aunt and I, very delightedly, accepted the invitation. It was a small town—Liberty, Indiana. When I came to my aunt, she knew that I had had an unhappy childhood, and she said, "Now, Ethel, you're welcome to have boy friends in our home, but there are two boys in this town that I don't want you to date, and one of them comes from a very fine family, one of the best. But he's in all sorts of scrapes because he drinks too much." Four months later, I married this guy. I'm sure his family felt that it was a marriage that—well, I was a girl from the wrong side of the tracks—definitely!

I felt that his family were accepting me because it was good sense. I could do something for their Russ. But they didn't do anything for me to build up my ego. And Russ didn't tell me he'd stop drinking, and he certainly didn't stop. It went on and grew worse and worse. We had two daughters. I was sixteen when we were married and he was seven years older. I remember one instance when he took off and went down to Cincinnati and was gone a week on a drunk.

Finally, it got so bad that I left him and went back home and took my two children with me. I didn't see him for a year, or even hear from him. That was seven or eight years after we were married. I was still bitter because I felt that drink had completely ruined my childhood and my married life, and I hated everything pertaining to it. I was about twenty-five then, and I had never touched a drop.

I got a job in the woolen mills in Ravenna—very hard work. I looked much older than I was, I was always large, and I went back to work in this job. I kept my children with me. At the end of a year, the children got a card from their father, which I still have and cherish. He said, "Tell Mommy I still love her." I had gone to an attorney to see about getting a divorce during that year.

Then he came into town on the bum. He had taken up light work, and he had a safety valve and a pair of spurs and the clothes on his back, and that was all. I welcomed him with open arms. I didn't realize how I still felt about him. He told me that he would never drink again. And I believed him. As many times as he would tell me that, I still believed him. Partially so, anyway. He got a job and went back to work.

He stayed "dry" for thirteen years! Dr. Bob often said that it was a record for what he felt was a typical alcoholic.

We built up a splendid life. At the end of those thirteen years I never dreamed that he'd ever take another drink. I had never taken one. Our oldest daughter got married; they were living at our house. Our other daughter was in her last year of high school, and one night the new son-in-law and my husband went out to a prize fight. I never was concerned any more, anywhere he went. He hardly ever went to anything like that without me. We were together all the time, but this night I got up and saw it was late. I heard my son-in-law coming upstairs, and I asked him where dad was. He had a very peculiar look on his face, and he said, "He's coming." He *was* coming, on his hands and knees, up the stairs. As I look back, I was very broken up about it. But I don't believe now that it was with any deep feeling of resentment that I said to him, "The children are raised, and if this is the way you want it, this is the way we'll have it. Where you go, I'll go, and what you drink, I'll drink." That's when I started drinking.

We were the most congenial drinkers you ever saw. We never rowed or fought. We had the grandest time ever. We just loved it. We'd start out on the craziest trips. He'd always say, "Take me for a ride, Ma." So, sometimes we'd end up in Charleston, West Virginia, or here or there, drinking all along the way. These vacations became quite something, and he always had two weeks vacation the first two weeks of every September.

One year we got as far as Bellaire, Ohio. We always started out on the Saturday before Labor Day. I'm pretty near afraid of Labor Day yet. One Sunday afternoon, the only time I ever got picked up for drunken driving, I got picked up in Bellaire. They threw us in the jail. I wasn't nearly in the condition I had been in many times to be picked up. I really wasn't very high. They called the Mayor in so we wouldn't have to stay in there over the holiday. He took his one hundred and seventeen dollars and let us go, and we proceeded. That to me was the greatest humiliation, to think that I'd finally landed in jail. My husband said that I said, "Can you imagine them giving us that jail fare?" And he said, "What jail fare?" And I said, "Well, they brought a pitcher of coffee, and a sandwich wrapped up for me." And he said, "That wasn't jail fare. They didn't give me anything to eat. Somebody must have taken pity on you and gone out and got it for you." And another thing, it's a wonder they didn't throw us back in because I could become very dignified and sarcastic. As we left, and they were escorting us across the bridge into Wheeling, I, with great dignity and sarcasm, told them if their wives were ever visiting in Akron, and they, too, were looking for their route signs as I was, that I hoped that I could extend to them the hospitality that had been shown to me in Bellaire.

The next time vacation time rolled around that

was a bitter lession to us. Of course, this year we were drinking heavier and heavier and we decided on staying home and being sensible, doing a little drinking, and painting the house. So, on that Saturday before Labor Day, I got drunk and set the house on fire—so we didn't have to paint it. I think that was the last vacation before sobriety.

I hated myself worse and worse, and as I hated myself I became more defiant towards everything and everybody. We drank with exactly the same accord that we finally accepted A.A. We comforted each other.

My defiant attitude became worse. There was a very religious family that lived down the road from us, and we were on the same party line. I'd hear them on the phone having prayer meetings and so forth, that sort of talk over the phone, and it completely burnt me up. They used a sound truck some. It would stop out in front of our house, and I still believe those people sent it! They'd sit out there and play hymns and I'd be lying in there with a terrific hangover. If I'd had a gun I'd have shot the horns right off the thing, because it made me raving mad.

It was just about this time, in 1940, that we met up with A.A. Russ read a piece in the paper, and he kind of snickered, and said, "See here, where John D. has found something to keep him from drinking!" "What's that?" I said. "Oh, some darn thing they've got here in the paper about it." We talked about it afterwards, and we felt that there might be some time we'd need it. It was a thought that there might be some hope for us.

One morning after a terrific drinking bout, I was in a little bar near our house, and I shook so that I was very much ashamed, because I was getting the shakes worse and worse. I sipped the drink off the bar because I couldn't hold it in my hand, but I was still a lady, believe it or not, and I was deeply ashamed. There was a man watching, and I turned to him and said, with a defiant air I carried with me all the time, "If I don't quit this I'm going to have to join that alcoholic business they're talking about." He said, "Sister, if you think you're a screwball now, all you have to do is join up with that. I'll get you the password, and I can find out where they meet because I know a guy that belongs. But they are the craziest bunch! They roll on the floor and holler, and pull their hair." "Well, I'm nuts enough now," I said to him. But right then the hope died that had been in my heart when we read about John D.

Time went on and the drinking got worse and worse, and I was in another barroom, down the road the other way, a small one, and I took my glass—that morning I'd been able to lift it from the bar—and I said to the woman behind the bar, "I wish I might never take another drop of that stuff. It's killing me." She said, "Do you really mean that?" I said, "Yes." She said, "Well, you better talk to Jack." (Jack was the owner of the place. We always tried to buy him a drink, and he always told us he had liquor trouble—couldn't drink.)

She said to me, "You know, he used to own the Merry-Go-Round. He used to drink, and then he found something that started up in Akron that helped him quit drinking." Right away, I saw it was the same outfit this other guy told me about, and then again hope died.

Finally, one morning I got up and got in the car

and cried all the way down to the M.'s—the people who owned the bar—and told her I was licked and wanted help. I thought, "No matter how crazy they are I'll do anything they say to do." I drove these three or four miles down the road only to find that Jack was out. (This was funny. They owned this joint, she ran it, and he sold for a brewery. That was his job. And he'd been dry a year. I don't think Jack was hospitalized. I think his entry into A.A. was through spending some hours with Dr. Bob at his office. He brought many people into A.A. through his barroom.) Mrs. M. said she would send Jack over as quick as he came in.

He came with two cans of beer. He gave my husband one and me one about ten-thirty on the eighth day of May in 1941. He said, "There's a doctor here in Akron. I'm going in to see him, and see what can be done." Dr. Bob was in Florida, but Jack didn't know that.

That was our last drink of anything alcoholic. That nasty little can of beer! At two-forty-five that morning I thought I would die. I lay across the bed on my stomach with nothing but pain and sickness. I was scared to death to call a doctor. I thought when people did what we did that they just locked them up. I didn't know that anything was ever done for them in a medical way. So I stayed awake.

Men from A.A. started coming out to the house the next day. I paced the floor with a bath towel around my shoulders, the perspiration running off me. An attorney sat at the side of the bed where I was lying, and he sat on the edge of his chair and looked as innocent as a baby. I thought, "That guy never could have been drunk." He said, "This is my story"—real prim. And I thought, "I bet he's a sissy. I bet he never drank." But he told a story of drinking that was amazing to me.

Jack brought the *Saturday Post* with Jack Alexander's story. He said, "Read this." Jack didn't seem to have too much of the spiritual understanding. He said, "I think this will tell you more. This is based, really, on the Sermon on the Mount. Now, if you've got a Bible around . . ." One of our gifts from the family was a very lovely Bible, but we'd let the bulldog chew it because we weren't too interested in it. I had a little Testament, which was very small print. When you have a hangover and can't even sit still, try to read small print! Russ said, "Mother, if this tells us how to do it, you'll have to read it." And I'd try, but I couldn't even see the letters. But it was so important that we do the things we were told to do! Jack said there was a meeting in Akron every Wednesday night and that it was very important that we go. Jack said, "Now you start and go to these meetings, and then you'll find out all about it." I don't think that there was anything said about religion. I didn't know anything about the Sermon on the Mount.

I had the Big Book ("Alcoholics Anonymous") that had been brought to me. Paul S. had just called me, and I remember he stressed reading the Big Book. I was reading it for all that was in it, and I said to Russ, "We can't do this. We couldn't begin to." And Jim G. had such a wonderful sense of humor, and when he came I was in tears, and I told him, "I want to do this, but I can't. This is too much. I could never go and make up to all the people I've done wrong to." He said, "Let's put the Big Book away again, and when you read it again, turn to the back and read some of the stories. Have you read those?" No, I was all interested in this part that told you how to do it. That was the only part I was interested in. And then he got us to laugh, which was what we needed. When we went to bed my sides ached, and I said to my husband, "I thought I would never laugh again, but I have laughed."

"Well," I said to dad, when the A.A. people kept coming with those lovely cars and looked so nice, "I suppose the neighbors say, 'Now those old fools must have up and died, but where's the hearse?' "

On Wednesday night Jack M. said, "You meet me at the Ohio Edison Building, and I will take you to the meeting." And we went down through the valley, and I remember reading about the Ku Klux Klan and how they burnt crosses, and I thought, "God alone knows what we are getting into this time!" I didn't know what they were going to do because he didn't tell us much. So we came to King School. And they introduced me to Miriam and Annabelle. They told Annabelle to take me under her wing, and I shall never forget how she sort of curled up her nose and said, "They tell me you drink too." I often think how that could have turned some people away, because there were no other women alcoholics there then. And I said, "Why sure, that's what I'm here for." And I was glad, and I have been ever since, that I said that. And I wasn't resentful toward her, either.

There was a young fellow who led the meeting and that was a beautiful thing to me. He talked about his wife taking his little boy away from him because of his drinking, and how he got back together with them through A.A., and we began feeling grateful right then that all these things hadn't been taken from us. They opened with a little prayer, and I thought it was very fine that we stood, all of us together, and closed with the Lord's Prayer.

I'd like to say here how important it was to us then that we do all the little things that people said were important, because later when Russ was so sick that I had to hold him up, they had a meeting out at the house. When we closed the meeting with the Lord's Prayer, Russ said, "Mother, help me stand." This was after his illness. We were in A.A. three and a half years when he was taken from me. We had never missed a Wednesday night at King School for a year. We had that record.

I always feel that our God consciousness was a steady growth after we became associated with A.A. And we loved every minute of that association. We had big picnics out at the house with A.A. We had meetings at each other's homes and, of course, that was a grand place for people to get together out there; they seemed to think so too.

I give a great deal of credit to Doc and Anne for changing our life. They spent at least an evening a week in our home out there for weeks and weeks. Sometimes saying very little, but letting us say. Russ used to be very much pleased because he'd say, "I think Dr. Bob thoroughly enjoys coming out here. He can relax and it's quiet."

At that time they didn't let us know that people ever had trouble. I mean slips. I remember sometime, it was possibly six months after we had been going steadily to King School, that we were coming home from a meeting and saw a car along the way, and a fellow in back drinking a bottle of beer. And Russ said, "I would have sworn that was Jack M." The next morning his wife came dragging him in before Russ went to work, while I was getting breakfast. It had been Jack M. We wept and Russ didn't go to work.

Jack had been sober about a year and a half. His wife was cussing him, raving at him, "I just brought him over to show you what kind of a guy he is! He wants to go to the hospital, and I'm not paying for the hospital again!" We were so mad at her because she talked to him that way. Russ said, "Don't do another thing today but help him. *Do* something for him! If he thinks he needs to go to the hospital, I'll pay for him." She said, "He's not going to the hospital, whether you pay for it or I pay for it, he's not going!"

In the spiritual strength I had found, because of A.A., I felt that I had made a complete surrender, that I had really turned my life over that summer. I thought I had done that until Russ' second collapse, and the doctor told me very candidly that he wasn't long for this world. I knew then that I hadn't made a complete surrender, because I tried to bargain with the God I had found, and I said, "Anything but that! Don't do that to me!"

Russ lived a year longer than they expected him to live, and in that year he was in bed for at least six months. I can't express what A.A. meant to us during that year. Before the end finally came, I had, I guess, made the surrender because I finally had been able to say that I would not mind too much. And I realize that there was one salvation for me. Thank God I had no desire for a drink when he died.

There were two women in the St. Thomas Hospital at that time in a room. (Russ was buried on Friday, and on Sunday afternoon Hilda S. had invited me there to dinner Sunday night, and I didn't think I could do it. I knew Doc and Anne were going to be there, and all of them thought it would be good for me, but the first thing I did was to go to St. Thomas and try to talk to those women.) I sat down on the side of one of their beds, and I started to weep, and I couldn't stop, and I was so startled, and I apologized again and again for it. And that woman told me long after that was the surest proof to her that this program could work. If, on Sunday, I could be there, trying to think of something that would help her with this problem, then we must have something that could work. I felt it certainly must be very depressing to her that I should sit there by her bedside and cry.

I feel that one of the things that I still have to guard against is that I used to be set in my way about what I considered the old-time A.A. I have to tell myself, "Other things are progressing and A.A. must too." We old-timers who get scattered and separated and then witness the construction of services to get in more people and to make this thing function, we think that A.A. has changed, but the root of it hasn't. We are older in A.A., and we're older in years. It's only natural that we don't have the capacity to change, but we ought not to criticize those who have.

There's another thing I would stress. I think it's awfully hard on people, especially if they're new people, to hear these long drawn-out talks. I don't ever remember that I was bored myself when we first came in, and they came out to the house and talked to us about these things. I ate up every bit of it, because I wanted to find out how to stay sober.

Before I stop—I always was a great talker—I want to say that nobody will ever know how I miss Annie's advice about things. I would get in the biggest dither about something. I hadn't been in too long when one of the men's wives called me one Sunday and told me she didn't think I had any part of the program. Well, I wasn't sure I did, and it was awful foggy, and I wept and asked her what she thought I ought to do about it. She said she didn't know, but that I sure showed plain enough I didn't have any part of it. I didn't think I was going to get drunk right then, but I remember how comforting it was when I called Anne and told her. I was crying, and I said, "Alice says she knows I don't have any part of the program." She talked to me and laughed about it and got me all over it. Another thing that was helpful to me. I used to think I was cowardly because when things came out pertaining to the program that troubled me, I said to her many times, "Annie, am I being a coward because I lay those things away on the shelf and skip it?" She said, "I feel you're just being wise. If it isn't anything that's going to help you or anybody else, why should you become involved in it, and get all disturbed about it?"

So there you are. That's my story. I know I've talked too long, but I always do. And, anyhow, if I went on for ten or a hundred times as long I couldn't even begin to tell you all that A.A. has meant to me.

HOME BREWMEISTER

An originator of Cleveland's Group No. 3,
this one fought Prohibition in vain.

Strangely enough, I became acquainted with the "hilarious life" just at the time in my own life when I was beginning really to settle down to a common-sense, sane domesticity. My wife became pregnant and the doctor recommended the use of port or ale ... so ... I bought a six gallon crock and a few bottles, listened to advice from amateur brewmeisters, and was off on my beer manufacturing career on a small scale (for the time being). Somehow or other, I must have misunderstood the doctor's instructions, for I not only made the beer for my wife, I also drank it for her.

As time went on, I found that it was customary to open a few bottles whenever visitors dropped in. That being the case, it didn't take me long to figure out that my meager manufacturing facilities were entirely inadequate to the manufacture of beer for social and domestic consumption. From that point on, I secured crocks of ten gallon capacity and really took quite an active interest in the manufacture of home brew.

We were having card parties with limburger and beer quite regularly. Eventually, of course, what with all the hilarity that could be provoked with a few gallons of beer, there seemed to be no need of bridge or poker playing for entertainment. The parties waxed more liquid and hilarious as time went on, and eventually I discovered that a little shot of liquor now and then between beers had the tendency to put me in a whacky mood much quicker than having to down several quarts of beer to obtain the same effect. The inevitable result of this discovery was that I soon learned that beer made a very good chaser for whiskey. That discovery so intrigued me, that I stayed on that diet almost entirely for the balance of my extensive drinking life. The last day of my drinking career, I drank twenty-two of them between ten and twelve a.m. and I shall never know how many more followed them until I was poured into bed that night.

I got along fairly well with my party drinking for quite some time, but eventually I began to visit beer joints in between parties. A night or so a week in a joint, and a party or so a week at home with friends, along with a little lone drinking, soon had me preparing for the existence of a top-flight drunkard.

Three years after I started on my drinking career, I lost my first job. At that time, I was living out of town, so I moved back to the home town and made a connection in a responsible position with one of the larger companies in the finance business. Up to this point I had spent six years in the business and had enjoyed the reputation of being very successful.

My new duties were extremely confining and my liquor consumption began to increase. Upon leaving the office in the evening, my first stop would be a saloon about a block away. However, as there happened to be several saloons within that distance, I didn't find it necessary to patronize the same place each evening. It doesn't pay to be seen in the same place at the same hour every day.

The general procedure was to take four or five

shots in the first place I stopped at. This would get me feeling fit, and then I would start for home and fireside, thirteen miles away. On the way home numerous places must be passed. If I were alone I would stop at four or five of them, but only one or two in the event I had my mistrusting wife with me.

Eventually I would arrive home for a late supper for which, of course, I had absolutely no relish. I would make a feeble attempt at eating supper, but I never met with any howling success. I never enjoyed any meal, but I ate my lunch at noon for two reasons; first, to help me get out of the fog of the night before and, second, to furnish some measure of nourishment. Eventually, the noon meal was also dispensed with.

I cannot remember just when I became the victim of insomnia, but I do know that the last year and a half I never went to bed sober a single night. I couldn't sleep. I had a mortal fear of going to bed and tossing all night. Evenings at home were an ordeal. As a result, I would fall off in a drunken stupor every night.

How I was able to discharge my duties at the office during those horrible mornings, I will never be able to explain. Handling customers, dealers, insurance people, dictation, telephoning, directing new employees, answering to superiors, and all the rest of it. However, it finally caught up with me, and when it did, I was a mental, physical, and nervous wreck.

I arrived at the stage where I couldn't quite make it to the office some mornings. Then I would send an excuse of illness. But the firm became violently ill with my drunkenness and their course of treatment was to remove their ulcer, in the form of me, from the payroll, amid much fanfare and very personal and slighting remarks and insinuations.

During this time, I had been threatened, beaten, kissed, praised, and damned alternately by relatives, family, friends and strangers, but of course it all went for naught. How many times I swore off in the morning and got drunk before sunset I don't know. I was on the toboggan and really making time.

After being fired, I lined up with a new finance company that was just starting in business, and took the position of business promotion man, contacting automobile dealers. While working in an office, there was some semblance of restraint, but, oh boy, when I got on the outside with this new company without supervision, did I go to town!

I really worked for several weeks, and having had a fairly wide acquaintance with the dealer trade, it was not difficult for me to line up enough of them to give me a very substantial volume of business with a minimum of effort.

Now I was getting drunk all the time. It wasn't necessary to report to the office in person every day, and when I did go in, it was just to make an appearance and bounce right out again.

Finally this company also became involved and I was once more looking for a job. Then I learned something else. I learned that a person just can't find a job hanging in a dive or barroom all day and all night, as jobs don't seem to turn up in those places. I became convinced of that because I spent most of my time there and nary a job turned up. By this time, my chances of getting lined up in my chosen business were shot. Everyone had my number and wouldn't hire me at any price.

I have omitted details of transgressions that I made when drunk for several reasons. One is that I don't re-

member too many of them, as I was one of those
drunks who could be on his feet and attend a meeting
or a party, engage in a conversation with people and
do things that any nearly normal person would do,
and the next day not remember a thing about where I
was, what I did, whom I saw, or how I got home.
(That condition was a distinct handicap to me in trying to vindicate myself with the not so patient wife.)

Things eventually came to the point where I had
no friends. I didn't care to go visiting unless the parties
we might visit had plenty of liquor on hand and I
could get drunk. Indeed, I was always well on my way
before I would undertake to go visiting at all.

After holding good positions, making better than
an average income for over ten years, I was in debt,
had no clothes to speak of, no money, no friends, and
no one any longer tolerating me but my wife. My son
had absolutely no use for me. Even some of the sa-
loon-keepers, where I had spent so much time and
money, requested that I stay away from their places.
Finally, an old business acquaintance of mine, whom I
hadn't seen for several years, offered me a job. I was
on that job a month and drunk most of the time.

Just at this time my wife heard of a doctor in
another city who had been very successful with
drunks. She offered me the alternative of going to see
him or her leaving me for good and all. Well . . . I had
a job, and I really wanted desperately to stop drinking,
but couldn't, so I readily agreed to visit the doctor she
recommended.

That was the turning point of my life. My wife accompanied me on my visit and the doctor really told
me some things that in my state of jitters nearly
knocked me out of the chair. He talked about himself,

but I was sure it was about me. He mentioned lies and deceptions in the course of his story in the presence of the one person in the world I wouldn't want to know such things. How did he know all this? I had never seen him before, and at the time hoped I would never see him again. However, he explained to me that he had been just such a rummy as I, only for a much longer period of time.

He advised me to enter the particular hospital with which he was connected and I readily agreed. In all honesty, though, I was skeptical, but I wanted so definitely to quit drinking that I would have welcomed any sort of physical torture or pain to accomplish the result.

I made arrangements to enter the hospital three days later and promptly went out and got stiff for three days. It was with grim foreboding and advanced jitters that I checked in at the hospital. Of course, I had no hint or intimation as to what the treatment was to consist of.

After being in the hospital for several days, a plan of living was outlined to me. A very simple plan that I still find much joy and happiness in following. It is impossible to put on paper all the benefits I have derived . . . physical, mental, domestic, spiritual, and monetary. This is no idle talk. It is the truth.

From a physical standpoint, I gained sixteen pounds in the first two months I was off liquor. I eat three good meals a day now, and really enjoy them. I sleep like a baby, and never give a thought to such a thing as insomnia. I feel as I did when I was fifteen years younger.

Mentally . . . I know where I was last night, the night before, and the nights before that. Also, I have no fear of anything. I have self-confidence and assurance that cannot be confused with the cockiness I once possessed. I can think clearly and am helped much in my thinking and judgment by my spiritual development which grows daily.

From a domestic standpoint, we really have a home now. I am anxious to get home after dark. My wife is glad to see me come in. My youngster has adopted me. Our home is always full of friends and visitors. (No home brew as an inducement.)

Spiritually . . . I found a Friend who never lets me down and is ever eager to help. I can actually take my problems to Him and He gives me comfort, peace, and happiness.

From a monetary standpoint . . . in the past few years, I have reduced my reckless debts to almost nothing, and have had money to get along on comfortably. I still have my job, and just prior to the writing of this narrative, I received an advancement.

For all these blessings, I thank Him.

Too Young?

Sergeants, doctors, girl friends — everybody seemed to be picking on him. But he couldn't be an alcoholic at his age, could he?

I am a twenty-four-year-old alcoholic. I started drinking about age thirteen. Since I didn't do well in school, I quit and joined the Army at age seventeen. While I was in basic, I got high off booze almost every night. Usually, the next morning I would be quite sick. But who wasn't after drinking that much?

One morning when I was feeling really bad, I was put on K.P. and the head cook wanted me to go out and scrub the garbage cans. I halfway washed them, and he told me to do them again, and I did, and he yelled at me to do them again, and I picked up one of the cans and threw it at him and told him to do them himself. He turned me in to the company commander, but I got off the hook, and that was all that mattered.

Somehow, I made it through basic and then laid off the booze for about three months, because I was in school at night. If I could lay off it, that meant I didn't have to worry about a drinking problem, I thought. An alcoholic *can't* lay off the booze—right? (Now I know the answer—wrong.)

I got orders to go to Vietnam, and I spent most of the year over there either drunk or sick with a hangover. When I came home from Nam, I met a girl I'll call Karen. We got along fine for about two weeks, until she told me where to go and to take my damn bottle with me. So I took my bottle and went and drowned my sorrows.

Next, I was sent to Arizona, where my drinking picked up some more, and I started having blackouts, and I was thrown in jail for speeding and drunken driving. It wasn't long before I quit caring how I looked or what my job performance was. Finally, I reenlisted to go back to Nam. The same as before, I stayed drunk pretty much of the time. I was sent to a psychiatrist, for they didn't think it was normal for me to want to kill my platoon sergeant or to attempt suicide twice.

When I came home again, the only thing I had left to love was the bottle. Karen didn't want to see me anymore, and neither did two other girls I'd been going out with. But I met a real wonderful girl I'll call Jean. We got engaged, and we were happy—Jean with me, and me with the bottle and Jean. From my post, I'd go spend weekends with her. After about three months, no more weekends. I called her every night from a local bar, and often she was not at home. "It can't be my drinking," I thought, "because I can stop any time I want to. I just don't want to."

I began taking drinks in the morning to get started. Other days, I had to miss work because I was still too drunk to stand up. Everyone was against me—I'd show them I didn't need them. I got orders to go to Germany, and everyone in Germany was against me. They passed me over for promotion twice. The third time, after almost five years as an S.P. 4, I finally made sergeant. No one seemed to care if I made it or not. I'd show them—I'd get drunker!

I couldn't think straight anymore. Most of my conversations were meaningless to everyone but me. I couldn't remember what had been said five minutes ago. I usually passed out when I hit the bed. I'd wake up covered with sweat. I heard voices when no one was around, and I saw things that weren't there. Then one day, whammo! I was in the hospital, hysterical. What had happened? Was I having a nervous collapse? The doctor asked about my drinking, but I wouldn't talk to him. "I'm not crazy," I thought, "and I can't be an alcoholic—I'm too young."

When I was released from the hospital, I went back to my unit, and nothing had changed. They were all picking on me. I had to get a drink, and then another drink, and then. . . .

I realized I couldn't quit. But I couldn't go on with it, either. I talked to the first sergeant and the battalion commander, and they got me in contact with an A.A. member. I was sure I wouldn't belong in an A.A. group—they were all old men, I thought, and all skid-row bums. But I was in such deep trouble that I decided to try A.A. anyhow.

After having a few drinks, I went to a meeting—and the people there were *not* all old men and definitely not skid-row types! All of them were so nice to me that I figured I must be careful—they were bound to want something, being that nice. I couldn't trust them. The next meeting I went to, I didn't have any drinks beforehand. I sat and listened and heard the first speaker say, "I am an alcoholic." I couldn't admit that I was. But after hearing their stories, I *knew* that I was, and I admitted it.

I still couldn't make it through the nights without drinking, so I went back into the hospital, this time to a rehabilitation center. I went to A.A. meetings twice a week. When I got out of the hospital, I continued making the meetings. I found out that the people in all

A.A. groups were as nice as the people in the first one. I also found out that all they wanted was to help me get sober and to stay sober themselves. A.A.'s Twelve Steps showed me the way to sobriety if I wanted it. I wanted it!

I started to take A.A. seriously, and A.A. gave me a new way of life. After a time, my mind began to clear of the fog that had covered it. My memory slowly returned. I felt better mentally and physically. Once I did have a slip—tried drinking again—but the A.A.'s tell me not to worry about yesterday, because nobody can change it, and not to worry about tomorrow, because it hasn't come yet. Live twenty-four hours at a time, they say. And it works. I'm sober today. Like I said, I'm a twenty-four-year-old alcoholic—and I'm happy.

THOSE GOLDEN YEARS

All the joys of retirement lay ahead for this movie publicist. Safely pensioned, with no job to protect, at last he could drink as he pleased.

*U*ntil I took Social Security and a pension at the age of sixty-eight, after forty years in motion-picture-studio public relations, I had successfully hidden even any hints of approaching alcoholism. Two years later, a month beyond age seventy, I was crying for help from A.A.

Through studied sneaky-drinking, I'd become a senior citizen without having lost a day's work because of booze. I had never even been told by a superior that maybe I was drinking too much. I still had a wife and family, a home and a car, my driver's license, and a proper amount of insurance. No jail booking, drunk-driving citation, barroom fight, or even a tumble off a barstool. I had been far too busy building, protecting, and maintaining an image of respectability and all the other business pluses.

I was aware of symptoms of impending dependence, and I told myself I had gotten out of the rat race just in time to head off any booze problem. Now, no longer under pressure, I could safely guard against loss of control.

If reasons for covering up are strong enough, secrets can be hidden from the world. I had suppressed tendencies to overindulge and thus reveal my "moral weakness," because false pride was so dominant. I'd worked hard to be tops in my profession. For a decade, I'd headed up a forty-publicist department. My guild had elected me president twice and later given me a "man of the year" award. I'd been on the board of governors of the Academy of Motion Picture Arts and Sciences for six years. I was "too important" to show any indication of being a drunk. Away down deep, I was motivated into dishonest behavior because I was a people-pleaser. Aren't we all?

My drinking career started late. A square from ul-tra-dry Kansas, I did not taste grog until I had finished college, done a stint on newspapers, married, become a father, and been in studio publicity two years.

Then, one night, my whole pattern for drinking was set. I was assigned to keep media guests happy at a Halloween party given by a major star in his plush home. I was thirty-two, a babe in Boozeville. There was a bar, and what I tasted spelled sheer heaven. No-body but me got smashed. I threw up. I felt disgraced and humiliated—a man who couldn't hold booze—a social disaster.

I vowed that never again would any important per-son whom I wished to please and impress ever see me drunk. Although I did drink, it always was with cau-tion—unless I was alone. All hidden drunks aren't at home in housewives' dresses. And I was able to go on the wagon for long periods of time—once for four years, to cure an ulcer.

After such often-painful vigilance (and numerous phony stints of abstinence), retirement naturally cre-ated an impulse to live without restraints. The need to uphold a façade had been irksome. Now, with the ar-rival at retirement, it was gone. I could let down the bars.

I believe that the release from people-pleasing restrictions gives retirees more motivation to drink than boredom does. Every breadwinner, whether trying to impress a boss or to hold customers in his own business, is fettered by people-pleasing.

Retirement rids the potential alcoholic of many shackles. Gone are time cards to punch, alarm clocks to obey, nosy rumor-mongers and talebearers to evade. No more snoops or big shots breathing down our necks. No more business pressures. No monkeys on our backs. No prickling consciences to needle us with guilt feelings. We're free at last to do our thing, to live uninhibited lives, to drink when and how and where we wish, when we want to and when we need to. We even can be rebels for the first time in our lives.

I was keenly aware that my all-important security, which I had been constantly afraid of losing for four decades, no longer was endangered. Nobody could take away my retirement income. Only death could wipe out that security. And retirement is a time for thinking, not of death, but of living—at long last. I soon was to ask myself, "What living?"

Many retirees embrace alcoholism while secluded in motor trailers, rest homes, leisure-world bungalows, mountain cabins, or beach cottages, or even in penthouses, on yachts, and inside Palm Springs cabanas. They daily pass into oblivion, alone or with mates. (My addiction bloomed within a small apartment I shared with my wife, a heart patient.) Happy, happy senior-citizen existence!

Hidden old-drunks can pass out on their beds and snooze unreproached, under the guise of taking those vital retirement-age naps. Even obvious intoxication is excused by younger people as something "he's earned the right to do," and they say, "After all, who's he hurting?"

So long as a retiree woos his bottle at home, he stays out of public trouble. Unlike his skid-row brother, he isn't heckled for sleeping in alleys or doorways. Unlike the drinking driver, he avoids facing judges. He seldom is a disgrace.

But for him, financial security or even affluence can be a tragedy. He has few worries, fewer warnings. He'll never read in his "sweetness and light" senior-citizen publications anything but the joys of lolling in the rocking chair, angling on the riverbank, or bowling on the green. He may even read in a newspaper that one out of every seven drinkers will become alcoholic, but he rarely is told that it holds true for *all* ages—or that the tolerance to alcohol (and other drugs) decreases steadily, year after year, in the bodies of all persons.

Boredom sets up every retiree for two chief dangers: obesity and alcoholism. So oldsters are advised to develop interests, find hobbies. A friend of mine, a golf nut, rushed out on retirement to play every day. Three months later, he hated the game and found solace in the bottle. He's now in A.A. and works as a volunteer for the local alcoholism council.

Boredom was no worry to me when I went out to pasture. The movie racket had kept me too long from writing those novels, articles, short stories, and scripts on which I had copious notes. Creativity at the typewriter would keep me busy and alert, I said.

My alcoholism-prone mind, however, reminded me that all great authors had needed a stimulus to build up inspiration and inventiveness before each day's work. That, of course, was a shot of booze. Since I started out eager for early-day efforts, that meant guzzling before noon. In so simple a manner did my morning drinking begin.

By the law of averages, some efforts came out well. I did some things I liked, and even sold some. But the percentages started tobogganing, and it was often a shock to read over some of the pages when sober. My writing career was described in the couplet "Alcohol gave me wings to fly,/And then it took away the sky."

The drinker's mind is full of uncertainties and insecurities. We "instant perfectionists" also are hypersensitive, alas. How hurt I was when editors bounced back my ideas quickly and my best friends opined that my output needed a lot of rewriting.

What alcoholic can live with rejection? How devastating, too, are the subsequent feelings of inadequacy and self-pity. There's only one answer—liquid comfort. The unwillingness to admit failure requires even further friendly intake. It becomes vital, also, that others not know of our defeats, nor suspect our loss of confidence. A people-pleaser beaten down? No way! While I sought the comforting arms of alcohol, I knew this was a sign of weakness on the part of a longtime-successful old codger with white hair, the image of dignity. I was unwilling to bare my secrets to those who might display scorn. The fear, of course, necessitated a program of hidden alcoholism.

I had no need to hide in closets, bathrooms, or garages. I could hide my alcoholic stupor behind pretense. Seated at the typewriter, I faked deep thinking or portrayed creativity by key-tapping. Hiding behind a newspaper, magazine, or book, I really saw nothing, but simulated deep interest.

The radio was my good friend. Lying on the divan, "getting in the mood" to write, I cried openly or inwardly, as I listened to sad songs. "I'll Never Smile Again"—how perfect. But the saddest, and thus the most consoling, drifted through from the country-music station—stories of broken hearts, wasted lives, lost loves, sung plaintively. One night, I hit the jackpot. In succession came "What Made Milwaukee Famous Made a Loser Out of Me" and "I'm Drinking My Christmas Dinner All Alone."

Somehow, I managed to read pieces on alcoholism. I knew about A.A. I agreed it was great stuff—for those who needed it. If ever I got that bad . . . The word "insanity" came through clearly—and repugnantly. That let me out.

Yet I recently recalled that each morning I used to talk to the bottle when I took it down from the closet. I would take a gulp, then warn the jug not to try to entice, lure, or seduce me into having more than one "medicinal" jolt. How futile! I always succumbed to its seduction.

No matter how often I had gone into and come out of alcoholic lows during the day, the pattern bounced me out of bed each night about 2:00 a.m., shaking and hurting in the agitation that always follows a drug's sedation. Not wishing to disturb my wife, I slumped in a big red-leather chair and suffered. I was sure those who needed a bit of the hair of the dog really were alcoholics. I would not start that. I'd just take a couple or three barbiturates to get back to sleep—*eating* my alcohol.

A lot of lost dreams, empty futures, and crazy things of the past went through my mind. One night, I was struck with the memory of a line Alan Ladd used in "Shane," a movie that I'd worked on. He'd told a villain, "The trouble is, old man, you've lived too long." How that line echoed through my mind! I knew why I identified. It was *my* line, the story of *my* life. I'd lived too long and become a loser, dependent on booze. Well, at least I could drink myself to death. Real soon. Then everyone would be sorry for me.

Two nights later, self-pity went even further. I sat up in the big red chair, suddenly thinking, "My God, with my kind of lousy luck, I might not die soon! I could go on living and hurting ten years longer, or more." I decided to quit drinking. When I found this impossible, I became scared for the first time.

Crises were emerging rapidly. It was a month beyond my seventieth birthday. Death seemed the only way out. I had forgotten "If ever I get that bad, I'll try A.A." There was an upper cupboard full of empties. Best that they not be found after I'd had my last drink on earth. I was gathering the cache for disposal when my wife woke up and caught me at it. She had not known the extent of my consumption. She gasped. I foresaw another heart attack. I went into action. Hauling her to the divan, I sat with her and began to talk, frantically but clearly—and making sense.

Where were all those words coming from? They surprised me. I told her that I was an alcoholic, victim of a disease, that there was no cure, only arrestment through total abstinence. I told her I had to go to A.A. It was the only hope I had.

Spiritual experience? Whatever it was, it brushed all the heavy burdens off my back.

I did go to A.A., two days later, walking in alone. And I have not had a drink since that night.

Out of those forty years as a movie press agent came one blessing that granted me a blind faith in the program. I had worked so long in a profession where fakery, deceit, and untruths are tools of trade that I instantly recognized honesty when I heard it, from the mouths of A.A. members.

They described what had happened when they went out and tried drinking again, and I knew they were sincere in saying that it could happen to me. That always has been good enough for me.

When I retired, I said I'd never be bored. A.A. has not let me down there. How full it has kept my retirement years—the five I've lived since the first two lost in traveling a rocky road to hell, before I made a U-turn.

Not long ago, I was lunching with another retired publicist. He was close to tears in describing his boredom without an activity. He said, "How I envy you for whatever you've found." He did not know it was A.A., and it was useless to tell him, for he doesn't have our disease.

I tried to encourage a search for some new goal. But I couldn't help thinking, "You poor guy. I feel so sorry for you. You're not an alcoholic. You can never know the pure joy of recovering within the Fellowship of Alcoholics Anonymous."

LIFESAVING WORDS

*For this officer in the Indian Army, going on the
wagon was not enough; attempts at control failed.
The answer came to him by mail.*

Three years and three months of sobriety, without
a slip, has meant a lot to me, my wife, and my
family. It has meant life. The encouragement received
in the early days, especially from the A.A. General Service Office, made a tremendous difference to my sobriety. The regular flow of all the literature, which I keep
meticulously and which, of course, I study, has been
wonderful. I have never attended an A.A. meeting, so
it is essentially the literature that has kept me on the
A.A. program.

I returned to my home in Lucknow, India, at the
end of November last year from a vacation in one of
the most famous beauty spots in our country, a mountain resort 6,800 feet up, with a wonderful lake. The
place is Naini Tal, in the foothills of the mighty Hi-
malaya Mountains, and it has some very significant
memories for me.

I finished high school here in an American-spon-
sored Methodist public school, known as Philander
Smith College. I eventually became a schoolmaster, but
gave up the profession to join the Indian Army. After
training, I was commissioned as a first lieutenant.

The army made a difference to me. It was here I
came to know properly what alcohol was. It finally got
such a hold on me that I was completely at my wits'

end, not knowing what the result would be. I have been of a very religious outlook all my life, but that made no difference once John Barleycorn got the better of me.

Eight years ago, my wife and I decided to spend a vacation in Naini Tal, the mountain resort. In those days, I was doing a staff appointment in army headquarters in New Delhi. This was my first long vacation of sixty days since I had joined the army. During this vacation, in the months of September and October, I decided to go on the water wagon. I succeeded in this attempt for approximately fifteen months with only a couple of slips. However, I am an alcoholic, so I always looked forward to the day when I would be able to drink again.

At Christmastime next year, I convinced my wife that I had alcohol under control and that I would do controlled drinking over Christmas and the New Year. I did. The result was as usual. In a short time, it became uncontrolled drinking. During the next three years, I tried often again to give it up, but failed miserably.

Then I saw an A.A. advertisement in a newspaper, and I wrote to the address it gave. The reply came, putting me in touch by mail with my sponsor in New Delhi. Following this, I had a short vacation, during which time I read as much literature as my sponsor could send me. I have read systematically since then, and A.A. literature has kept me sober.

Last year, I decided on an A.A. vacation in Naini Tal. I read, studied, and meditated on every bit of A.A. literature in my possession. Studied the Big Book again. Took down notes for reference purposes. The difference between the two vacations was this:

On the first, though on the water wagon, I looked forward to my next drink. I went on the wagon more to placate my wife than anything else. On the second, I knew—as I know now—that if I remained away from the first drink, then I had not to worry about the hundredth one. And I knew this: Once an alcoholic, always an alcoholic. I owe everything to A.A.

A TEEN-AGER'S DECISION

Just three years of drinking pushed a shy, lonely
young girl to the depth of depression. Out of sheer
despair, she called for help.

I had my first drink when I was fifteen and my alcoholic potential had ripened me to the point of necessary escapism. I needed alcohol from that night on, and it in turn used me, ruling my life for three years.

I never drank socially; I drank as often and as much as I could. My eventual goal was to drink myself to death. All my life, it seemed, was spent on the outside looking in. I had been unhappy, lonely, and scared for so long that the discovery of liquor seemed to be the answer to all my problems.

But it began to be an awfully painful answer as hangovers, blackouts, trouble, and remorse set in. My parents' car had a strong attraction to fences, and one night I blacked out and drove the car down a bank, ramming the steel fence around someone's backyard. By the time I figured out what had happened, I saw two flashing red lights atop squad cars, sedately coming around the corner.

I certainly wasn't my shy, quiet self that night—as I was informed the next morning. It was a pretty blurry night. I could hardly see at all, and my memory kept eluding me. I do recall lying on a cold cement floor and shredding into little bits several pieces of stolen identification cards, and washing my face in the toilet bowl trying to sober up, and screaming hysterically while clinging to bars too high to see out of, and cursing everyone that came near me.

Naturally, this experience didn't stop me. It only became another excuse to drink. I lost my driver's license, was made a ward of the court, and was put on probation (not to mention the fact that I might have killed three friends and myself). None of this really impressed me. Soon, it became apparent that my schooling was interfering with my drinking. Without hesitation, I did the only logical thing—ran away from home. I was in the fourth quarter of my senior year at high school, and my mother was quite sick in the hospital.

Can you picture two girls hitchhiking their way to Las Vegas from Washington State? We did, and spent a month boozing it up, popping pills, and smoking marijuana; taking shelter where we could, which included a veterinary hospital one night; accepting meals from anyone; actually begging; stealing anything we were in need of, which was about everything.

This escapade also ended up in the clutches of the law, and my friend was institutionalized for eight months. I had turned eighteen during the trip, and I despondently returned home by jet (on Daddy's bankbook) to a pair of miserable, hurt parents.

It was then that I began to hate myself, and drank primarily to ease my conscience and forget. The more I drank, the worse it got and the more I had to drink. Every day became that much harder to live through, and I began to take a look at myself. What had happened to the shy, lonely churchgoing wallflower? I had never been very happy, but now it was unbearable.

I'd managed to drink my way through all my friends. I had no one in the world to talk to. With increasing guilt and never-ending depression, I was too weak to continue this day-by-day suicide.

Thank God I knew of A.A., so I called. I had no idea what would happen—I just knew I didn't want to live if life was going to go on like it was.

Today, I'm counting my blessings instead of my troubles. When I walked into the friendly atmosphere of my first A.A. meeting, I knew I was where I belonged. Here were people who had thought and felt as I had. Here was the understanding I'd been searching for all my life. These people were my friends, and I felt their sincere interest in me. With these new and enlightening doors opening up to me, I was able to make the eventual decision to stop drinking, a day at a time—because I, too, was an alcoholic. And with this came the only real freedom, the freedom of truth.

My sponsor used to say to me, "If I could only paint you a picture of how beautiful life can be without booze . . ." I wanted so badly to see the picture as it was in her mind. Well, now I'm living it and trying to paint it for others. A.A. has become a way of life and living for me. It has brought about a revelation of self, the discovery of an inner being, an awareness of God.

I wouldn't give it up or trade it for anything. And the only one who can take it away from me is me—by taking that first drink.

Rum, Radio and Rebellion

*This man faced the last ditch when his wife's voice
from 1,300 miles away sent him to A.A.*

"*Y*ou an alcoholic! I don't believe it."

"Sure, I've seen you tight several times, but you're no alcoholic!"

"You kidding—you an alcoholic?"

Many times have I heard the above expressions since I have been in A.A., and many times I have had to reply "Definitely I am an alcoholic, and while it may be hard for you to believe, it is not hard for me, for I have learned many things about alcohol and myself that would, perhaps, be difficult for you to understand."

As these words are written at fifty-three years of age, with over nine years of A.A. behind me, with all its wonderful teachings, I haven't the slightest doubt about being an alcoholic.

I have always considered myself one of the lucky members of our fraternity. Lucky because my excessive drinking never got me in jail, or hospitalized, nor did it ever cost me a job. As a matter of fact, when I came into Alcoholics Anonymous I was close to being at the peak of my career. I certainly was, as far as my living standard was concerned. However, what I had gained materially on the credit side of my ledger, I have since learned was more than offset on the debit side by egotism, resentment and dishonesty.

I was born in Cleveland, Ohio, the only child of a

prominent dentist, and a very proud mother. They were neither poor nor wealthy, but far better off than the average couple. I had every advantage a child could have, private schools (several of them), dancing schools, two colleges, coon skin coats, automobiles, a listing in the social register and all the rest. All of which could turn out but one thing—a very popular, but spoiled, brat.

In the various schools I attended, it was always a case of just getting by. Too many outside activities to do much studying. I was active and did well, however, in school publications, dramatics (which came in handy during my drinking career), and Greek letter societies. I had no trouble at all in being elected to the two drinking societies at my college.

I had run away from school to join the army in World War I, but missed it by one day since the Armistice was signed the very day I landed in Atlanta to sign up with Uncle Sam. As usual, I ran out of money, and, as usual, I wired my father for funds to come home. He answered by wiring that I could stay there until I earned enough to get home. It was a terrible blow at the time and I thought he was pretty much of a heel, but of course it was the finest thing he could have done for me under the circumstances. It took me a year to make it home. I went to work in Birmingham for a newspaper at fifteen dollars a week. Prohibition came along, and with it my first taste of moonshine. I didn't particularly like it, but I loved the effects, and managed for the next twenty-five years to drink anything and everything, either handed to me or purchased, at the slightest excuse.

When I did make it home in 1920, I re-entered school and caught up with my class in a few short months—I actually did a year's work in three months, proving much to the disgust of my dad that I could do it when I wanted to.

All I can remember about the Roaring Twenties is that I drank a great deal, thought I was having a grand time, managed to get to Europe for a few weeks, was very proud of the dozens of speak-easy cards entitling me to an entree in the better joints between Cleveland and New York, took on a wife, and built a home in a fashionable suburb of Cleveland.

High living, a great many fair weather friends, the 1929 stock market crash, and a couple of years of Depression, soon relieved me one by one of my worldly goods, including my wife. In this I was greatly aided and abetted by one John Barleycorn. Like all alcoholics endeavoring to run away from themselves and their environment, I decided to go to New York. This was at the height of the Depression and the end of Prohibition. Neither of these circumstances was very helpful to my type, since I had not learned to face realities.

The next few years in New York can be described in a very few words. Drinking—and more drinking. I got behind in my rent, but never in my drinking. Looking back, it is surprising to me now that I managed to keep working and have enough money to squander at the various spots in the big city. By this time I had become associated with the fast growing and fascinating business of broadcasting. I was working for a Chicago firm that represented several large radio stations. It was my job to sell time on these stations to advertising agencies in New York. It was also my job to entertain the owners of these stations when they came East on business—or the pretense of business. This phase was right down my alley; I had my master's degree in the art of making "whoopee."

I was living in a small room on West 53rd Street right off Fifth Avenue, when I met a young lady who eventually was responsible for altering my entire way of living. She was studying fashion design, was living in the same rooming house, and was from my home town of Cleveland. I made little headway in my first few meetings with her. She was intent on her studies, and kept her distance. By persistence and salesmanship I managed to see more and more of my new friend, and because of her sympathetic nature she tolerated my company. Her influence and companionship managed to lessen my drinking to some degree. After several months of acquaintance I asked her to marry me, but was politely refused. I asked this question weekly for the next couple of years.

In January 1938, I had the opportunity to go to northern Vermont to manage a small daytime radio station that was up against it financially, and was about to fold its antenna. The challenge intrigued me; also it was another opportunity to run away from myself and the "fast life of the big city." Once again I asked my girl to marry me and join me in this new venture. At this time, however, she had an opportunity to go to Salt Lake City on a new project for the government, but she did promise me that if I would curtail my drinking and buckle down to hard work she would give serious consideration to my latest proposal and maybe join me at a later date when I got settled. With new hope in my heart and new resolutions I set off for Vermont.

My work kept me busy the first few months on the new job. It was strictly a one-man operation and I knew I had to tend to my knitting to make a go of it. Furthermore, I knew that I was looked upon as a city slicker from New York, and I had to be pretty cautious among small town, conservative Yankees. One of the things I needed badly was business for the station. New programing was beginning to build an audience, but sponsors were pretty scarce. I got around this by joining the local Rotary Club, and through this association with the business men of the community my little station began to grow. It also was the beginning of another cycle in my drinking. It started when I joined a few of the men for cocktails before the noonday Rotary luncheon. Before long I was at the luncheon meetings an hour before the others, that old and familiar trademark of every alcoholic. Since the radio station was getting on its feet, it didn't require so many nights of evening work, and that permitted leisure time for drinking. After all—wasn't I entitled to it? I sure had been working awfully hard of late. It wasn't long before I became a five o'clock alcoholic. During this time I faithfully was writing my girl in Utah. Of course I kept her posted on how well the station was doing and wrote convincing letters of how well I was doing with the liquor problem. My salesmanship was still good, for in the fall of 1938 she called me from Salt Lake and finally agreed to take me on for better or for worse. We were married in Montreal in November.

Proud of my little station and of my new bride I settled down to a happy married life. It was to be short lived, for on the day before Christmas I completely disillusioned my wife and ruined our first Christmas by coming home from the Rotary lunch dead drunk. It was the first of many such experiences that became the only cause of harsh words, tears and heartaches in an otherwise truly beautiful marriage.

In 1940 another good opportunity came up and we moved to Pittsburgh where I was to manage two radio stations under the same ownership. My business reputation had reached from Vermont to Pennsylvania, but, thank goodness, my drinking reputation had not. Once again I was back in big-time operations, and along with them, big-shot complexes. It didn't take long for me to fall in with a fast crowd who had their lunch in the men's bar of a leading hotel. I graduated there from a five o'clock alcoholic to a noon-day one. By hook or crook I usually managed to sober up before I reached home, but always "terribly tired" from a "hard day's work," and just having to have one or two before dinner. My wonderful wife did everything to play along with me. She was tolerant beyond all belief. I did everything to make her an alcoholic too. She tried reasoning with me, endeavored to work out various drinking schedules, in fact all the tricks were practiced faithfully for a short time somewhere along my shaky road to unhappiness. The inevitable always happened. I would follow certain drinking schedules or diets faithfully for a few days, and then somewhere along the line would over-train and upset the apple-cart. On more than one occasion my wife would threaten to leave me. Time after time, I would beg forgiveness on bended knees, with tears rolling down my cheeks, and promise I would never again drink too much. And deep in my heart I really meant what I said because I loved her more than anything else in the world, yes—even more than liquor. It was hard for her to believe in my love by my actions. Even I couldn't understand it, because I did love her so. How could I continually break my promises? Soon I was to discover the answer.

In the very early spring of 1944, my frustrated wife couldn't take it any longer. After another of my "never again episodes" she packed up and left for her parents' home in Florida. Her parting words were "I am not leaving you because I don't love you; it's because I do love you. I can't bear to be here when you lose the respect of others, and above all—when you lose your own self-respect."

For a few weeks I toed the line. I was going to prove to her that liquor wasn't necessary in my life, and above all that I still loved her more than anything else in the world and that I wanted her back. This routine was short-lived too. I began hitting the bottle again, and with it self-pity, resentment, loneliness and remorse set in deeply. Why should this happen to me—hadn't I provided a good home—wasn't I making a good living—didn't I just get a substantial raise that had put me in the upper bracket class? Sure I still loved her, but hang it all, she was unreasonable! I had given her everything a wife could ask for. The more I thought like this the more I drank to submerge my sorrows. One Saturday noon I staggered home with every intention of showing her. I would end it all, and then, by George, she'd be sorry! I entered the house, opened a new bottle of whiskey and sat down to drink myself into the right frame of mind to get in my car, start the motor and close the garage door behind me. A few hours later I came out of a complete stupor in our living room with a flash of sanity. Looking directly at me was a large oil painting of my wife, and her very words seemed to shout at me—"I am not leaving you because I don't love you; it's because I do love you. I can't bear to be here when you lose the respect of others, and above all—when you lose your own self-respect." This was about ten p.m., and the time here is important.

It had happened to me and I had to do something about it. Thank God that in spite of my heavy drinking my mind was clear enough to make a decision then and there. I had read and heard a little about A.A. and so, groping for the phone book, I found the A.A. number and with hope in my heart eagerly telephoned. I heard a lovely voice, and a sympathetic ear listened to my plea. I was told that someone would call on me shortly, to sit tight and not take another drink. Sure enough in a couple of hours two men were at my door and for the first time I heard some facts about liquor and my problem that sounded sensible to me. They told me their stories, which were much more rugged than mine—yet what they said made sense, and the way they put it was easy for me to understand, with an understanding I had never had before. I promised my two sponsors that I would attend their meeting the next Tuesday evening. I kept away from liquor and eagerly waited.

My first meeting gave me a great deal of hope and lots of willing ears for my tale of woe and for my questions. After a few meetings I decided to drive to Florida unannounced to see my wife and tell her about my newfound friends and association. I was certainly a complete surprise when I arrived at her family's home, but because I arrived on the wings of a tropical hurricane there wasn't much she could do but let me in. That night she too had new hope because I had made sure she would know what I was doing about my drinking by packing every bit of A.A. literature I could put my hands on right on top so she couldn't help but see it when she opened my bag.

I stayed on in Florida for three weeks, enjoying our reunion, a newfound health and a deeper love than I had ever experienced before. We came back to Pittsburgh as happy as a bride and groom. We attended meetings together, and mutually enjoyed our newfound friends. In September of this same year I went to New York alone. I thought this was a good time to experiment with liquor. Of course, it didn't work. I tried a few drinks my last night in the city before coming home. Luck was with me, for I made my train, but I arrived home the next morning with a new kind of hangover. I had done something terrible! I had not only let my wife down but also a lot of other wonderful people who had helped me. Of course, more than anything else I had let myself down, but I didn't realize how much then—as I do now. I didn't say a word to anyone about my lapse. I went back to my group meetings, but not wholeheartedly, and I often skipped them with the excuse that I was too tired. It was worrying my wife a little, but she had the good sense not to take me to task about it or goad me into going. I got through the holidays all right until New Year's Day. We had some people in, and I was making drinks in the kitchen, when I suddenly decided to hoist the bottle for a quick one. I had just raised the bottle to my lips when my wife opened the door and froze me completely in my tracks with "Happy New Year, dear." I didn't take the drink. I was scared—would she leave me again? Later I told her I had not taken the drink and that I was all right. When our meeting night came around the next evening, I went—"for her sake" I told her. I said I was okay, but if it would make her feel better I would go "as tired as I was after the strenuous holidays." She told me not to bother going "for her sake"; she told me in a nice way that it didn't make any difference to her—and that really scared me—so I went.

A lucky break, at least some will call it lucky, was in store for me at my group that night. Attending his fourth or fifth meeting was an old friend I had not seen for twenty years. He was full of his newfound life of happiness and sobriety. His enthusiasm and keen interest in A.A. fired my spirits again. I attended my weekly meetings with regularity, re-read the Big Book, attended other group meetings, gave leads when asked to and did some Twelve Step work whenever I was called upon to do so. In other words, I began contributing, and so, naturally, I began to get something more. A whole new world of happiness and love began to unfold before my eyes, a truly new way of living.

One night at the dinner table my wife said that tonight was my first birthday in A.A., and that the group would have the usual ice cream and cake for the "one year man." Now I was on the spot. I had never told a soul about my lapse in New York. For the next couple of hours a terrible battle went on between the good gremlins and the bad ones, one faction urging me to tell the truth, the other telling me to sit tight and say nothing. I had no trouble making the right decision when I saw my wife open her purse at the meeting that night and deposit a cute little angel in the middle of my birthday cake. When I was called upon for a few words I had to tell my friends that I wasn't one year old in A.A. that evening but only a "nine month baby." With that utterance I again made a wonderful discovery. I had thrown off a big lie that had been burdening me down for months. What a wonderful new feeling, what a wonderful relief!

I could end my story here, but for the new man I would like to add a few words. You'll read and hear a great deal about the spiritual part of our program. I haven't written anything about that part of my story, but I believe in a Greater Power which I call God and I ask for His wisdom and guidance daily. My first spiritual experience in A.A. came quite early to me. You will recall that I said the time that I got the idea out of a clear sky to call A.A. on a certain night was at about ten. While I was in Florida trying to convince my wife with all the A.A. literature that she should come back to me, she went over to her desk and picked up a clipping she had taken from the *St. Petersburg Times* about A.A. It was the first she had heard or read about it and she said she had considered sending it to me or trying to have someone in Pittsburgh send it to me so I wouldn't know where it came from. However, knowing me, she thought it was a foolish idea, that I wouldn't be interested. But for some reason—she just didn't know why—she just had to hold onto that clipping, with its thin hope. She said she cut this clipping from the paper at about ten on the same night, and at the same time as I called A.A. in Pittsburgh—some 1,300 miles away.

To the new man I would also like to say that this program is not for sissies for, in my humble opinion, it takes a man to make the grade. It is not too difficult nor too easy to grasp. I have had many more reasons to drink since I have been in A.A. than I had in all the years of my drinking. I've had more problems but, thank God, I have had the teachings of A.A. with which to face them. And, believe me, I thank God that

I found out about A.A. before I had to beat my brains out—before I had been hospitalized, jailed or lost a job. When I hear the more rugged stories of alcoholics who became sicker than I did with this affliction, I humbly thank God for showing me "the handwriting on the wall."

In meeting me casually, I don't think my strong belief in "The Man Upstairs" shows, but I have no other explanation for the many good things that have happened to me since I have been in A.A.—they came to me from a Greater Power. These words may be difficult for you to understand now, but be patient and you'll know what I mean.

If I were asked what in my opinion was the most important factor in being successful in this program, besides following the Twelve Steps, I would say Honesty. And the most important person to be honest with is Yourself. If there is something in my story that rings a bell with you, then *do* something—now! I repeat, I am one of the fortunate members of A.A.—a lucky guy who is very grateful.

ANY DAY WAS WASHDAY

This secret drinker favored the local Laundromat as a watering hole. Now, she no longer risks losing her home, her self-respect, or her laundry.

*I*n my drinking days, I found the ideal spot for the alcoholic housewife: the neighborhood Laundromat. There, I could be a proper mother and wife while drinking up a storm. At the Laundromat, I was undisturbed by barflies with questionable and unwanted intentions. Also, I believed I was the image of all domestic virtues, secluded in my washday (any day) refuge.

My childhood was shrouded in the fumes of alcohol. Dad's image for me was that of a big Irish oilman who came up through the school of hard knocks and so had to be a two-fisted drinker. My mother was a lovely, sweet woman, whose only weakness was my father. We lived a kind of seesaw existence in the early days. It was never boring, but I developed a feeling of deep insecurity. At times, when I noticed other families, I felt something was very wrong with ours. As my father climbed the ladder of success in the oil-field business, his drinking also climbed. I thought he merely had a "weakness." My mother said so, again and again.

When I was nineteen, I married a fine man who had never known an insecure moment in his life, let alone the trials and tribulations of booze. He and I had a large family—six children, to be exact. We went out occasionally, and I would take a drink to ease the tensions of daily life. It was fun at first, since I never had indulged before. I had no qualms, because I felt the source of a drinking problem was all in how weak one was, and I wasn't like my dad (I thought).

Then my father fell down a flight of stairs on one of his lost weekends, at the peak of his career, and died. It left us dazed, because he had seemed so indestructible. After his death, my mother soon picked up drinking where Dad left off, and in a very short time she died of cirrhosis of the liver. And I still felt it was a weakness—plus, in her case, adverse circumstances.

Very soon after I lost Mother, my five-year-old little girl was killed by a neighbor's car. I felt this was the final blow. Within a few months, I was admitted to a state hospital for the mentally ill. A few months after that, I was released and left the world of insanity, only to return to the world of alcoholic insanity.

I couldn't drink at home, because my husband frowned upon this. (In fact, every time I saw him he had a frown on his face.) So that's when I discovered the Laundromat. I would gather up all my soiled clothes, as much as I could cram into a grocery cart, and be off.

Near the Laundromat, I would buy one bottle of pop and a few bottles of beer or wine, and go into the rest room, empty the pop bottle, refill it with the booze, and proceed to do my laundering. So innocent, so discreet! The only drawback was, I always knew how I arrived there, but somehow, between the rest room, the rinse, and the fluff-dry, I never knew when or how I got home. I lost a lot of shirts that way, and sometimes I was minus a whole wash. All this while, I wondered whether I could do laundry for the neighbors as a part-time job. That way, I could spend most of my time at the Laundromat!

Before too long, my husband (who seemed to prefer his shirts dirty) put his foot down, declaring that our family might have the cleanest clothes in town, but that I hadn't been out of the same old dirty slacks and blouse for a week. He said he was through and would seek a divorce. With that, he told me to leave, because I was unfit as a mother, a wife, and a laundress.

I knew he was right, except for the last statement. So, with mixed feelings of humiliation, anger, and fear, I decided to look for an answer. My sister-in-law took me to a place she had heard about the helps women like me. I had nowhere else to go, and I knew something was terribly wrong, and the reason had to lie within myself. At a women's halfway house, I became associated with Alcoholics Anonymous and became aware of alcoholism as a disease, not just a "weakness." Slowly, my life seemed to unfold before me, shedding insights on childhood resentments, jealousies, and fears that had mushroomed in adulthood, and also on the self-pity that I had wallowed in at every opportunity. I saw at last that I had the same disease my father had, only I was being given a chance to live, not die.

I went to many meetings and met many beautiful people. One night, a few weeks after joining the Fellowship, much to my surprise and delight I saw a familiar but no longer frowning face. It was my husband, and he was learning, too. We soon resumed our marriage, even moved away from the street of sad memories and found a new home. But what is more important is that I found a new life in Alcoholics Anonymous. I'm very active in A.A. work and active at home, too, with my family. I still wash clothes, lots of them, but I no longer lose them at the Laundromat. That's right! During three years in A.A., I haven't lost so much as one shirt.

A FLOWER OF THE SOUTH

Somewhat faded, she nevertheless bloomed afresh.
She still had her husband, her home, and a chance to
help start A.A. in Texas.

I know that if I do daily what I have done for these last thirteen and a half years, I will stay sober. I didn't know that when I came into A.A. I knew that I wanted to try A.A. and if that didn't work, I didn't think anything would. I wish I could tell you how and why A.A. works, but I don't know. I only know that it does—if you desire it with your whole heart and without reservation. I think that no one comes to A.A. until he's tried everything else. As I grow in A.A., I realize that a person with as much self-will as I had, as hard a head and as diseased an ego, had to try everything that I could think of, butting my head against every stone wall before I was ready to come in. The only thing I have really to offer you is my own story, telling you just what sort of a drunk I was.

I came from a family where alcohol was socially acceptable. I lived in New Orleans where, at that time, cocktail parties, dances and night spots were almost the order of the day—or rather the night. I can't remember a dinner at home that we didn't have white wine or claret on the table. We always had cordials after dinner and I know my sister and my brother and I loved crème de menthe. So I was used to it, but I didn't know what the effect of alcohol was because I always had wine, usually with dinner, but always with a lot of ice and about two tablespoons of sugar in it. Drinking it with your meals, you didn't feel it.

I believe the first time I ever realized what alcohol would do for me was at my own wedding. I was an extremely sensitive person and so self-conscious that I hurt all over.

The night that I was married I had a big church wedding. But I couldn't enjoy anything; I was scared to death. Scared that my dress wasn't going to fit right, that the church wasn't going to be filled, that I'd fall flat on my face walking up the aisle; in fact, I was afraid I wasn't going to be a prima donna in the place where I should be. You didn't carry a little orchid up the aisle in those days; you carried a great big bouquet, like a funeral spray, and you didn't have your picture taken until just before you went to the church. As self-conscious as I was, I had to pose for those pictures, holding this huge bouquet. By the time all this was over, I was really in a terrific state, and my father taking in things said, "Miss Esther is about to faint. Get her something to drink." The servant he turned to was our old cook, and she liked to drink. Emma ran out to the kitchen and came back with a water glass full of bourbon and made me drink it down. The church was just three blocks from our home. I got right into the car and they drove me over, and just as soon as I got to the church they started the wedding. As I started down the aisle, that bourbon went right through me. I walked up the aisle just like Mae West in her prime. I wanted to do it all over again.

I don't think that I was conscious of what had happened to me, but I think that it registered subconsciously. It was really medicinal that night, that whiskey, and it was a medication after that. As long as it eased situations socially, it helped just fine, but somewhere along the line, it backfired. When I crossed that line, I don't know. Something went haywire and I got to depend on it so I could do nothing without it.

For some reason I can't remember, it finally dawned on me that I had a problem, and yet nobody was very critical about it except my family, and that was only because I decided, after seven years of marriage, that I would divorce my husband. I did divorce him in July. It only took a month to get a divorce in Texas. Then I went home. I was free, white and twenty-one and I had a time for myself. I put my poor mother and father through agonies but, finally, I couldn't stand living with them and having them watch everything I did. I had no feeling of security, and I knew that I had done a very stupid thing, so I went back to Texas and remarried my ex-husband. Then we moved up to Oklahoma. That was when all the boys and Esther got drunk and the wives didn't. They would talk about it. That went on for about three years, and then we moved back to Texas again. I really started drinking then.

Frank, my husband, would come home day after day and find me passed out. Or he would leave on a trip and by the time he came home, I'd be passed out. So finally, he said to me one morning, "Esther, why do you do this?" I said, "Well, I don't know why." I had been reading a lot about psychiatry and I thought, "Maybe if I talk to a psychiatrist he can find out what is happening, and then I can drink like a lady." Frank said, "If you'd like to talk to a psychiatrist, I'll see a doctor and find out who to go to here." Frank left to find the doctor and I got drunk.

Frank found the doctor, but the doctor didn't want

to take an alcoholic. He called me that because I was drinking too much. So I got drunker and drunker, and then, suddenly, I woke up in the booby-hatch.

I had never been inside of an insane asylum and I really thought I was going to a private hospital. I woke up in this bare room with nothing around me but bars; they wouldn't let me smoke and treated me, well, like I *was* nuts. I knew this, and right away I got furious and would not even talk to the doctor in the place. I wanted to go home. But they kept me there—I was supposed to stay a month, but they only kept me there seventeen days. I know that I was terribly screwed up inside, but I came out much worse. I could not identify myself with the people with whom I found myself and there was no understanding, and I can't stand confinement anyhow. Because of this state of confusion and frustration I had hysterics on the seventeenth day for the first and only time in my life. So the doctor let me go home on one condition. He asked if I would cooperate with him after I went home, and if I would have a trained nurse stay with me for at least two weeks.

I was so happy over getting home that I changed overnight, but not enough. In six years of worry, I hadn't learned anything. I was crazy about my doctor. I cooperated with that man one hundred percent! That is how dishonest I was with myself. I know now that I asked questions and told him that I wanted to learn, but I told him only what I wanted to believe about myself. The questions he asked me that I didn't answer honestly, I thought were none of his business. I could see no reason why they should have any relationship to this problem of getting drunk every now and then. So it drove me deeper into the psychosis or neurosis that I had, and that I hated deep down in my heart. I resented the fact that Frank had done this to me, and I just didn't know what was going on. Life was pretty miserable.

About this time, at Christmas, after being under this doctor's care, we decided that there wasn't anything more to do. Every time I got drunk, my husband would send me to a nursing home. He hesitated to send me back to that hospital. I think I disrupted the hospital.

Anyhow, after Christmas my husband gave me a cocker spaniel who is, I think, just as notorious in A.A. as I am. Frank had to go to New York, but because I had a dog, we had a duplex, and I thought—if only we had a house! A duplex apartment isn't any place to raise a dog. So I located a house, and I thought we ought to move into it immediately, but Frank was horrified, because he never knew what was going to happen to me. He always thought that maybe I was safer in a building where there were other people. He said that because of my drinking, he shouldn't leave, but that he had to go to New York for two weeks. Then he said I couldn't possibly move on the first of February because I couldn't stay in that place by myself. He said, "If your father will come out and stay with you, you can have the house." So I called my father and he said, "Yes," he'd come out and stay with me for that time. I loved my father dearly and I adored my dog, and I'd gotten this new house and Frank had just given me a new fur coat and I was thrilled to death. So Frank went to New York and despite all these things, I got drunk.

My father, as I have said, was very indulgent and loved me dearly, and knew how to get around me. He talked me into taking the Samaritan Treatment. He even had the people come out, and tell me what kind of a room I was going to have, and that he could come and see me, and that the dog could come and see me. So I took the Samaritan Treatment. I guess there are plenty of other graduates of this treatment around. There are no easy ways to sober up, but that's the most excruciating. I took that treatment three times and it didn't work—at least, for me.

There was a doctor in our church congregation who was interested in my case, and he thought it was a vitamin deficiency. So I went down to him quite a few times a month and had him shoot me full of the stuff; and then I went across the street to a little drug store to take a glass of beer or two beers, and then stopped at the liquor store to get myself a pint and go home. You know those vitamins just don't keep you sober!

We moved once more, to Houston; my husband thought maybe a change of environment would help and I'd be all right. There was nothing else left to try. We had tried everything. The only thing that I could do would be to call the doctor to help sober me up. I wouldn't go to the hospital because I wanted my dog there, so I had to have a trained nurse. The only time my dog would have anything to do with me was when I had a hangover, and when I was so sick he was the only one who would have anything to do with me at all.

I have told you some of the funny things, but not much of the shame and degradation. I fell down and knocked out my front teeth. I dropped a two-quart water bottle on my big toe. I couldn't walk, having it in a cast, and the doctor left the cast on three weeks longer than was necessary because he never found me sober enough to take it off.

One afternoon, the year after moving to Houston, I got as drunk as a skunk, and while I do not walk very straight sober, you should see me when I'm drunk! I was just as drunk as I could be, getting ready to take an afternoon walk. I got into slacks and out I went, weaving with the dog. A patrol car passed. The cop must have seen the condition that I was in because he decided to take me home. When he picked me up, I must have gotten sassy and told him that he couldn't do that, so he took my dog home and took me to jail! As I said before, I don't like to be fenced in, and with those bars you don't get hotel service. They phoned my husband that I was in jail and in such terrible shape that they didn't know what I would do to myself; and they realized that jail was no place for me, but that he was to wait a while before he got me, because at the time they called him to come over for me I was beating a tin cup against the wall. I wanted a cigarette and room service, which I didn't get. So I was in just a few hours. But somewhere during that time, I remembered going back on the bunk and crying my eyes out. I think that is when I hit bottom.

My husband couldn't tell whether I wanted to do something about my drinking. I was as defiant as anybody could be because I was scared. I didn't know which way to turn. So when he came for me, as he walked down the stairs, I could see him through the bars, and he was signing for me; I looked at him and said, "Don't you sign anything in this place!" I was going to sue the city for what they did to me. But Frank turned around and looked at me and said, "Esther, remember you're in jail and not at home." I don't want anybody ever to look at me like that again. The contempt and disgust that was in his face and thoughts! I think I actually read more contempt than was really there because just a week before someone had sent him the *Saturday Evening Post* article on A.A., and there was some glimmer of hope in it for him.

There was something else that I could try—A.A. But Frank was frightened to death to give it to me, because I resented everything he said and did. So he waited another week or two and I don't think I stayed sober hardly at all. Frank was out of town, and I remember that he'd gotten in this one night and found me drunk. The next morning he came into my room and said, "Esther, I'm not going to lecture you anymore, but I want you to read this article. If you will try this thing, I'll go along with you. If you don't, you will have to go home. I cannot sit by and watch you destroy yourself."

When he left I thought, what is this crack-pot thing? I took two or three drinks so my eyes could focus, and I could see that horrible picture of the awful drunk on the first page; he couldn't get the drink to his mouth, he had a towel around his hand and he needed a shave. But, from the very first paragraph on, something happened to me. I realized that there were other people in this world who behaved and acted as I did, and that I was a sick person, that I was suffering from an actual disease. It had a name and symptoms, just like diabetes or T.B. I wasn't entirely immoral; I wasn't bad; I wasn't vicious. It was such a feeling of relief that I wanted to know more about it and with that, I think for the first time, came the realization that there was something horribly, horribly wrong with me. Up to that time, I was so completely baffled by my behavior that I had never really stopped to think at all.

So, as I have said, I don't know how or why A.A. works. I only know that it first reached me through the *Saturday Evening Post* article. There was no one I could call. I know that when Frank came home, I said, "I want to try this thing," and he said "There's a post office box to write to in New York." It was the A.A. General Service Office in New York that I wrote to, and that office has always meant a lot to me. Today, because of A.A.'s growth during the intervening years, it is of course much bigger than it was then.

I wrote on a Saturday. I was shaking so, I asked my husband to write the letter for me, but he said no. This was something I had to do all by myself. So I wrote this letter in very shaky handwriting, and in just one week came back a letter with A.A. literature from New York. They sent me the regular letter they send to everybody else, but along with it, Ruth Hock, the non-alcoholic secretary, wrote a longhand note because she could see from the letter that I really needed help badly. That personal touch did help me too.

That was on Saturday and my husband was leaving town Sunday night. He said, "Wait until I get back and I will go with you to see this man." (That was the man the A.A. office had referred me to.) So Frank left town, and by Monday morning I had been sober for that whole week. I wanted to try A.A. with my whole heart and soul. I had learned an awful lot about myself in that one little article. Monday morning I was feeling just like a million dollars—all I needed was half a pint! So I got a half pint and at midnight that night, I called the number I had been given, but the man who had started the group was in the hospital, so I didn't know what to do. The letter from A.A. had said this man would see me—there weren't any women.

I stayed drunk from Monday until Friday, and I call that my spill into A.A. I'm glad I had it then. In spite of knowing that my drunkenness was a symptom of the things that were wrong with me, and that I could never drink again, I thought I couldn't yet give it up, although I was going to try. I never want to forget that last drunk as long as I live. It was one of the worst I ever had. It was the first time in my life that I could not get a lift out of what I was drinking; and so one Friday night, at five minutes to six, I had half a water glass of warm gin, and that is when I first asked God to help me.

There are so many to whom I feel deeply grateful; to my husband (and best critic), whose generous love, compassion and understanding have helped me along the way; to those before me in A. A. who inspired the first article I read, and the friend who sent that article to Frank; to Ruth for her personal note, and the first A.A. to talk to me; to my Bishop, whose loving and believing spirit inspired me; and to all the members of the Houston Group who were so patient, kind and helpful—and to countless others.

In my second year in A.A. we were transferred to Dallas. However, I threw myself into Twelfth Step work, and what I feared would be a calamity turned out to be the most blessed of blessings. My work with other alcoholics has led me, day by day, into ever wider and richer experiences.

I wish I could tell you all that A.A. has done for me, all that I think and feel about A.A., but it's something that I have experienced and have never been able to put into words. I know that I must work at it as long as I live; I know that it is only by working at it that I can stay sober and have a happy life. It is an endless career.

It has changed not simply one department of my life—it has changed my whole life. It has been a fellowship with God and man that has held good wherever I've turned and whatever I've done. It is a way of life that pays as it goes, every step of the way, in compensations that have been wonderfully rich and rewarding. It has made life a thousand times easier and simpler than did the endless compromises and conflicts by which I lived before. It pays daily in more harmonious relations with my fellow men, in ever clearer insight into the true meaning of life, and in the answering love and gratitude wherever and whenever I have been the instrument of God's will in the lives of others. In all these ways I've experienced, in ever growing measure and beyond all expectations and rewards, a joy which I had never before imagined.

The words of Dr. Bob and Bill are with me all the time. Dr. Bob said, "Love and service keep us dry," and Bill said, "Always we must remember that our first duty is face-to-face help for the alcoholic who still suffers." Dr. Bob tells about keeping it simple and not to louse it up. It's the last thing I ever heard him say, and I think there are some of us who, at times, try to read extra messages and complexities into the Steps. To me, A.A. is within the reach of every alcoholic, because it can be achieved in any walk of life and because the achievement is not ours but God's. I feel that there is no situation too difficult, none too desperate, no unhappiness too great to be overcome in this great fellowship—Alcoholics Anonymous.

CALCULATING THE COSTS

A retired Navy man looks back over twenty years of drinking, to add up his A.A. "initiation fee."

A few times at meetings, I have heard this statement: "Members of A.A. have paid the highest initiation fee of any club members in the world." The statement fascinates me because of its simple verity. It is also stated that we will never be able to figure out how much we have spent on alcohol. True! However, a rough estimate of one alcoholic's initiation fee seemed possible. Namely, mine. (I can't know how much others of our Fellowship have paid financially and, even more important, mentally and physically.)

Drunkalogues and statistics can be boring, but it is necessary to delve a little into each in order to come up with some kind of rough estimate. It is bound to be rough, because who can say exactly how much of that green blood—commonly known as money—was dissipated on dissipation? So please accept these humble calculations as, if anything, an underestimation. After all, upon coming out of a week-long or ten-day drunk, it was hard enough to figure up just how much that one drunk cost, let alone trying to calculate the cost of approximately twenty-five years of active alcoholism. But, as it was with drinking, this project will be entered into with enthusiasm and optimism—and probably wind up the same way, depressed.

Twenty-five years of drinking! My drinking career extended from age eighteen to forty-three. Eighteen

343

will be used as the starting point, because my drinking before was limited by age, the law, and money. I displayed alcoholic tendencies actually from the age of fourteen, when I started to steal wine from the family jug, siphoning it off one drink at a time so it wouldn't be missed, not drinking it immediately, but saving it until about a pint was accumulated, so that I could get drunk. Even at that age, I had learned that one drink was not enough. I had to have enough to get drunk on, or what was the use?

At eighteen, I got my first steady job. Twelve dollars a week. This eliminated one of the limiting factors, the financial. Age and the law were still against me, but laws were not as strictly enforced in those days as they are now, and I discovered that as long as I had the green blood, there was always a way to get alcohol, either from a nondiscriminatory bartender or from an older friend who would be glad to purchase the joy juice for the privilege of sharing it. At this time, the price of booze in the bars was fifteen cents a shot and ten cents a beer. I found out fast that the cheapest way to get drunk was on shots with beer chasers at two bits a crack.

Saying these sprees were limited to one a week (they were not), and saying that the average spree was ten of these drinks (sometimes more, sometimes less), we come up with the first boring statistic: two-fifty per week out of twelve dollars. To keep it in round figures, let's say twenty percent of my income went for giggle gurgles. After a few more estimates as to income and expenditures for booze over a few sample years, taken at random, I conclude that this twenty percent stayed fairly constant. As income increased, the price of liquor increased proportionately. I graduated from shots and beer chasers to Scotch and sodas. (It was the beer and cheap whiskey that was making me so sick. Where have we heard this before?)

At age twenty-one, I enlisted in the Navy for two reasons: (1) to avoid being drafted into the Army, and (2) out of a burst of patriotic fervor inspired by the advent of World War II and as the result of an all-night drinking binge which found me sitting on the doorstep of the Navy recruiting office when the chief petty officer arrived to open for business at nine o'clock Monday morning. In the back of my mind, I probably thought, "They won't take me as drunk as I am." But I was wrong.

Two weeks later found me being sworn in, and the first payday in the Navy made me realize I had found a home. My first pay was ten dollars, pay for recruits at that time being twenty-one dollars per month. But my board, room, and clothing were free, and I could spend the whole ten bucks on booze. So I spent twenty years in the Navy.

Now my drinking was limited by only one factor, the enforced periods of dryness caused by lengthy tours at sea. The short tours could be taken care of by sneaking enough whiskey aboard ship so that it could be rationed out until another supply could be laid in. The only other occasionally limiting factor was that I might run out of money before the next pay day rolled around. But I was a careful and cunning alcoholic, and this didn't happen very often.

So I believe that twenty percent is a very conservative estimate of the amount of income I blew. For an estimate of salary from the twenty-one a month to start with, to over $400 per month upon my retirement after twenty years in the Navy, I believe that an average income of $2,000 a year over this period is low, but, as I stated earlier, an underestimate is best.

Some simple mathematics and more statistics: $2,000 a year for twenty-five years is $50,000, twenty percent of which is $10,000.

Alcoholics being the argumentative lot that we are, the A.A. membership will undoubtedly come up with a few who will dispute these figures. So please bear in mind, and I would like to emphasize, that this is a very rough estimate. Like most statistics, it doesn't prove anything—just satisfies a little curiosity engendered by the wail "Oh, those initiation fees" that prompted this investigation.

Incalculable are the intangible initiation fees that A.A. members have paid: the sick, sick hangovers, the remorse, guilt, broken homes, jails, and institutions, and the mental anguish in general that has been generated over the years. Only god as we understand Him can calculate these. But now, with His help and grace, this child of His has paid his initiation fee for good, as long as he remembers to stay away from the first drink (the one that does all the damage) one day at a time.

Stars Don't Fall

A titled lady, she still saw her world darkening. When the overcast lifted, the stars were there as before.

$\mathcal{M}$y alcoholic problem began long before I drank. My personality, from the time I can remember anything, was the perfect set-up for an alcoholic career. I was always at odds with the entire world, not to say the universe. I was out of step with life, with my family, with people in general. I tried to compensate with impossible dreams and ambitions, which were simply early forms of escape. Even when I was old enough to know better, I dreamed about being as beautiful as Venus, as pure as the Madonna and as brilliant as the President of the United States is supposed to be. I had writing ambitions, and nothing would do but that I'd write like Shakespeare. I also wanted to be the queen of society, with a glittering salon, the bride of a dream prince and the mother of a happy brood. Inside, I went right on being a mass of unlovely self-pity, queasy anxiety and sickening self-debasement. Naturally, I succeeded in nothing. Until I reached A.A. my life was a shambles; I was a mess, and I made everybody near and dear to me miserable. I had to go through extreme alcoholism to find my answer.

There was no material or external reason for this. I was born in a castle—the family home, in Europe. My father had a title; there was plenty of means in the family. When I was a baby, my mother brought me to

America, and I never again saw my father. But again, the living was easy. My family, on my mother's side, was brilliant, gifted and charming. They were ambitious, successful, strong and famous. They inherited wealth and acquired more.

They did the best they knew how as far as I was concerned. It took me three psychoanalysts and several years in A.A. to really get this through my head.

Up to my early thirties, when my drinking had become a major problem, I lived in large houses, with servants and all the luxuries that I could possibly ask for. But I did not feel a part of my family or a part of the set-up. I got a good non-academic education; my intellectual curiosity was encouraged. I learned how to hold a terrapin fork. Otherwise I got nothing out of it.

Before I started to drink seriously, I tried a couple of other escapes. At eighteen I ran away from home. Showing all the courage and ingenuity that I had not used in a positive way, I covered my tracks and hid from my family so successfully that they did not find me for months. I went out to the West Coast, waited on table, washed dishes and sold newspaper subscriptions. Like most sick people before me, I was implacably selfish, and chronically self-centered. My mother's heartbreak, or the unpleasant publicity I had caused did not bother my pretty head. After eight months, the family found me. Their telegram was kind and nice. But I was afraid. I was still untrained for any work but washing dishes and waiting on table. So I married a nice, well-meaning young newspaperman, so as not to have to go home. It did not occur to me that marriage might be a job, too. We came back East and met both families. His were good, simple Quaker folk who accepted me with love. But I did not fit into this pattern either. The birth of a daughter filled me with new fears. Responsibility again. Her father became both mother and father to her. At the tender age of twenty-three, I got a divorce. My husband was made miserable by this, but I had already made him and myself miserable. He got half custody of our child, but later kept her during most of the school terms. It was the only real home she knew. I resented this, but I did nothing constructive about it.

Now I had done some living but I hadn't learned a thing. This was where I started my first drinking lessons. Up to this time it just hadn't occurred to me to drink. My Quaker mother-in-law, bless her heart, used to set the Christmas pudding ablaze with lumps of sugar dipped in rubbing alcohol. But now I was a young divorcee, leading a Washington social life. My family always bought the best, and the embassies were flowing.

I think I had the physical allergy right away. A drink never gave me a normal, pleasant glow. Instead it was like a tap on the head with a small mallet. I was a little bit knocked out. Just what I wanted. I lost my shyness. Five or six drinks and I was terrific. Men danced with me at parties. I was full of careless chatter. I was so amusing! I had friends.

I got a novel written. It was all about Scott Fitzgerald's little lost debutante, abused, misunderstood and running wild. The book was published, but the reading public said—So what? I did not see that the book dripped with self-pity. I only saw that I had not become Mrs. Shakespeare.

I met a wonderful man. He was the dream prince, the answer. I, who did not know how to give love, was head over heels "in love." I wanted him to love me and make up to me for everything. He was brilliant and ambitious. He was well behaved, and idealistic where women were concerned. But he noticed that I was not a good mother to my child, that I relegated her to nurses when she was with me. He saw that I was unsettled, living away from my family and renting houses here and there. A house in Virginia, during the fox hunting season; a little chalet in Switzerland during the summer or a place on Long Island—each house complete with cooks, butlers, maids. Above all, he noticed that I drank a good deal, often got tight in his company and told him naughty stories. He did not like naughty stories, so I made them naughtier. He finally decided that he did not love me enough, and soon he told me so and said he was engaged to another girl.

He has since become famous and distinguished, an asset to his country. I saw him recently and he told me that he had always felt guilty, because, after our separation, I had become a serious alcoholic. With ten years of A.A. behind me, I was able to tell him that I'd have been an alcoholic, no matter what; that I had been a sick person, unfit for marriage.

Even then I knew in my heart that I was unfit for the very things I wanted most, a happy marriage, security, a home and love. But when this happened to me, I declared to friends that I would get drunk, dead drunk that very night, and stay drunk for a month. A normal person, hit with adversity, can go on a drinking spree and then snap out of it. But I got drunk that night and stayed drunk, getting increasingly worse until I found A.A. ten years later.

That first night I blacked out at a large dinner party. In the morning, because I was young and healthy, my remorse was worse than my hangover.

What had I said? What had I done? I experienced my first real guilt and shame. This was in Virginia, where I had rented a house with stables and a swimming pool, and the fall fox hunting had begun. The people I knew rode hard, and some of them drank hard. Many of them carried a flask and sandwich case, strapped to their saddles so they could stay out all day. But whereas my horse was always equipped with a flask, I merely endured the fox hunting so I could start drinking at lunch time. I would pull out early, and go to the hunt breakfast and the flowing bowl of milk-punch. By two-thirty in the afternoon I was always tight.

During these years, I did acquire some good friends. A few stood by me, at least in their hearts, throughout the whole of my drinking career. Others have come back, others I have lost. But at this time, I began gravitating toward the really hard drinkers, hanging around with them more and more. My old friends showed distress. Couldn't I drink less? Couldn't I stop, after a few? It was nothing to my own inner distress, my self-reproach, and my self-loathing, for was I not bearing out all the horrible things I had always suspected of myself?

I accepted a big tax-free income from the family, but I didn't like it when they told me how to live. I went to Europe to escape them, so I thought. I was really trying, once more, to escape from myself. Imagine my surprise when I came to, in Europe, and discovered I had brought myself along! I rented a beautiful apartment on the banks of the Seine in the winter, and a chalet in Switzerland in the summer. I read sad poetry, cried, drank red wine, wrote sad poetry, and drank some more. I also wrote another novel, all about Scott Fitzgerald's poor, misbegotten, unloved, tipsy little debutante. Even the critics kidded me about this one. I had worked the previous summer on a New York fashion magazine, a job I really enjoyed. I was now with the Paris office. I stayed with them until I got drunk and had a row with the Paris editor.

During this period I married again. This was an Englishman who, at least at this time, drank as much as I did. What we had in common was alcohol. On our honeymoon in Egypt, he cuffed me around quite a bit, and subsequently he hit me some more. I can't blame him. My tongue had become increasingly skilled at venomous home truths. He had not developed this art and had no recourse but his fists.

We went through the two years of deadlock required by the English divorce laws. During this time, you are supposed to behave yourself, but I took a little wine-tasting tour through France, all by my lone, with car and chauffeur. Tasting the best of burgundy at a famous restaurant one night landed me passed out on a park bench in the public square. I came to and found a man leaning over me. When he reached for me, I rose and smote him. He, in turn, kicked me so I fell to the ground. Bruised, and deadly ashamed, I told no one. I began, here and now, to fear the answer to the question—what is the matter with me? I had already been to one analyst at home. We had not gotten anywhere. Was my mental state more serious than he said? Was I insane? Was that it? I did not dare to think. I drank and kept on drinking.

Drunk or sober, I was hectic, unpredictable, irresponsible. At a large party in Geneva, with people from many countries represented, the kind of party that is "protocol" in the extreme, I swayed, laughed hysterically, made naughty remarks in an unhushed voice, and was finally led from the scene. My friends were understandably hurt and angry. Why had I done it? Why? I could not tell them. I was afraid to think why. Now I hid when I wanted to drink. I drank alone or with someone, anyone who would stay and drink with me. I passed out frequently in my home, alone.

An American doctor in Paris said I had an enlarged liver. He also said, "You are an alcoholic and there's nothing I can do for you." This went in one ear and out the other. I did not know what he meant. An alcoholic cannot accept the news that he's an alcoholic unless there is a meaningful explanation given, and an offer of help, such as you get in A.A.

I returned from Europe a while after that encounter, and I never went back. Things were no better with the family, so I moved to New York. Here, also, I had good friends, but I became more and more separated from them. Why did I have to have at least three cocktails to sit through dinner? Other girls whom I had known all my life asked for one weak scotch after dinner. Sometimes they'd put it on the mantel and forget it. My eye would be glued to that glass. How could anybody *forget* a drink? I would have three quick strong ones in order to endure the evening.

My first analyst said, "You are becoming more and more of an alcoholic," and sent me to another analyst. This good and gentle man, a brilliant research doctor, got nowhere with me fast. I was accepting help with one hand and pushing it away with the other. The liquor counteracted the help I was getting.

Meanwhile I had found another escape. This one was a dandy. It combined running away from my world, and drinking all I wanted to. I had met a bunch of gay young Bohemians who lived in the Village, and were sowing their wild oats. They were all kids, most of them younger than I was. All of them have since settled down to jobs and good marriages. None of them were alcoholics, but at this time they were drinking as much as I was. They introduced me to beer in the morning to kill hangovers. This was the life! I was the center of attention, just what my sick ego craved. They said I was so funny, and told me, with shrieks of laughter, what I'd done the night before. Ribaldry was the substance of the conversation, and I set out to be the funniest and most ribald of them all.

They woke up with hangovers, but with no remorse. I woke up filled with secret guilt and shame. Underneath, I knew this was all wrong. Now it was semi-blackouts every night, outrageous behavior, passing out in some friend's Village studio or not knowing how I got home. The horrors of increasing hangover sickness to occupy the entire day; nausea, dry heaves, the rocking bed, the nightmare-filled mind.

At this stage, I began a daily mental routine. I must drink less, I would tell myself. Or: If I'm really a genius, I must produce a great work, to show why I *act* like a genius. Or—this is a little too much! I'd better taper off. I must use self-will, self-control. I must go on the wagon for a while. Drink only beer or wine. I used all those well-known phrases. I also thought that I must have *power over myself.* I was an agnostic, so I thought. My new friends made fun of God and all the orthodox beliefs. I thought I was the captain of my soul. I told myself that I had power over this thing. One day soon, the analyses would reveal why I drank and how to stop.

I did not know that I had no power over alcohol,

that I, alone and unaided, could not stop; that I was on a downgrade, tearing along at full speed with all my brakes gone, and that the end would be a total smash-up, death or insanity. I had already feared insanity for a long time. Certainly, when I was in my cups, I was not just drunk, I was crazy. Now my whole thinking was crazy. For, after those daily self-punishing sessions with myself, after the vows to stop, I would change entirely as evening came on. I would get wildly excited and look forward to another night of drinking. The remorse would turn inside out, and become anticipatory pleasure. I was going to get drunk again—Drunk!

My child was being exposed to all this. She was also the victim of my scolding and incessant nagging. I was really scolding my mortal enemy, the inner me. My poor child could not know this. Her father, quite rightly, wanted to put her in a school. When I protested, his lawyer, my lawyer, and my third and last analyst had a conference. She was duly sent to school, away from me.

This new analyst was a woman doctor, one of the best in the country. She did all she could to help this situation and to protect my child. She was endlessly patient as we looked together for an answer. She, more than the others, showed me what ailed me basically, why I was immature and insecure. But I was not able to make use of this knowledge until after I became sober. A.A. had to stop my drinking first. Then I was able to do something about me.

There were a couple of good things. And again these were things that I really profited by after I sobered up. I saw that my Village friends, all of whom had small jobs, were living happily on about a tenth of my sinecure. It had never occurred to me before that I could live simply and be independent of my family. So I did the right thing in the wrong way. I had a drunken quarrel with my family, denounced them and left them forever. They were awfully good about not cutting me off. It was I who had to tell the bank, after a certain time, to refuse all further deposits. I had saved my allowance. I now had quite a nest-egg. I had a tiny trust fund, and I moved into a small apartment where I learned to cook, keep house, and do the things that normal people do. I learned a whole new sense of values. I wrote and sold some short stories. These things were carried out in moments of less severe hangover or short stretches on the wagon. But the money I had saved up went for cases of liquor. I was, when drunk, just as undisciplined and erratic as ever. My new friends had a social conscience. They were bright and well read, they held various political views. In the course of drunken arguments, I found my own views and a sense of responsibility as a citizen. I tried volunteer activity. But my attempts at community service ended in a drunken and abusive row with a fellow volunteer.

By this time I had ceased to be the life of the party. I became a menace, the fish-wife, the common scold. I took everybody else's inventory. Finally my new friends told me, one by one, that I could not come around any more.

Now came the black and endless dismal night. I went to bars alone to drink. There was one Village bar in particular for which I formed an obsession. I had to go there every night. I rarely remembered getting home. The bartenders took care of me, not out of brotherly love, but through enlightened self-interest.

An obstreperous woman in a bar is a nuisance, and they wanted no trouble with the police. On the other hand, I was a marvelous customer. For three generations my family had had a charge account in one of the big New York hotels. I stopped at the cashier's any hour of the night on the way to the bar and cashed a check. In the morning I would wake up with a dollar or two. I suspect that those bartenders would wait until I had shot my wad, then call a cab and send me home. This too is how the nest-egg went.

So here, in this dive, this hangout for dead-end alcoholics and neurotics, here was I. In a sick people's place, myself among the sickest. I despised the other barflies and, naturally, they loathed me. In my cups I used to tell them off, giving them lengthy advice on how to lead the right life. They got so they moved their barstools when they saw me coming. The bartenders too, treated me with contempt. Yes I, the queen of them all! The glittering society belle, the modern Shakespeare, the happy wife, the loving and beloved. I, who had dreamed these sick dreams, now reaped the nightmare. What I had secretly believed myself to be all along, this I had become. I was not beautiful or good, as I had yearned to be. I was fat, bloated, dirty and unkempt. Most of the time I was covered with bruises from "running into doors." I wore a man's raincoat, turned inside out, a present from a friend, for now my funds were low. I could not live on that tiny trust fund and still drink all I wanted to. My tweed suit, once a very good one, was shapeless and baggy with bare places worn in the elbows from leaning on the bar.

Once, in a strange gin mill, I stole a bottle from behind the bar. The bartender, a tough Irishman, came around and "gave me the elbow," which means that he raised his elbow and smacked me in the face. I literally hit the sawdust. Luckily a friend was with me, who dragged me out, screaming and cursing, while the bartender threatened to call the police. But I never got into jail. I didn't get into a sanitarium either. I wanted to die and often I would think of ways. I would walk up and down under the 59th Street bridge, trying to get up the nerve to go up there and jump. Once, when I called my analyst, and told her I was contemplating death, she came over and tried to get me into a sanitarium. Frightened and shamed, I refused, and sobered up temporarily. I was not mugged or manhandled. I did not resort to semi-prostitution for the price of drink. But all these things *could* have happened. The sanitarium *should* have happened. I was not fit to be on the loose, and there was no one to commit me.

I think now that a God, in whom I did not believe, was looking after me. Perhaps it was He who sent my analyst to a psychiatrist's meeting at which Bill spoke. In those days, psychiatry and A.A. had not gotten together as they have since. My analyst was one of the first to learn of A.A. and to make subsequent use of it in her work. Having heard Bill speak, she was instantly sold. She read this book that you are reading now. She asked me to read it.

"These people all had your problem," she told me.

Anybody who had my problem was beneath contempt!

I read the book and God leapt at me from every page. So this was a group of reformers! What intellectual interests could we have in common? Could they discuss literature or art? I could just hear their sweet,

pious talk. Nobody was going to reform me! I was going to reform myself!

I returned the book to my analyst and shook my
head. But now a strange thing happened. In my cups I
began to say, "I can't stop." I said it over and over,
boring my fellow barflies. Something in the book had
reached me after all. In a sense, I had taken the first
step. My analyst pricked up her ears.

"Why don't you just go down and see Mr. W.?"
she asked. "See what you think."

I now said a lucky and wonderful thing. I said,
"O.K."

In those days the A.A. Foundation was down in
the Wall Street district of New York. As I went in I
was dying of mortification. They would all stare at me
and whisper! Oh, poor self-centered, sick little me. I
did not reflect that half the office was composed of
A.A. members, and that I was as unexciting as any
client in any office.

Bill was tall, grey-haired, with the kind of asym-
metrical good looks and pleasant easy manner that in-
spire confidence in the shaken and afraid. He was well
dressed; he was easy going. I could see he wasn't a
quack or a fanatic.

He did not take out a folder and say, "What is the
nature of your problem?" He said to me, gently and
simply, "Do you think that you are one of us?"

Never in my entire life had anyone asked me "Are
you one of us?" Never had I felt a sense of belonging. I
found myself nodding my head.

He now said that *we* had a physical allergy combined with a mental obsession, and he explained this
so that I saw for the first time how this could be. He
asked me if I had any spiritual belief, and when I said

No, he suggested that I keep an open mind. Then he called Marty and made an appointment for me. I thought, "Aha, he's passing the buck. Now comes the questionnaire." I did not know who this Marty was. I did not want to go and see her, but I went. A friend of Marty's, another A.A. let me in. Marty was late. I felt like a gangster's moll about to be interviewed by the Salvation Army. The strange A.A. put me at ease. The apartment was charming; the shelves were full of books, many of which I myself owned. Marty came in, looking clean, neat, well-dressed and, like Bill, she was neither a bloated wreck nor a reformer. She was attractive; she was like the friends I had once had. Indeed, she had known my cousin in Chicago. Years of drinking and general high jinks had cut her off from old friends. She too had gone to cheap bars to drink. With more physical courage than I had possessed, she had twice tried to take her life. She had been in sanitariums. Her luck had been worse than mine, but not her drinking. I, who had feared questions, now began trying to interrupt and tell *my* story. I couldn't get a word in edgewise! Marty was smart. A load weighing a thousand pounds came off my back. I wasn't insane. Nor was I the "worst woman who ever lived." I was an alcoholic, with a recognizable behavior pattern.

I went to my first meeting with Marty and some other girls. I was sold, intellectually. But my life, even sober, was all askew and so were my emotions. In those days there was only one big meeting a week in New York. On non-meeting nights I was lonesome, or so I told myself. I went to several Village bars, and drank cokes or tea. I had been on the wagon when I came to A.A. and this sobriety-tension eventually popped. Not understanding the twenty-four-hour plan, or not wanting to, I began drinking and was off-again on-again, during that first month.

A fellow A.A., called Anne, who had helped me, went on a terrible bender. Priscilla, an A.A., who, like Marty, has become one of my greatest friends, decided that I was a stubborn case. Since they could do nothing with Anne either, Priscilla suggested that I go and look after Anne. Now, I am big and weak, but Anne was bigger than I and strong. Her idea of fun on a bender was to hit sailors and insult cops. We were to go up to our A.A. farm in Kent, and I spent the evening before riding herd on Anne. I was so busy keeping her out of trouble, and so scared she'd swing on me, that I had my last two drinks that night. The farm, in those days, was primitive. There was no central heating, and this was the dead of winter. Anne and I went up in ski clothes and fur coats, and it was so cold we slept in them. I tried to wash a little, but Anne refused to wash at all. She said she felt too horrible inside to be pretty on the outside. This I understood. This was how I had looked and acted a few short weeks ago. I completely forgot about myself in trying vainly to help Anne, whose misery I understood.

On the train going back, Anne's one idea was to get to the nearest bar. I was really scared. I thought it was my duty to keep her from drinking, not knowing that if the other fellow is really determined to drink there is nothing you can do about it. However, I had phoned New York from the farm, appealing for help, and there in the station to meet us were two A.A.'s, John and Bud. They were a couple of normal, sober, attractive men. They took Anne and me to dinner. We, who were dirty, bedraggled and in ski clothes. They did not seem ashamed to be with us, these strangers.

They were taking the trouble to try and help. Why? I was astonished and deeply moved.

All these things together brought me into A.A. I got off the so-called wagon, and on the twenty-four-hour plan. I had never had the physical courage to shake it out before.

John and Bud became my friends. John said, "Keep going to meetings." And I did. He himself took me to many of them, including the ones out of town.

Except for one short slip, during the first eight months, which was an angry "the world can't do this to me" reaction to a personal tragedy in my life, I have been sober for twelve years. I, who could never stay on the wagon for more than a week. The personality rehabilitation did not come overnight. In the first year there were episodes such as kicking Priscilla in the shins, getting the lock changed on the desk in the A.A. Club, because I, as secretary, didn't want the Intergroup secretary "interfering," and taking an older woman member out to lunch for the express purpose of informing her that she was "a phony." All the people involved in these flare-ups took it with remarkable grace, have teased me about it since, and have become good friends of mine.

A.A. taught me how not to drink. And also, on the twenty-four-hour plan, it taught me how to live. I know I do not have to be "queen of them all" to salve a frightened ego. Through going to meetings and listening, and occasionally speaking, through doing Twelve Step work, whereby in helping others you are both the teacher and the student, by making many wonderful A.A. friends, I have been taught all the things in life that are worth having. I am no longer interested in living in a palace, because palace living was not the answer for me. Nor were those impossible dreams I used to have the things I really wanted.

I have my A.A. friends, and I have become reacquainted with my old friends on a new basis. My friendships are meaningful, loving and interesting because I am sober. I have achieved the inner confidence to write quite unlike Shakespeare, and I have sold a good deal of what I've written. I want to write better and sell more. My spiritual awakening in A.A. finally resulted in my joining a church some years ago. This has been a wonderful thing in my life. I consider that I was taking the Eleventh Step when I joined this church. (This was for *me*. Many good A.A.'s never join a church, and do not need to. Some even remain agnostics.)

Every day, I feel a little bit more useful, more happy and more free. Life, including some ups and downs, is a lot of fun. I am a part of A.A. which is a way of life. If I had not become an active alcoholic and joined A.A., I might never have found my own identity or become a part of anything. In ending my story I like to think about this.

GROWING UP ALL OVER AGAIN

A "good boy" reached adulthood and success without achieving maturity or fulfillment. Defeated by alcohol and pills, he found the way to a new life.

I was twenty-eight years old. I had been elected president of a civic club. I was a deacon and a Sunday-school teacher. I had a lovely wife and three children. I had just begun a dental practice in a beautiful new office. I had completed a three-year tour in the Navy. My wife was in the Junior League, and I was on the board of directors of the local center for the mentally retarded.

No one could have told me then that I had not earned all my success, nor could anyone have told me that I was an alcoholic and a drug addict. The only thing that bothered me was a queasy feeling I had in the pit of my stomach. It hinted to me that everything was phony. I had accomplished all the right things that our society expected, and I had no real peace of mind nor gratitude. I was nothing more than a spoiled, indulged, and talented brat.

In less than two years, I lost my practice, my home, my wife, and my children. I tried the church and psychiatry and finally came to A.A. The last time I drank, when I was twenty-nine, I drank for only four days, yet I threatened to kill my children; I beat my wife at home and on the church steps; I mistreated a child in my office; and I ran to a hospital for mental illness to avoid jail.

I am one of the growing number of A.A. members who are second-generation. In fact, I was taken to A.A. by a woman whom my father had taken to A.A. thirteen years earlier. I neither drank nor smoked until I was nineteen years old. I was an honor graduate in high school, and I was a "good boy" to whom mothers pointed when their sons went astray. Awarded a scholarship to a famous old Eastern college, I began to drink at the end of my freshman year, and by junior year, I had to transfer to an easier state university to keep my grades up. Oddly enough, the dentist who started A.A. in Amarillo, Tex., benevolently arranged my admission to dental college. During my first year there, I married.

Fear, love of dentistry, and an imitation of my father's periodic drinking pattern took me through dental college soberly, except for the few parties and vacations in those four years. I graduated with honors, but could not feel any real responsibility as a father or a husband.

Then came my tour in the U.S. Navy, part of it being two years in the Philippines. My life there was a nightmare of periodic binges on alcohol and pills, adultery, unhappy hours at the dental office, seeing my wife give birth to our second child and have several miscarriages, living in a turbulent household, and making continual attempts to be the respectable dentist, husband, father, and community leader.

A return to the United States provided effective as a geographical cure, and a period of sobriety ensued, with the help of the church. When I went back to my hometown to go into private practice, I experienced another brief lull in my addiction to alcohol and drugs. But it did not take long for the pressures of living to bring out my immaturity and my insecurity. I depended on optimism and ambition to live in society; when I began to tire, I had to depend on chemicals instead to keep going.

I came to A.A. simply because there were no other doors of help open to me in my hometown. In A.A., I have had to be torn down and then put back together differently. No one could live such an irresponsible, immature life as I had without consequences. A.A. made it possible for me to face the consequences of my past actins. After I came to A.A., I was divorced by my wife; I lost my practice; I was legally restrained from seeing my children; I went broke; and the dental society threatened me with the loss of my license. Only A.A. kept me from running away.

My A.A. experience has been active: three meetings a week, many tapes, many A.A. conferences, much work on the Twelve Steps, and much work with other alcoholics and their families. A.A. has given me a new wife, a beautiful stepdaughter, a new practice, a new home, and a new relationship with my four children. Most important, A.A. has enabled me to go back and start growing up all over again in all areas of my life. Truth and sincerity do not come easily to me. Admitting that I am wrong or that I do not know is difficult for me.

My gratitude to A.A. grows deeper each day I am sober. My second wife is a young A.A. member, too, and what a terrific adventure this is for us! All the statistics are against me. I am a young alcoholic with a drug problem, a doctor, the husband of an alcoholic, the son of an alcoholic, and a man once diagnosed as a violent manic-depressive. Why am I alive, free, a respected member of my community? Because A.A. really works for me!

UNTO THE SECOND GENERATION

A young veteran tells how a few rough experiences pushed him into A.A.—and how he was therefore spared years of suffering.

*M*y eyes opened onto a hazy world. Two fuzzy objects came into focus. Slowly I realized I was in bed and that the objects were my feet, encased in a harness affair. I blinked slowly as I shifted my gaze to my arms. They also were held in some sort of strap arrangement.

Gradually consciousness returned enough to let me know I was in a hospital. I looked about the room. At one end of the bed, near the foot, was a printed card, and beneath that was a charted graph. I couldn't focus enough to make out the chart, but the card contained two words—"ACUTE ALCOHOLISM." Then it came to me. I was in a hospital. The place—Hawaii. I closed my eyes and tried to think

I remembered having had a little drink of whiskey with a can of warm beer as a chaser. Then something happened. What was it? I couldn't recall. I opened my eyes again and a shadow fell across the bed. Standing there was a gray-haired man—tall, trim and in uniform. There were gold bars on his shoulders.

Now I know. I'm in the U.S. Navy. This must be the doctor. He asked how I felt. I didn't reply. A corpsman stood beside him. The doctor motioned to the corpsman to undo my straitjacket and leg restraints. I moved about a little. The doctor sat down beside the bed and asked me how I felt.

"Do you know why you're in here?" he queried.

I could tell him a lot of reasons why I am here in an alky ward at the age of twenty. I don't know how I got here this trip, but it doesn't matter very much. I'm an alcoholic. Don't mince words. I'm a rummy. I can't control my drinking any more. It controls me.

I remembered back to high school when I was fifteen. We all had lockers. The other pupils kept books, pencils, paper, gym equipment and such stuff in their lockers. I did, too. I also kept beer. At fifteen I was strictly a beer drinker. I didn't graduate to the hard stuff until I was sixteen. The other kids would light out for the hamburger huts or ice cream parlors, the pizza joints or bowling alleys, after football games and dances. I didn't. I went to saloons where I could get drinks.

I didn't give a whoop about anything scholastic. I got a job after school pumping gas and worked until ten or eleven at night. I was the kid of the crew. I tried to mimic the talk, ideas, moods and even the drinking of the older men. It hurt to be considered a kid. I talked out of the side of my mouth, as they did. I smoked as much, tried to drink as much, and do everything they did, only more so.

I found I could boost my income by figuring out a lot of cute little tricks that the boss wouldn't be likely to notice—filching money from the Coke machine, short-sticking customers on oil, and selling oil I'd drained out of other cars.

School was getting to be one big bore. I was skipping classes about two days a week and doing no book work whatever. I was failing in everything. The principal had no alternative but to expel me. I beat him to it. I quit, when I was just past sixteen.

I had a drinking problem on my hands even at that time. So did my parents. They both drank like fish. They had been drinking for many years and were getting progressively worse. Home life didn't mean much to me. They were kind when they thought about it, but that wasn't often. I wanted love and affection but I didn't get it. I did as I pleased most of the time.

I wasn't burdened with parental guidance and I didn't want any. I ran away for the second time, with another lad. We got to Omaha, from my home in Chicago. We headed out of town walking—no money, cold and hungry. It was late at night. We spotted a church in a small town. We broke open a window and got inside. We started to light matches to see, but the draft blew them out. So we rolled old newspapers together and made torches to find a good soft pew and get some sleep. My torch blazed madly and the pew caught fire.

We heard some yells outside. A busload of basketball players had been passing and saw the flames. They summoned the fire department and the sheriff. I spent the next three days in a cell. My dad, who was a newspaper man and had some connections, had meantime put a stop on me, and I guess that report went all over the country. We were identified and I was put on a train for Chicago. The sheriff bade us goodbye very happily. I still think dad paid him something to let me go.

Back home again! Drinking conditions at home were even worse than before. I would rather have stayed in jail except I didn't like bologna and cold potatoes for breakfast. I got a job with the newspaper my dad worked for. I liked it and soon moved into the photo department, which was what I wanted to do. "Ace crime photographer," that's me.

About this time I got my first crush on a girl. I teamed up with a cute little blonde with whom I was working at the office, and for about a year we were inseparable. Beaches, parties, dances, movies—everything. Here was the lost love I'd missed at home. I was drinking quite a bit of whiskey now. She didn't like it, but I thought it made a man of me. Once in a while I stayed home for a night, to see how my folks were doing. They were doing very well—at least a fifth apiece a day, except on dad's days off when they did some serious drinking.

I was now nearly eighteen. I enlisted in the Navy to escape the Army draft. It looked as if the war would be over any day, but I had to go anyhow. I planned to stay home the night before I left, but my folks got so drunk I walked off early in the evening and spent the night with my girl, getting very drunk myself. Next morning I was sworn in, feeling no pain. I went into the Navy in fine style. I was drunk. Three years later I was discharged in the same way.

At Great Lakes Boot Camp I latched onto a soft billet. My job was to make out the guard schedules and thus I was exempt from ordinary recruit training activities. This went on for thirteen weeks, the first eight of which I wasn't allowed visitors. But my dad pulled some strings and got in to see me after three weeks. He and mom smuggled in a couple of pints to me. This was fine, but it was just an extra dividend, for I'd made connections by this time and was buying a bottle a day from the cook. I stayed in the barracks all day, "making out guard schedules," and getting mildly plastered from the jug under my desk. I applied for photo school at Pensacola Air Base and made it. While waiting to depart I was selected—by giving a CPO five dollars—to be bartender in the Navy Chief's Club. At night I tended bar.

While I was at Pensacola my dad became dangerously ill and almost died of pneumonia plus a heart attack. I got emergency leave for twenty days. Mom and I drank every waking moment because we felt so sorry for dad. I tried to control her drinking by pouring her whiskey down the sink before I'd leave for the night, to get drunker myself.

I don't know why I didn't fall out of the open cockpit of some of those planes I flew in while taking aerial pictures. I didn't. And when this six-month school was over I applied for duty in Hawaii and pulled it. I wanted to get as far away from home as possible.

Pearl Harbor was a breeze of nine months, a gay Hawaiian paradise, drinking under the palms, listening to the surf beat on the shore, a bottle of whiskey near at hand. I was becoming a solitary drinker, but I didn't care. I was transferred to Kaneohe Bay, across the hump to the windward side of Oahu, to the aviation base. This was wonderful. I talked the Old Man into letting me live in the photo lab instead of the barracks, and for eighteen months nothing interfered with my drinking. The boys at the Post Office used to bring me my jugs; mail couldn't be opened for inspection at the gate. This was an ideal set-up.

I was only twenty now, but I was a man. Wasn't I drinking more than a quart every day? I knew I was hitting the skids, but what of it? Didn't I come from a family of drinkers? There wasn't much I could do about it, and I didn't want to do anything anyway.

About this time my folks found A.A. It solved their problems and they started living a sane life again. They wrote me many long letters about it. I thought it was fine for them. They really needed it. But I knew I'd never get that way.

I seldom left the base anymore except once in a while when I felt the need of talking to some girl. Then I'd get a pass to Honolulu. Meanwhile the letters from home were telling about how much my folks wanted to make up to me for some of the things I'd missed. I hadn't told them about my drinking, but I guess they knew. I'd reply and some of my letters they saved. To this day I haven't been able to decipher what I wrote to them.

One night I was sitting in the lab alone with a fifth and a case of beer listening to dreamy Hawaiian music on the radio. Slowly a pile of pineapples started to build up on the table. They got bigger and bigger and nearer and nearer, as if they were going to fall and crush me. Two of them leaped from the table and crashed into my head. I was knocked to the floor, swinging madly at the faces on those pineapples. I swung, I swore, I started throwing beer cans at the advancing hordes of pineapple faces. I cut my hands, my face, my legs. Then I collapsed. I had D.T.'s.

The doctor was still sitting beside my bed. My past had slipped before me in a twinkling. The doctor said I'd been brought into the hospital like a madman, crying, raving, ranting, swearing, completely in the throes of delirium tremens.

I was released in a week, a week of hell with no drinks. I told the doctor my parents' drinking history and blamed them. He was interested and said he'd help me all he could. He even went to bat for me before the court martial that inevitably followed and, as a result, I drew only thirty days—fifteen in solitary.

Two months later I was discharged. I was supposed to come home on a troop ship, but I talked the base commander into flying me home. We were supposed to take off at noon, but were delayed until six p.m. I spent the time in a nearby tavern, was loaded on the ship, went to sleep before take-off, and the next thing I knew someone was shaking me and telling me we were over San Diego.

I went to Tijuana that night and landed in jail. Drunk and causing a brawl, they said. Heck. All I'd wanted was one more drink. I was escorted back to San Diego next morning—by the Shore Patrol, but I was discharged on schedule.

I headed home for the most wonderful experience of all time—meeting my "new" parents—mom and dad looked different than I had pictured them. They had color in their faces, sparkle in their eyes and love in their hearts. It was a glorious homecoming. Dad got out a jug for me and poured welcome home drinks. I took it easy, because they didn't know about me. But I was soon drinking as heavily as I had been.

I would drink all night in bars, come home about five a.m., down a good big glass of whiskey straight, and tumble into bed. Or maybe I'd come home wild drunk, singing and raving about what a fine place home was and what grand parents I had since they joined A.A.

Sometimes I'd make it home and go to sleep at the wheel of my car, for all the neighbors to see next morning as they left for work. I paid nine hundred dollars for a second hand car on my return. I lost it many times and mom and dad would drive me around until I found it. I spent eighteen hundred dollars fixing up that car in the first year I was home, after four bad smashups. Why I wasn't killed or how I got home I don't know.

The end came the next year. I'd lost my car again, pawned my wallet and all identification papers for a bottle, and gotten home somehow. Again I went into a mild form of D.T.'s, but with no pineapples this time. The folks called a doctor and he knocked me out with sedatives. I'd heard a lot about A.A. and met a great many A.A.'s during that year at home, but I hadn't thought of it for myself. I'd thought of it in an offhand way, of course. But I didn't want to stop drinking— not at twenty-two. I merely wanted to cut down. And the folks said A.A. was for people who *wanted* to quit, otherwise it wouldn't work.

But as I came out of this second bout with D.T.'s, I knew I was licked. I'd packed more drinking into seven years than many a heavy drinker does in a lifetime. And I'd proved I couldn't handle it, time and again. That doctor in the Navy hospital told me I wouldn't live five years if I didn't quit. I'd fooled him thus far. But for how long? "I've got to stop if I want to live," I told myself, and if I don't want to break my parents' hearts and maybe jeopardize their own carefully built-up and hard-fought-for sobriety.

"I'll do it," I told myself. "I'll do it. I'll join A.A. if it kills me. Mom has said the only requisite to start is willingness. Well, I'm willing, if it will curb this awful desire to drink, this fear of not having a drink, this feeling of always being alone, scared, deserted, sick. Dear God, I'll do anything! Only show me how."

That is how I came into A.A. There was a red plush carpet to welcome me, but even so it wasn't easy. I'd acquired a new girl, a lovely girl who knew of my problem and had tried to help me. A week after my decision to join A.A., she called it quits. Three days later I lost my job. This combination nearly threw me. I thought, "If this is A.A. why not go back to drinking, kill myself with booze in the next three years the doctor had given me, and call it a bad job?"

But I didn't. I attended meetings, I talked to my folks; I talked to younger people they had gotten in contact with to sponsor me. And somehow or other I stayed sober.

I joined A.A. at twenty-two. I'm twenty-six now and I haven't had a drink since I made my decision. At that time life to me was spelled "w-h-i-s-k-e-y." Today I think of life in terms of happiness, contentment, freedom from fear and despair, sane thinking, ability to face problems as they occur, the opportunity to help other alcoholics and to be decent.

Were I to revert to drinking, even now, I wouldn't give anything for these four years in A.A. They have been the happiest of my life. I have been helped morally, spiritually, mentally and materially through A.A. I used to think, "Why live without whiskey?" Now I know I can't live without A.A.

Four years ago I had nothing but a jumbled, mad existence. Today I have all that anyone could ask. I have a lovely wife who understands my problem and helps me with it. I have two wonderful little boys. I have a good job. I have kind and sympathetic parents. I'm buying my home. I owe no one—except A.A.

A FIVE-TIME LOSER WINS

The worst of prison treatment couldn't break this
tough con. He was serving time on his fifth felony
conviction when a miracle happened.

*F*or me, as for most alcoholics, it was "Eat, drink,
and be merry, for tomorrow you die." But, of
course, I couldn't die. I painfully awakened each time,
mentally, physically, and spiritually sick. Nothing
could pull me out of the abyss but more alcohol. Later
on, it took alcohol fortified with other drugs to pull
me up. Still later, even alcohol and chemicals together
could not lift me.

There are many things worse than dying, but is
there any death worse than the progressive, self-
induced, slow suicide of the practicing alcoholic? The
alcoholic suffers death many times over. Alcohol
wrings the guts out of life, eats into the brain in such a
way as to make the alcoholic blind to the truth. I served
twelve years in prison, never suspecting that without
alcohol I would not have been in prison at all. Had it
not been for A.A. in prison . . . I'll never know, but my
educated guess is that I would not be alive today.

You see, I am a five-time loser, which means five
felony convictions (not including the cases beaten). I
served time in four penitentiaries and several prison
camps, including a maximum-security camp.

The two years I spent there, I was incorrigible, and
the records bear this out. Also, I was insane at times—
according to society's yardstick. But when I cracked

my leg with a sixteen-pound sledgehammer in the rock hole, I was fighting the system, using my body. Same thing when I let lye and water eat away at four of my toes and my foot for five hours. I was an agitator, a troublemaker, and many men as bitter as I was followed me.

I do not want to digress into the dynamics of penology. However, one thing I am certain of: Inmates in prison who attend A.A. have their chances of remaining free greatly enhanced—this is a proved fact. Of course, an inmate must begin living the A.A. way "inside," if he is to stand a chance "outside." Intake of alcohol changes one's personality—even the healthy personality. If my personality is inadequate, antisocial, or full of kinks and I alter it with alcohol or any chemical, bingo! There go my good intentions, fear of consequences, will to care, responsibility for my behavior. What else can I do except what I have always done in the past?—act as my old self and return to prison. It is estimated that two-thirds of the men in prison were under the influence of alcohol and/or drugs when they committed their offenses.

Yet prisoners often can't identify with many A.A. members' drinking stories. Well, this is understandable. Most of us did not stay out of prison long enough to run the alcoholic gamut—to develop the ongoing kind of alcoholism or alcoholic drinking you hear about in A.A. talks.

We always, or nearly always, had good intentions when we were released from prison. But with the first drink, our good intentions dissolved; our personalities changed. We reverted to the old way of life we knew— a life full of anger, vindictiveness, resentment, fear, dependence, denial, self-will, irresponsibility. And we found ourselves back in prison, where our personalities became even more warped.

Sobriety and a plan for living that produces a personality change and a spiritual awakening are imperative. Through A.A., many receive the needed change and awakening just by trying to live by A.A. principles and associating with A.A. people. We do this by going to many A.A. meetings with an open mind and a desire to live the good-feeling life without chemicals—liquid or otherwise.

Through A.A., we can experience freedom from self. After all, it was self (you, me) that stood in our own way, that ran the show and ran ourselves into bankruptcy, that hurt the ones we loved. All Twelve Steps of A.A. are designed to kill the old self (deflate the old ego) and build a new, free self.

I would rather talk about the good things A.A. has taught me; I feel that hitting on just a few sordid points should be sufficient to let those of you in institutions know where I came from.

In a prison in my native state, I spent eleven months in solitary confinement, bouncing in and out of the "hole" (a bare concrete-and-steel cubicle) about five times during those eleven months. Each ten-day period in the dark hole, I was fed bread and water daily, with one full meal on the third day only. I thought that was bad until I hit the hole at a prison camp; it was just wide enough and long enough to lie down in. There, I received several soda crackers and water daily, and before I could have my third-day meal (again the only meal in ten days), I had to drink a glass of castor oil or mineral oil, depending on the cruelty of the person who was doing the dispensing. Ten days of this treatment the first time knocked me from 200 pounds to 130, and I seldom stayed out of the hole long enough to gain back my weight.

I wore stripes and chains. Shackles were permanently fixed to my ankles. There is really nothing to dressing with chains and shackles on, once you learn the technique of putting inside-out pants through the shackles.

I was one of those bad cons nobody can reach. The first time I remember seeing or hearing of A.A. was twenty years ago. They were having a large A.A. meeting in the prison auditorium. (Two large red A's stand out in my memory.) In those days, I trusted no churchgoer, and thought A.A. was for weaklings. I didn't even try to understand. I didn't know I was an alcoholic and (like most men in prison today) could not relate alcohol to any of my past troubles.

Four years later, I was taken to my first A.A. meeting out of prison, in Los Angeles. For the next five years, I was in and out of A.A. in Los Angeles, Phoenix, and San Francisco. Finally, I threw away all my books and decided never to return to A.A. I was living, but I was dead.

I left California and came back to my native state. I had been in several hospitals for alcoholism. Then I committed my last offense. Three weeks after an armed robbery in which one person received a superficial flesh wound (I could have killed someone!), I was apprehended. I woke up in jail, sick, withdrawing from alcohol and speed, already a four-time loser, and now a fifth felony charge against me. This was the end of my world.

Fortunately, I received only fifteen-twenty years, and I went back to my alma mater (where I had spent so much time in the hole). I was forty-four years old; my life had been wasted. I sank into total despair. I hit my bottom. However, I still would not attend A.A. in prison. I nearly reverted to my old, incorrigible self— had trouble with a couple of other prisoners, was planning an escape. If I failed, they would throw away the key, and I would never get out again.

Then the miracle happened. While I was taking inventory in the cold-storage locker one Sunday, a wooden sign bolted to the inside door stopped me in my tracks. It was the Serenity Prayer! The words jumped out at me. I suddenly remembered one of my first A.A. meetings, where I heard, "If you are an alcoholic and if you continue to drink, the end is death or insanity." They hadn't mentioned the living hell before death.

Yes, I knew what the Serenity Prayer was—A.A. had taught me. It was to be my lifesaver—the final catalyst. (I am looking at it now in my bedroom—a copy that was presented to me a couple of years ago by the A.A. group in that same prison.) During the twenty-four hours after running into the Serenity Prayer, I think I took the first three Steps for the first time. I surrendered totally. I began to sleep, to relax, to accept my plight. I started going to A.A. in prison at the group's next meeting.

When I had served only eighteen months of my sentence, this ex-incorrigible was placed in honor grade. (God works through people.) Then I was transferred to the honor-grade unit, where I spent the most painful year of my life. It is painful to grow, and without the help of my "civilian" A.A. companion, big Gene, I might not have survived that critical year of adjustment. This A.A. friend took me into his home when he had me out on pass. He and his wife more than accepted me; he listened to all my woes; both of them treated me as a human being.

Shortly thereafter, I was selected, with eight other inmates out of the 10,000 in the state's prisons at that time, to attend a school designed to take former "management problems" like me and convert them into paracounselors. After nine months of training, all the rest of my class was paroled and went to work in the Department of Corrections. I was not eligible for parole, until—with God's help, I'm sure—the governor cut five years off my sentence. I was paroled when I had served less than three years. Then I, too, went to work as a counselor in Corrections. One would have to understand the correctional machinery to see what a miracle this really was.

After a few months there, I went to County Mental Health as an alcoholism worker. Now, I have been an alcoholism counselor for over a year and am off parole. I go back to my old alma mater occasionally to give A.A. talks, and—just think!—the warden is my friend. I count my sobriety date from the day I began going to A.A. in prison, not from the date of my last drink. Being dry is not being sober.

Three weeks ago, my phone rang, and a voice I hadn't heard in over twenty-three years spoke. It was my ex-wife, and she said my twenty-seven-year-old son, who has completed his Marine Corps training and graduated from college, wanted to see me privately, was getting married in three months, and wanted me at the wedding. I haven't seen my son since he was three and a half years old. He doesn't know me, nor do I know him. I thank God I am to see him this month. At the wedding, I hope I will also get to see my daughter and their mother. My daughter was one and a half years old when I last saw her. I attempted nearly two years ago to make some amends and contact my children, but it wasn't God's time yet.

Nothing that has happened to me do I deserve. I'm talking about the good things that have happened. I owe everything to A.A. and God. I take credit for nothing. I will be fifty years old next month, haven't seen my son or daughter yet, nor my daughter's two children, my grandchildren; but I am grateful. It is all like a dream.

Forgive me—I cannot write further about this latest turn of events, anticipating seeing the family I deserted so long ago. Besides, I can only live today. I must be ready and willing should I never see them. This is difficult, but it is the only way it has worked for me.

I am still arrogant, egocentric, self-righteous, with no humility, even phony at times, but I'm trying to be a better person and help my fellowman. Guess I'll never be a saint, but whatever I am, I want to be sober and in A.A. The word "alcoholic" does not turn me off any more; in fact, it is music to my ears when it applies to me.

God bless all you people in A.A. and especially you fellows in prison. Remember, now you have a choice.

PROMOTED TO CHRONIC

*This career girl preferred solitary drinking, the
blackout kind, often hoping she'd stay that way for
keeps. But Providence had other ideas.*

I wasn't always an alcoholic.
    In fact it has been only within the last fifteen
years that I changed from a fairly normal, controlled
drinker into an alcoholic. I don't mean that I went to
bed one night a normal drinker, and awoke the next
morning an alcoholic.

It wasn't that simple.

I started drinking socially and at parties and proms
when I was about twenty years old. I didn't like it particularly at first, but I did like the effect I got from it. It
made me feel quite grown-up and mature, and I think
another added attraction was the fact that so far as my
family was concerned, it was forbidden, and it had a
special attraction for that reason. After a while I really
did enjoy drinking and what it did to me, and I became dependent upon it for every occasion. Eventually
the day came when I was dependent upon it even
when there wasn't any occasion. When I didn't have
anything else to do—a dull evening at home—I'd
sneak a few drinks upstairs in my room, and that began to be a habit.

Then I went on my first week-long bender of solitary drinking, locked up in a hotel room, because my
family opposed my coming marriage. I figured that
perhaps if I went ahead with that marriage, which I

was sure was right for me, that would be the answer to my drinking problem. I thought I would be quite happy and never would I drink too much again. So—I tried that.

(I think my first feeling of fear came with my first week's solitary drinking, locked up in that hotel room. The hotel management, knowing that something was wrong, sent for a doctor. The doctor, apparently realizing that one thing that I certainly needed was sleep, left a bottle of sleeping pills there and in my drunken state I took them all, instead of the one or two he had prescribed. If it hadn't been for an alert hotel maid, I might have died then. From that time on, fear was with me because I realized that not only would I not *remember* what happened to me while I was drinking, but apparently I couldn't *control* what happened. And there didn't seem to be anything to do about it.)

Having passed over the border line, the next five years were filled with fear, failure and frustration. Tragedies during those years that were caused by my drinking, such as the breaking up of my marriage, the death of my child, other things—had little restraining effect. In fact, sometimes they served as good excuses to drink more, to forget. It was in Washington, D.C., that this transition took place, and that the really bad part of alcoholism began happening.

The last Christmas I spent in Washington, fourteen years ago, comes to mind. Only a few days before Christmas I went to the dentist for a periodic checkup. X-rays showed that a couple of teeth had to come out. I hadn't been drinking much about that time, for I had begun to realize that there was something abnormal about my drinking, although as yet, I didn't realize that it was so out of control. On the day set for the extractions, on my way to the dentist's I felt a little nervous, so I had a couple of drinks, and after the teeth were out I was *very* nervous, so I had a few more.

When I got home my mouth was very painful, so I got an ice-bag and went to bed. The next day the ice-bag and I were still in bed—but we had a bottle too! My pattern of drinking at that time had reached the point where once I really started, I would retire to my bed and drink myself into oblivion. The rest of that week is pretty hazy.

And so it went. I remember vaguely violent quarrels with my husband, his finding my liquor supply time and time again and throwing it out. And then my waiting until I was sure he was asleep, and stealing money from him to replenish the supply.

Then I remember him coming into my room one night with a friend, and telling me to get dressed—we were going away.

I fought and struggled, but to no avail. I was taken out of the house and put bodily into a waiting car with nothing on but a robe and gown. We were on our way to New York, where he planned to leave me with my sister. On the way I tried, and I mean really tried, to throw myself out of the car. Finally they stopped and bought me a bottle; they knew so well that would keep me quiet.

We pulled up in front of my sister's house just as dawn broke. There was a long discussion between my husband, my sister and her husband. It was obvious even to me, in my drunken state, that I wasn't wanted. My parents were due for the holidays that day, and she didn't want them to find their drunken daughter there. So we turned around and started back to Washington. I was too weak and exhausted to even try to throw myself out of the car. The trip back was completed in one of those dead, awful silences.

My husband helped me into the house, packed himself a bag, and gave me some money. He said he didn't care what I did with the money, but there was going to be no more until I was completely sober. He said he was finally and completely through—that he never wanted to see me again.

I was frightened—terribly frightened, and in about three days I was sober. On the day before Christmas I telephoned him and told him I was sober and asked him to come home. He said he'd see. I waited all the rest of that day and paced the floor all that night.

At noon on Christmas Day I called my family in New York, wished them a Merry Christmas, and assured them everything was fine with me. I almost broke down and cried when I talked with them but I didn't. It was the one redeeming act of that Christmas.

Then in a couple of hours, when there was still no word from my husband and no sign of him, I had the feeling we alcoholics all know. "What's the use? What's the sense in trying to do the right thing?" There was that awful alcoholic loneliness.

I went out to a restaurant, found a booth way back in the rear, and started drinking. All afternoon I sat there and drank and played Bing Crosby's recording of "Silent Night" over and over again on the juke box. To this day I can't hear that song without remembering that awful Christmas.

What happened afterwards I don't know. I completely blacked out. The next recollection I have is of my husband coming into my room (I later found out it was on New Year's Eve) accompanied by two policemen. This time I didn't put up any fight because I knew why they were there and where I was going, the psychopathic ward of the City Hospital, where I had been once before.

Did that stop my drinking? Temporarily, but not for long.

Things went from bad to worse, and since I had finally and completely failed at the job of being a wife and a mother, my marriage ended. And then I went back home to live with my parents, and the merry-go-round started again—only this time I didn't have to worry about waking up behind bars in a psychiatric ward.

Instead, I started going to a nice private sanitarium which, after the first visit, turned out to be more like a country club than anything else. After the first two or three days you were allowed the run of the place and it was a lot of fun. Also, after that first visit I learned I could refuse to sign myself in unless they gave me a glass of whiskey in one hand and a glass of paraldehyde in the other. This easy method of sobering up would last at least three days.

There were doctors and psychiatrists there who tried to help me, but at that point I wasn't having help from anyone. I didn't want help. I had decided I was no good—never would be any good, and the sooner I could drink myself out of this life, the better.

My visits to that sanitarium went on for nearly three years, until in March of 1944, my father died and I was too drunk to attend his funeral. At that point everyone decided something drastic had to be done. They held consultations and discussions, and finally decided to give me the "Conditioned Reflex" treatment. I won't go into detail about that, but I can assure you it's no fun.

The idea behind it is that, having taken the treatment, your system is so "conditioned" that the mere sight or smell or taste of alcohol produces a violent reaction, and you become ill. But it didn't condition this girl's thinking.

You may wonder why, since I was having all this trouble, and was having to seek the assistance of others, A.A. hadn't come into the picture. Actually it had, way back in 1940.

The same doctor who had sent me to the psycho had asked my husband, "Why don't you send her to this Alcoholics Anonymous?"

My husband said, "What is A.A.?"

At that time there hadn't been any publicity such as we have now. Even the Jack Alexander *Saturday Evening Post* article hadn't been written, and there was only a tiny group of people in Washington.

So the doctor said, "I really don't know too much about it, but they tell me it is a bunch of drunks who get together . . ."

My husband interrupted, "She's bad enough now without getting mixed up with a bunch of drunks."

And so, in those following years, whenever A.A. was mentioned I would have no part of it. In my screwed up mind I kept thinking I could have gone to A.A. way back there in 1940, and perhaps saved my marriage and home. I even wanted to—but I wasn't allowed to, so I won't go now.

Finally, however, in November of 1944, at long last I went to A.A.

And A.A. took this wreck of a woman and brought her back to life.

Why did it work for me when all other agencies

had failed? Was it because they told me in A.A. that I was an alcoholic?

No, I had known that.

Yes, I even knew I was a "chronic alcoholic."

On one occasion when I was serving time in my favorite drying-out place while I was having a session with the psychiatrist, she left my case history on her desk when she was called away from the room. Sly and crafty, I thought now I'll find out what they think of me here, what they "have on" me, what I've said coming in here drunk. There at the top of the folder was my name, age and address, and underneath were the words, "Periodic Drinker." Only they had been scratched out and over them was "Chronic Alcoholic."

As an indication of just how confused and mixed up I was, just as soon as I could I left the office and hurried around to tell other patients that I was getting better. I had been promoted from a periodic drinker to a chronic alcoholic! I honestly didn't know the difference. A.A. didn't teach me I was an alcoholic; rather it taught me that because I was an alcoholic my life had become unmanageable.

It seemed to me that those A.A.'s to whom I talked knew all about me. It is true that the doctors and nurses in the various institutions I attended knew too. But the difference lay in the fact that the A.A.'s knew from their own bitter experience.

In other words, the kindest doctor in the whole world, and I had one such, couldn't help me because I always felt, "You can't know about me—you can't possibly know—you don't even drink!"

But to another woman, the first woman I met in A.A., I could talk. In all the sanitariums and psycho wards I had never met a single woman who said she was an alcoholic. They were always there because of a nervous breakdown, or for a "rest cure"—any reason except because of drinking.

(I've met some of these same women since in A.A.) But by listening and talking to these A.A.'s—talking to them as I had never talked to anyone in my whole life, I saw that it was my *life* that was unmanageable—not just my drinking. With their help I also saw that certainly, because of some of the things I had done during the years, I was bordering on insanity, and so facing the record, I tried to believe that a Power greater than I could and would restore me to sanity.

The other of the Twelve Steps of Alcoholics Anonymous seemed insurmountable to me at first.

But the older members in A.A. told me, "Easy does it." In the light of subsequent events it became evident that I took their advice far too literally, for, after some months of happy sobriety I drank again. Had I tried honestly and sincerely to practice the Twelve Steps I would have seen from my continuous moral inventory that I was getting off the beam—I would have found that there were some active resentments in my life, a terrific amount of self-pity. But more important, I would have found that once again I was sitting in the driver's seat—I was running the show.

The Higher Power to whom I had turned, and who had sustained me, had once again been thrust into the background, while my emotions were running my life and, as always, my emotions ran me to the bottle.

It came about in this way.

When I first came into A.A., the woman who was my sponsor was the first woman I had ever met who admitted that she was an alcoholic. And she was a charming, delightful, lovely person. She gave me such hope and inspiration that I set her right up on a pedestal. And so for three months this one woman was my A.A. I went to meetings, I spent a lot of time at the clubroom, but it was all centered in this one woman. But she couldn't carry me forever. She realized that, and the way I felt, and so for my own good she gradually began to pull away. Of course I had the sensitive, hurt feelings of the alcoholic. I thought, "Oh well, these people are just like all the people I've known all my life. They build you up with a lot of false hopes and promises, and rush you around here and there and then, all of a sudden, it's gone." And when she broke a luncheon date with me one Saturday, after I had been in A.A. for about three months, I said, "I'll show *her*! She can't do that to me!" And I got drunk.

Well, you know who I showed. I showed myself. And I landed right smack back in that sanitarium that I had gone to so often. While I was there I realized that I had missed something. I realized that I was trying to pin everything on an individual—not the book or the group or the Higher Power, or anything else. So I concentrated and studied the book during that time, and I liked a lot of the things it said in there. I remember particularly one sentence that seemed to say, "This is for you." It read something like this: "Faith without works is dead. Carry this message to other alcoholics. You can help where no one else can." Here was a book that said I could do something that all these doctors and priests and ministers and psychiatrists that I'd been going to for years couldn't do!

That was over seven years ago, and thank God and A.A., I haven't had a drink since. During these seven years a thing called the Twenty-four-Hour Program—a gadget I used to think was only a snare to trap the newcomer—has come to mean much to me, not only as regards my drinking but in the whole pattern of my life.

I realize that all I'm guaranteed in life is today. The poorest person has no less and the wealthiest has no more—each of us has but one day. What we do with it is our own business; how we use it is up to us individually.

I feel that I have been restored to health and sanity these past years not through my own efforts nor as a result of anything I may have done, but because I've come to believe—to really believe—that alone I can do nothing. That my own innate selfishness and stubbornness are the evils which, if left unguarded, can drive me to alcohol.

I have come to believe that my illness is spiritual as well as physical and mental, and I know that for help in the spiritual sphere I have to turn to a Higher Power.

JOIN THE TRIBE!

From a Canadian reservation to overseas bars to New England lockups, an Indian traveled a long trail that finally led him home to A.A.

I proud to be son of Tall Man, American Indian, and member of A.A. for many moons. We all one as Great Spirit walks through A.A. like sun walks through day. This first story I ever write. Sorry for mistakes. Love has no words to spell or lines to start and stop. Our language has few words to say many things.

I was born a Maliseet Indian on reservation in Canada. Oldest of thirteen children. Was altar boy at church on reservation. Had first drink in young teens, but was scared of my father. So didn't drink much then. Now think I was alcoholic from first drink. Never forgot magic in firewater.

When I was twenty-one, my cousin come home from U.S. Army on leave. I stay with him at aunt's house in Maine. That night we drink beer at taverns. He had bottle of hard stuff. He gave me many drinks from bottle. Next thing I know, it was next day. First time I have blackout, but not last. My aunt had sharp words for me about drinking. I not listen to old woman.

I join Canadian Army, but could not run away from problem. Soon found wet canteens serve drinks to Indians in uniform. Went overseas on beer. Soon change to hard stuff. Then many blackouts for next two years. God must watch over me. Got into no trouble. Came home. Met father (Tall Man) at fork in road—one way to reservation, other way to State of Maine. We went to booze joint in Maine. Remember only first two drinks. Then I black out and get home four days later. Now I slide down mountain fast. Take many pledges, but break them.

I get arrested. I get arrested again. Judge say I go to jail next time. So I change counties in Maine. When counties run out, I move to Connecticut. Climb on water wagon for few months. Build houses for some cops—ha-ha. Soon I drink beer. Then hard stuff. Then I find jails in Connecticut, too. Cops say for me to call them, they get me out. I think they sorry they tell me this. Next two years, I call them many times. Last time in jail, I have two black eyes. Cops now sick of me, so they buy me one-way ticket to Canada. Pack my clothes and put me on train.

My brother and me find work on turnpike in Maine. I stay on wagon for while, but miserable. Then I drink again, but more miserable. I want to stop this bad life, but where to turn? Last time I drink, I go to room. Think about kill myself. Then went on bridge to jump. By Grace of God I stop, think two things: This would kill good mother and father; then remember boys talk about Indian fellow who been sober three years. I hear about A.A., but think it religion. I have a religion. But now I change if it bring good life.

I find Indian fellow. We talk long time. Tell him I want to get away from bottle and misery. How he do it? He say he take me to A.A. meeting. I go with him to first meeting, in small town in Maine. My sponsor say men who talk speak truth. Then I know we walk same trail. Have not take drink since.

I hear men say, "One day not drink. Not try no

drinks for Lent or for life. Just one day." This sound easy, so will try. They say call friend before I buy drink. Talk and meetings make me feel good. So I jump quick from First Step to Twelfth Step to help my brother, living with me. Two weeks later, he come to A.A. meeting. Came to believe. Have not drink since. We both happy.

After six months, we move to Bridgeport, Conn. Find same A.A., same Spirit. Year later, I go to Canada to carry message to Tall Man, but he not listen to son. He old, sick, want to be alone with bottle.

Miracles happen all time in A.A. Two years later, my brother take Tall Man to first A.A. meeting. Tall Man was blind, but soon he see. He stay sober. Start group on reservation and carry message, help start other groups all over Maritimes and New England. He was old, but now he grow young with new life in A.A. and travel all the time. When he speak from heart, big men cry. Words of truth and love are strong medicine. Tall Man die five years ago, a sober, peaceful, happy man. Maine newsletter *(Boomerang)* say: "With tireless devotion and humility, this venerable Indian gentleman traveled thousands of miles humbly pleading for sobriety. He planted many seeds, and it will be many moons before another rises to walk in his shoes." Tall Man now see Great Spirit in Big Group in sky.

To find work, I have travel much. At every place, I find A.A. group first. I keep it simple; go to many meetings; carry the message to those who listen. To me, program is spiritual. I feel Great Spirit at all meetings and when talk to A.A. friends. I know peace. "How?" they ask me.

I say, *"Just let it happen."* This sober Indian say to

sick, red-eyed alcoholic who want good medicine: "Put cork in bottle. No drunk hopeless if he want to follow guide along right trail. Go to A.A. meetings. Listen, not just hear noise. Get sponsor and phone numbers. Call friend in A.A. when bad thoughts come. Let group spirit of love and understanding protect you. Take my hand. Walk with me up Twelve Steps of A.A. to peace."

To Indians, I say: "Don't be afraid to join A.A. I once hear people say only Indians crazy when drunk. If so, A.A. full of Indians. Join the tribe!"

BELLE OF THE BAR

Waitress by day, barfly by night, she drifted down the years into jail. Then A.A. showed her the beauty of normal living, in a whole family reborn.

When I came unto A.A., I had no intention of quitting drinking—I figured I was doing all right. After all, I had been working for eighteen years, slinging hash, and I was managing. Mind you, I had absolutely nothing to show for that eighteen years, except a beat-up car that I hadn't even paid for, but I was doing all right. No clothes, no money, no home, no real friends to speak of, mentally and physically pooped, but I was doing all right!

Aside from being a common drunk I had a very serious pill affliction and all the garbage that goes with it—lying, stealing, cheating anybody and everybody, conning the people I could, and staying clear of the ones I couldn't.

Then a terrible thing happened. I ran out of people! Even my family didn't have much use for me. When they saw me coming, they locked up the silverware and everything else of value. I felt very lonely and hurt, because nobody understood me. I felt very sorry for myself and attempted suicide on many occasions, making sure there was always somebody within reaching distance to see that I didn't finish the job. Any time I tried to kill myself, I was either drunk or pilled-up or both—usually the last.

Once, I phoned my brother-in-law and told him I

was going to take a handful of pills (in fact, I already had) and I would slash my wrists if he didn't come over to stop me. Knowing that he was sober, I timed it just right, so I could do the slashing just before he hit the steps. It never entered my head that I would have been pushing up the daisies if he had decided not to come. He did come, and I landed in the funny farm for a while. When I got out of there, I lasted about fifteen minutes at home, before I headed for the drugstore and more pills, and then the bar.

Oh, I was beautiful in those days! Some drunken women really are, you know. If our hair is half-bleached (with dark roots), poker-straight, and not combed, this adds to our beauty. Then, of course, there are always the wrinkled slacks, which have been slept in and are so dirty, they could walk away by themselves. And we usually have some kind of grimy sweater that we think we look sexy in, even if we weigh ninety-five pounds soaking wet and are not wearing a bra. Some of us always remember our big mouths when it comes to a drink, but somewhere along the line, we seem to have forgotten about taking care of our teeth. This really makes for an attractive woman! Our shoes are no better than the average hobo's, and if we are fortunate enough to have a pair of stockings on, nobody notices the runs in them, because of our dazzling beauty and our dirty feet. (We don't have much time for bathing in our crowded schedule.) We are so beautiful that it is never too much trouble to get some poor stranger to buy us a drink. (Actually, he does it solely to get rid of us.)

You see how much work some of us have to do on ourselves when we finally come into A.A.! I really do believe it is much harder for a woman to gain back her self-respect than it is for a man. Men are supposed to be tough and rugged to start with, but if a woman becomes that way, it is pretty hard to get back the niceties of womanhood.

I drank from the age of twelve until I was thirty-two. I wasted twenty years of my life, and there is nothing I can do about that, but there is something I can do about now. I was very fortunate indeed not to have suffered any brain damage. For two years, I was also addicted to heroin. At one time, I was using twenty caps a day; I nearly died half a dozen times on the street. So I wasn't just tinkering around with it—I had to get in with both feet. This was the only period when I didn't drink, but that was hardly any consolation.

Finally, I was arrested and got six months for drugs. Since then, I have never been back to heroin. It is no problem to me now, but this is not good management on my part—just plain good luck.

To tell you a small part of what my mother's life must have been like: Three of her kids were in jail that year—two sons and a daughter. She must have been real proud of us, I'm sure. A couple of years later, we lost our elder brother in a house fire, because of pills and booze. We survivors are all in A.A. now, and my mother is in Al-Anon.

There is no cure for alcoholism, but it can be arrested in the program of A.A. We can have this new way of life—learning to live with our sickness and to be happy and content—if we are willing to change our way of thinking and be honest, first with ourselves, then with others. We are told to practice the Twelve Steps and Twelve Traditions to the best of our ability every day, one day at a time. It is suggested that we do not try to do a lifetime of repairs in one day.

I can't begin to tell you of all the benefits I have derived from this new way of living. I met and married a man in A.A., and I am the happiest I have ever been in my life. He is my best teacher; without him, I am sure I would never have made the progress I have. He has so much understanding, a real asset in sharing sobriety. He also cares; he really cares. This means a great deal to me, because I had always figured that nobody cared. How wrong I was! He has taught me that, in our new life, I am the most important person of all. For me, my sobriety comes before his or even before my feeling for him. He has also taught me that I must help myself first; only then may I be able to help others. I like to believe that I may have helped him, too.

It is so beautiful to get up in the morning not being hung-over and being able to remember where we were the night before. We are aware of the nice things around us, things we never noticed before in our drunken stupor. I planted my first flower garden this year and am actually excited to see the results. If someone had told me last year that I would be excited about gardening this year, I would have said he was off his rocker. If anyone had told me I would be enjoying a hockey game with my husband and my brother without being all boozed up, I would not have believed it. I went to church on Easter Sunday with my husband, and it didn't hurt at all. (And the church walls haven't tumbled down yet.)

I know the biggest word for me in A.A. is "honesty." I don't believe this program would work for me if I didn't get honest with myself about everything. Honesty is the easiest word for me to understand because it is the exact opposite of what I've been doing all my life. Therefore, it will be the hardest to work on. But I will never be totally honest—that would make me perfect, and none of us can claim to be perfect. Only God is. If I work on it every day, it will be easier to be honest with myself. Then getting and staying honest with other people will come automatically. I know I will be grateful for a chance to make amends to everybody I have hurt in the past.

THE PRISONER FREED

*After twenty years in prison for murder, he knew A.A.
was the spot for him . . . if he wanted to stay
on the outside.*

I began drinking as a kid, shortly after I reached
my fourteenth birthday. My father was alive, and
I had to do as he wanted, so I drank under cover. He
finally passed away, and the fear of him left me. I
didn't have to worry about him any longer. I rolled
along with the mob this way, that way and the other
way, but in those years nothing really bad happened to
me. That was still to come.

It started July 23. I went on a drunk. When I
wended my way home four days later, on the 27th,
there was a detective waiting for me. During the course
of that drinking, I had shot and killed one person and
almost completed the job on a second one. I was immediately arrested, arraigned in Homicide Court, held
without bail, and remanded to the old Tombs Prison to
await trial. I was indicted for the crime of murder in
the first degree. The trial lasted about a week, and
whether or not I was going to the death house was
anybody's guess. However, a verdict was brought in of
murder in the second degree. For that crime I received
a minimum of twenty years and a maximum of natural
life. In the meantime I had been indicted for the second
crime, attempted murder. I received an additional fifteen years for that, making a minimum of thirty-five
years and maximum of natural life.

On October 28th, I was sent to Sing Sing with a minimum of thirty-three and a half years to serve out of that thirty-five. There was no time for so-called good behavior, first-timers, or anything else. However, as time went on laws were enacted that reduced the sentence. I spent about six or seven weeks in Sing Sing, and was finally sent off to Dannemora in the Adirondacks. I have spent eighteen years in that institution. An ailment developed in one of my eyes, and I was transferred back to Sing Sing and operated upon. I remained there for about ten months, and then I was sent to a place called Wallkill, a so-called rehabilitation center.

I spent my last seventeen months in Wallkill, and it was there that I first got my introduction to A.A. When I had heard about it, it meant nothing but just two letters to me, but some friends of mine in the institution were very active in the program and really believed in it. They kept harping on it, that I go. One evening I decided to go because two of those friends were to speak. I rounded up a few more of my friends and off we went to the meeting, not for anything we would gain from it as much as to make a burlesque out of it. However, before the meeting got started, a group from the outside came in unexpectedly. I had enough decency so that I dismissed the idea of doing any clowning, and I did listen.

After hearing the first speaker I could tell myself that my own lot was rather mild. He had been in and out of Matteawan and many other mental institutions as a result of his drinking. He had gone through the windshields of cars a couple of times and was pretty well banged up. After the meeting was over and we had returned to the cell block again, I was asked how I was impressed. "Oh," I said, "that's not for me! Those poor stiffs probably went to a doctor and were told that if they quit they'd live three weeks and if they didn't they'd die in one." That was my attitude toward A.A. at that time. However, my two friends kept coaxing and cajoling to get me back again. Most of my attendance there was when people would come in from the outside. I clung to the outfit for the balance of my time, and finally I was released, after having spent twenty years and nine months behind bars.

I had an advantage in having an idea of what A.A. was about before coming out on the street. It wasn't anything strange to me, and I knew if I wanted to stay on the outside, that would be the spot for me. But after I passed through the gates I took a change of heart and mind. So instead of going near A.A., I just browsed around for that first month. Each time I would make a report to the parole officer he would ask me, "Have you been to an A.A. meeting yet?" I'd say, "No, I don't know where they're at or when they meet. I don't know anyone in the program." After I had made my third report, I stepped downtown, met some of the old crowd, and of course you know the answer.

I staggered home next morning. I couldn't tell you how I got there. When my mother opened the door, I almost fell in on my face. She asked me, was I going to do this to her all over again? That really stopped me for a little bit. I said, no I wasn't. She was the one who really helped me to make a go of that twenty years and nine months in prison. She's still alive today at the age of eighty-two.

So I went to an A.A. meeting the first chance I got, and I listened. I started prowling around with a couple of these A.A. boys, which kept me pretty busy and kept my mind off of downtown. I went along pretty well for the next ten months. Then instead of going out with A.A. again I went out with some of the other crowd and off again I went.

That woke me up. I've stuck pretty close to A.A. ever since then, taken it day by day, not biting off more than I can chew. The days have grown into a little better than four years of sobriety. I don't have any regrets. I don't miss any of the old crowd nor do I miss any of their parties. I have my ups and downs the same as the rest. It's no bed of roses, but somehow or other I've been able to make it, through the kindness of people in A.A. If something does come along that sort of upsets me, instead of walking in and throwing a buck at the barman and asking for a drink, I walk into a telephone booth, drop a dime in the box, and call somebody who was so kind as to give me his name and telephone number to meet such an emergency. I don't have any resentments. I had a rough lot, but I don't worry about that, after hearing the stories of many others. I think I am very lucky that there are people like A.A.'s and an A.A. program to hang on to and carry me through.

DESPERATION DRINKING

He was drinking to hold on to his job, to hold on to his wife, to hold on to his sanity. Finally, he was drinking to keep away those little men, and those strange voices, and the organ music that came out of the walls.

I'm fortunate because I live in an era when A.A. is available, and I'm able to take advantage of it. I'm grateful because that Higher Power led me to A.A. a little over three years ago, when I needed it very badly. My drinking pattern isn't very different from the average you find in A.A. After I came in I found I wasn't an exceptional drunk. I used to think I was. I also thought I was a brilliant drunk. I have my brilliant moments yet, but whenever the boys catch me at it they tell me so very plainly.

When we first come into A.A., many of us are confused because as a general rule we're at the end of our respective ropes, and we don't know what to do. It's like the fellow who came in A.A., and his sponsor said to him, "Listen, buddy, do you believe in a Higher Power?" And the guy said, "Heck, yes, I been married to her for years!" Yes, we find it rather confusing, but as we get around and get to know people in the group, they lead the way and all we have to do is to follow.

I started drinking rather early, at the age of sixteen. I didn't stick at social drinking very long. As I progressed and gained in capacity, I had blackouts. At first they were rather amusing, but a little later on they became serious. And so I got to the swearing off process. That and the morning drink came very early in my drinking career.

A former employer of mine said to me a little over ten years ago, "Pat, you seem to be one of those unfortunate people who at least once every six months must go out and roll in the gutter." That stuck with me for a long time. It was a thorn in my side, because I knew it was the truth, and I hated to hear the truth, especially about myself. So that pattern continued until I went into the Army.

The Army drinking alone covered a lot of territory. Like many of us who went into the service, I thought it would be a cure-all, a new life. But I came out of the Army just as big a drunk as when I went in, if not worse, because now I had a lot more resentments. I remember the day I came back to New York. It was my second arrival in New York. The first had been as a youngster coming out of Ireland. There was a great deal of difference. A lot of the boys had tears in their eyes, they were so happy to be home. For me, it was a little different because I couldn't help thinking about the past, and I saw the future more or less mirrored in the past. It wasn't pretty. Somehow or other I was coming face to face with myself, and I didn't like it. When I landed of course I hit a gin mill, and with three or four good shots under my belt the world began to go into that rosy glow.

I got married to the girl I'd left behind. She certainly wasn't in the dark about my drinking. She had been warned numerous times, not only by her family but by my own mother, that I was a hopeless drunk, that there wasn't anything anybody could do with me, that I'd never stop, and that eventually I'd break her heart. However, she had faith and she had hope (things I didn't have). We were married, and during the first nine months of that marriage I was sober. I was trying for her sake. But at the end of nine months we went to a party one night, and I took the first drink. No one had ever told me it was the first drink that did the damage. And I was off again.

The old pattern reasserted itself, but it was no longer once every six months. The intervals grew shorter. The binges were longer. They were harder to get off. I wasn't the type that could taper off. I had to stop cold. My last binge followed the previous one by two weeks. I had just come off a good one, and I went back on to the next one.

That type of drinking is not pleasant. It is no longer enjoyable. You no longer get the kicks. It is desperation drinking. I was drinking to keep away the shakes, drinking to keep away those little men and those strange voices and the organ music that comes out of the wall. I was drinking to try to hold on to a job, to try and hold on to my home, to try to hold on to my wife, to try to hold on to my sanity.

I had a habit of getting up just prior to the closing time of the saloons, about two or three o'clock in the morning. I'd get downstairs to the gin mill, get enough in to hold me until eight o'clock in the morning, then I'd go out and join that "misery parade" that so many of us know so well. You hit the street about ten minutes to eight, and you walk around the block, God knows how many times, waiting for that joint to open.

One morning I didn't wake up until after four o'clock. I wasn't a happy man that morning, but I'm happy now that it came about. Because as I sat on that bed, I knew that I was in a terrible spot and didn't know how to get out of it. The realization came to me that I had to stop drinking, that I *had* to find a way. Either that or end my life. That thought had come to me many, many times. I was afraid that sometime I would get half drunk and go through with it. Of course I really didn't have to worry on that score, because I wasn't the type that got half drunk.

I was at the end of my rope. I knew it, and I turned for help to someone upon whom I had turned my back for many years. I asked God for help. It was the first time that I had asked for help sincerely and honestly. And I got help. I went back to the old family doctor who helped me the first time I had the D.T.'s. At this point, I was no longer the wise boy. I went in there and asked him honestly if he could give me a cure. He just looked at me and said, "Pat, for you there isn't any cure." We talked for a while, and then he sent me down to the Alanon House over on the west side, and there I had my introduction to A.A.

It was a revelation to me to find that there were such people as those I found in Alcoholics Anonymous. It was a revelation when I read that First Step. It was very, very simple. My life had become unmanageable due to the excessive use of alcohol. I had drunk too often and too much. But somehow or other, with my old alcoholic brain, sitting there in that chair, I kept saying to myself, "I wonder if it'll work? I wonder if it'll work for me?"

Then I went to my first meeting. I was a very fortunate drunk. God has been good to me both in my drinking and in my sobriety. Because, thank God, since I came into this program I haven't had any trouble. Oh yes, I get the dry jitters once in a while, but that isn't anything to worry about. It passes away.

But I've never come close to that first drink. I took the advice of people I had heard at meetings, the people in the group. And I jumped in with both feet. Someone told me, "When you drank, you didn't get half drunk. You went all the way. In this program there aren't any half way measures. In here you must go all the way too." So I attended as many meetings as possible.

There are steps of recovery, of maintenance. Each one has its own place. We all use them differently. I found a great deal of friendship in this movement. I learned to pray honestly. When you come in here, you find the understanding that you need. A.A.'s Twelve Steps may confuse you when you read them over. But the more meetings you attend, the more people you meet at these meetings, the clearer the Steps become.

We must learn to walk before we can run. That's why we have these slogans. I use that "Easy Does It" every day, to slow me down a little. I have to watch myself all the time. So I don't jut take the inventory at night—I take it continually throughout the day. Before I step out and do anything, I stop and check it over first, and then let my conscience be my guide.

For me, A.A. has become a way of life.

THE CAREER OFFICER

A British officer, this Irishman that is, until brandy
"retired" him. But this proved only a temporary
setback. He survived to become a mainstay
of A.A. in Eire.

I am an Irishman and I was forty-nine when I joined A.A. I belonged to one of the Irish families who, more or less traditionally, sent their boys to the British armies.

I had a very happy upbringing at home. When I look back, I can't see anything that would have predisposed me towards being either a neurotic or a drunk. I went to a very good public school run by Jesuits. I got along well there. I was going to be sent to the Indian Civil Service, which, in those days, meant that people thought you had a certain amount of brains. I was very fond of music. I was one of the star singers in the choir and one of the leading violins in the orchestra. I liked games. There was nothing in my school life that I can look back on which was responsible for anything that happened afterwards.

Then I had a year in Germany at school that was, incidentally, when I got drunk for the first time. But that was just a mistake. I went out and drank some German wine and it went to my head. When I came back, I told the priest, the Chaplain of the place, exactly what I thought of him and he didn't like it. He reported to the Headmaster and the Headmaster was going to expel me. But I pointed out to him that as I was the first British boy who had been to the school, it wouldn't be very good advertisement for him, so I got over that all right. The term was nearly over and we parted on fairly friendly terms.

I had two years at Dublin University, and then in 1916, I got a nomination for Sandhurst, the British Military College. The war was on and it was a fairly short course, about eight months. Up to that time, drinking didn't really mean anything to me at all. In fact, I couldn't have told you the difference between sherry and brandy. But as soon as I got out on my own in France, I started drinking. At first, like everybody else, I could keep control when I drank, but if I did start to drink, even in those days, I was always one of the last to leave the party.

When the war was over, we had about a year in Germany, occupying the place. When I came home to ordinary garrison life in England, I found that I was drinking rather more than most people of my age. It didn't worry me very much, because at that time I could shut off for a couple of months without taking a drink or even wanting one, and without feeling that I was giving anything up. I should say there was less drinking in the Army than I thought at that time. Lots of the older people had taken to drinking quite a good deal more during the war, but the younger generation was, I think, about the same. In my own generation I stuck out, I can see that now, as being a very much heavier drinker than the average man. But as long as you did your work and didn't disgrace yourself, you were socially acceptable and nobody really intruded on your private life very much.

I was still very fit and good at games.

Then I went over again to Germany for four years

on an occupation job. I got a job by myself which suited me down to the ground, because there was nobody really to interfere with what I did, one way or the other, and I usually had my nerves in good trim when anybody was coming around to inspect. The gradual result was that I was drifting into making drinking one of the more important parts of my life. I was alone by myself in that job and for a long time.

Then I was sent out to India and from then on drinking just increased and increased, and I started having two or three day spells instead of just the ordinary concentrated one day. This was about 1926.

India lent itself to drinking then, if you were disposed to drink, because you lived in bungalows; you didn't live all together as you do at home in an Officer's Mess. We had a minor campaign or two and that helped distract attention from my drinking. By and large, I got through. I was still very good at games. I was up to international standards in one particular game, and that again covered quite a lot of my sins. Then a change in management took place in the regiment and the new O.C. didn't like me very much and I didn't like him, and he started to lie in wait for me. He didn't have to lie in wait very long, but fortunately by that time, I had acquired friends upstairs and they covered me for quite a time.

The Abyssinian war broke out just as things were going very badly for me, and I went off to Egypt on a job there. Strangely enough, right through to the end of my twenty-six years in the Army, I was still being offered very good and important jobs in spite of the fact that my superiors must have known that I wasn't thoroughly reliable. However, I kept that job in Egypt and Palestine for about two years, and then I changed over to the other battalion in my regiment. They weren't quite so up-to-date on my history and I got away with about four years with them. Then I had about six months on a small island in command of the troops there. I left because I had a contretemps with the Governor. I went to a dinner he gave one night, rather drunk. I buttonholed him after dinner and gave him a few tips on how to run his colony better and the result of that was about a fortnight or so later I was shipped back to my regiment. But on the other hand, I was terribly fortunate because that should have been a court martial offense and I should have been out on my ear. I was lucky again. I had three or four very uncomfortable months with my regiment then on the Suez Canal. The Commanding Officer only spoke to me when he wanted to tell me exactly who I was and what I was and how little I counted in the scheme of things and how glad he would be if I went away. Even at that, he spoke quite often.

Then Hitler's war broke out, and again, I was given a really important job on the Suez Canal, dealing with military shipping. I lasted at that for four months, chiefly on alcohol, because I never seemed to find any time to eat. At the end of that time, they shipped me back to my regiment again. I think the Commanding Officer was rather tired of this particular chicken coming back to roost so often because he very soon wrote in to the medical authorities to tell them that they had to get me into hospital, to be thoroughly examined for drinking. They brought me in and of course, they hadn't very much trouble in finding that I was an alcoholic. But that didn't mean anything to me. I didn't know what an alcoholic was. I was down in the Sudan by this time. They kept me in hospital for two months, and then they sent me up to Egypt, a three days journey. They sent me up with an attendant, and the attendant and I both arrived at the Egyptian Hospital rather the worse for wear. I was there for another couple of months and then, after a few more adventures in the East, I was shipped home.

About three months after that, my record reached home and I got a letter telling me I was retired from the Army, they put it very kindly, on medical grounds. But I knew that they knew what the medical grounds were, and that they had put a big black mark against my name. I was never to be allowed back. I had two or three feelings about that. In part, it was a feeling of intense shame at having to leave the Army during the war, but mostly it was resentment that this kind of thing should happen to me for, strange as it may seem, up to then I still thought I could control drinking. I thought, well, now that I've been put out for drinking, I'll just show them that they were completely wrong, so I went off on the biggest bout I had been on up to then, involving about a fortnight's blackout.

I was a civilian now. I was in a world that I knew nothing at all about, and I felt intensely afraid. I put myself into a home. I stayed there just long enough to work up a good resentment against the doctor in charge, who I didn't think was doing anything at all except collecting fees, and I left there fully determined that I'd never put myself in the power of medical people again.

I stopped off just to have one drink to see if it tasted the same on the way back to London, and that night I was carried back to bed again. So I decided I'd go back and live in Ireland to try the geography cure.

When I arrived back in Dublin, I had no friends

left. Everybody I had known in the old days had gone. This was in 1941. I had no work to do and I was at an age where it seemed too late to start anything new. In any case, I made myself believe that, so I just drifted about, existing on my retired pay, drinking, and living at home.

That went on for about six years. Things were getting worse and worse. I went to hospitals, I went to retreats and doctors, and finally my mother asked me to go and see a specialist of her own choosing. I talked to him for quite a long time and at the end, he said, "Well, you're not quite mad enough to be shut up for good yet, but you soon will be if you live long enough." That put a scare in me for about a fortnight. I was terribly afraid that I was actually going mad, if I hadn't gone mad already.

I couldn't understand myself. I was intensely unhappy the whole time, but I didn't seem to be able to do anything about it, and the worst part to me was the realization that all this was going to happen again and again until I died. I couldn't see that there was any way out of it, and I got absolutely despairing. My only hope was to try and get through what was left of life as best I could, but I could never visualize doing that without drinking. The thought of stopping drinking just never occurred to me.

As I say, this specialist put a scare in me for about a fortnight or three weeks, then I started my last bout, which went on and off for about three months. Finally, my mother came and said she had kept me at home for six years because she thought she could help me, but that now she had come to the conclusion that I wasn't even worth trying to help. I was to pack and go and get out of their lives for good. That was on the

28th of April, 1947. That morning was the first time I really realized where I'd got to in my life. I couldn't think of anything at all to do. It was no use talking of putting myself into a home, a hospital, or of going to see a doctor again, or of going to see a priest or anyone else. I had played all that out long ago. She really meant business this time. This was the only time in my life that I'd ever known my mother to be almost pitiless, but she couldn't be blamed for that.

Just as I was wondering what on earth I could do—I was too drunk even to pack a handkerchief—the memory of an A.A. write-up that I had seen in the *Evening Mail* flashed across my mind—and I thought to myself, this is something I haven't tried yet. So I did manage to get myself down to an A.A. meeting that night. Providentially, this was a Monday night when the Dublin Group met in those days, and my family agreed that if A.A. could do anything for me at all, that I'd be allowed to stay on at home on probation. But if I came back in the usual state, then I'd have to go off for good the next day.

Having made that bargain, I immediately began to feel I'd been trapped unto it and I went out and had some drinks—four glasses of gin, I remember. I was taking Benzedrine and paraldehyde quite impartially during the day then, and by the time I arrived at my first A.A. meeting, I was pretty drunk and certainly doped up to the eyes and completely jittery. I had been using paraldehyde more or less like ordinary drink for the last six years though, occasionally, I'd bounce back to Phenobarbital and things like that.

When I arrived at The Country Shop, which was a restaurant where they met in Dublin, I found about thirty-five or forty people in the room. It was their open night meeting, but of course I thought they were all alcoholics; I couldn't imagine why anybody else would want to go there, and my first reaction was, well, I've come to something that's not for me. People seemed to be carefully dressed, too happy, too normal. My mind was too screwy to be able to understand much of what was being said. But I did understand this eventually, that these people had been through a lot of drinking experiences just as I had, and had managed to make a job of it. What struck me most was that they all seemed to be quite pleased with having made a job of it and having stopped drinking. That gave me my first bit of hope. I thought that if these kind of ordinary people can do it, a man of my brains ought to find it much more easy, and I joined. I suppose I had reached my spiritual gutter that night, but I have never had what you could call a real urge to drink again.

Since I joined on that April night, A.A. has done more for me than just stop me from drinking; it has brought me back to life again. It has made me understand that I must be one of my world, that I cannot exist in any happiness as a rebel by myself. It has taught me that I can best keep my sobriety by sharing it out with others; that I must *bring* that sobriety to others who need it, in my own interest. It continues to try to teach me the real charity, the charity that gives time and good will and service, and not just money. It has shown me, through the tragic stories of so many other alcoholics, the utter futility of self-pity. It has taught me that success and failure are never final, and that neither count for very much in the final assessment of any man who has done his best. It has brought me back to a realization of my Maker and my duties to Him. It has made me very happy.

My mother lived on for five years after I joined A.A., the last two in complete blindness. Not least of my debts to A.A. is the knowledge that in that time when she wanted me most, I was there—and that I wasn't drunk.

HE WHO LOSES HIS LIFE

*An ambitious playwright, he let his brains get so far
ahead of his emotions that he collapsed into suicidal
drinking. To learn to live, he nearly died.*

I remember the day when I decided to drink myself
to death quietly, without bothering anyone, because I was tired of having been a dependable, trust-
worthy person for about thirty-nine years without
having received what I thought was a proper reward
for my virtue. That was the day, that was the decision,
I know now, when I crossed over the line and became
an active alcoholic. Perhaps a better way of saying it is
that, on that day, with that decision, I no longer
fought drinking as an escape. Rather, I embraced it—I
must in honesty admit it—with a great sense of relief. I
no longer had to pretend. I was giving up the struggle.
Things weren't going as I thought they should, for my
greater enjoyment, comfort and fame; therefore, if the
universe wouldn't play my way, I wouldn't play at all.
I, a man of steel, with very high ideals, well brought
up, an honor student and the recipient of scholarships
and prizes, a boy wonder in business—I, Bob, the author of this essay, looked and saw that the universe
was beneath my contempt, and that to remove myself
from it was the only thing of dignity a man could do.
Since, perhaps, suicide was a bit too drastic (actually, I
was afraid), dry martinis were chosen as the slow,
pleasant, private, gradual instrument of self-destruc-

tion. And it was nobody's business, nobody's but mine. So I thought.

Within a month, the police, the hospital authorities, several kind strangers, most of my friends, all of my close relatives, and a few adepts at rolling a drunk and removing his wrist watch and wallet had been involved. (There was a time, for about three months, when I bought a ten-dollar wrist watch every pay day—that is, every two weeks. Since it was wartime, I explained to the somewhat startled shopkeeper that I had many friends in the service whom I was remembering with a watch. Perhaps, without realizing it, I was.)

On that day of decision, I didn't acknowledge that I was an *alcoholic*. My proud southern blood would have boiled if anyone had named me such a despicable thing. No, it can best be explained in a little phrase I coined and sang to myself: "What happened to Bob? Bob found alcohol!" And having sung that phrase, I'd chuckle with amusement, turning into irony turning into self-contempt turning into self-pity, at the sad fate of Bob, that wonderful, poor little motherless boy who was so smart in school and who grew up to accept responsibility so early and so fast and who staggered under his burdens without a whimper until the time came when he thought he was too good for this world and so he ought to be out of it. *Poor Bob!*

That was one aspect of it, and a true one. There were several others. There was loneliness. There was the necessity for sticking to a job I hated, a dull, repetitive job performed in association with other men I had nothing in common with . . . performed for years on end, because the money was needed at home. There was the physical aspect; to be the youngest and the runt of the brood of children, to have to wear glasses very early and so to be teased, to be bookish and bored in school because the captain of the football team *could not* translate Virgil and yet was the school god while you, *you,* you little shrimp, were the school egghead, junior size and an early model.

There was the father one lost respect for at the age of eleven, because the father broke his solemn word in a circumstance where you, eleven years old, had assumed guilt when you were innocent; but the father would not believe you, no matter what; and to ease his suffering you "confessed" and were "forgiven," only—months later—to have your "guilt" brought up—only he and you knew what he was talking about—brought up in front of the stern grandmother. The sacred word was broken and you never trusted your father again, and avoided him. And when he died, you were unmoved. You were thirty-five before you understood your father's horrible anguish, and forgave him, and loved him again. For you learned that he had been guilty of the thing he had accused you of, and his guilt had brought suffering to his entire family; and he thought he saw his young son beginning his own tragic pattern.

These things were all pressures. For by thirty-five I had been drinking for a few years. The pressures had started long ago. Sometimes we are told in A.A. not to try and learn the reasons for our drinking. But such is my nature that I must know the reason for things, and I didn't stop until I had satisfied myself about the reasons for my drinking. Only, having found them, I threw them away, and ordered another extra dry martini. For to have accepted the reasons and to have acted on them would have been too great a blow to my ego, which was as great, in reverse, as my body was small.

In my twenties, I found Edna St. Vincent Millay's verse:

"Pity me the heart that is slow to learn / What the quick mind sees at every turn."

That couplet contains most of my reasons for drinking. There was the love affair which was ridiculous—"imagine that midget being able to fall in love!"—and my head knew it while my heart pumped real, genuine anguish, for it hurt like hell, and since it was first love, things have never been quite the same. There was the over-weening ambition to be the world's greatest author, when—at thirty-nine—I had nothing of importance to say to the world. There was the economic fear which made me too timid to take any action which might improve my circumstances. There was the sense of being "misunderstood," when as a matter of fact by my middle twenties I was quite popular, although I hadn't grown much bigger physically. But the feeling was a crutch, an excuse. It was my "secret garden"—bluntly, it was my retreat from life, and I didn't want to give it up.

For a while, for a long time, we can endure the intellect's being ahead of the emotions, which is the import of Millay's couplet. But as the years go by, the stretch becomes unbearable; and the man with the grown-up brain and the childish emotions—vanity, self-interest, false pride, jealousy, longing for social approval, to name a few—becomes a prime candidate for alcohol. To my way of thinking, that is a definition of alcoholism; a state of being in which the emotions have failed to grow to the stature of the intellect. I know there are some alcoholics who seem terribly, terribly grown-up, but I think that they are trying to make themselves *think* they are grown-up, and the strain of their effort is what is causing them to drink—a sense of inadequacy, a childish vanity to be the most popular, the most sought after, the mostest of the most. And all this, of course, is, in the popular modern jargon, "compensation" for immaturity.

I wish I knew a shortcut to maturity. But I wanted a cosmos, a universe all my own which I had created and where I reigned as chief top reigner and ruler over everyone else. Which is only another way of saying, I had to be *right all the time*, and only God can be that. Okay, I wanted to be God.

I still do. I want to be one of His children, a member of the human race. And, as a child is a part of his father, so do I now want to be a part of God. For always, over and above everything else, was the awfulness of the lack of meaning in life. Now, for me, and to my satisfaction, I know the purpose of life: The purpose of life is to create and the by-product is happiness. *To create:* Everyone does it, some at the instinct level, others in the arts. My personal definition, which I submit as applying only to myself (although everyone is welcome to it who wants it), includes every waking activity of the human being; to have a creative attitude toward things is a more exact meaning, to live and to deal with other human beings creatively, which to me means seeing the God in them, and respecting and worshiping this God. If I write with the air of one who has discovered the obvious, which is to say, the eternal truths which have been offered to us since the beginning, forgive my callowness; I had to find these things out for myself. Alas for us men toward whom Shaw hurled his cry, "Must a Christ be crucified in every generation for the benefit of those who have no imagination?"

My serious drinking covered about seven years. In those years I was in jail nine times, in an alcoholic ward, overnight, twice; and I was fired from three jobs, two of them very good ones. As I write these words, it seems incredible that these things should have happened to me, for they are, truly, against all my instincts and training. (Well! I started to cross out that last sentence, but decided to let it stand. What a revelation of ego and arrogance still remaining in me—as if *anyone,* instinct and training apart, *likes* to be in jail or in an alcoholic ward or fired from his job. After nearly eight years of sobriety in A.A., I still can set down such thoughts, "against my instinct and training," showing that I still consider myself a "special" person, entitled to special privileges. I ask the forgiveness of the reader; and from now on I shall try to write with the humility I honestly pray for.)

A pattern established itself. I never was a "secret" drinker, and I never kept a bottle at home. I'd visit one bar after another, having one martini in each, and in each hoping to find someone interesting to talk to. Actually, of course, I wanted someone to *listen* to me, because when I had a few martinis inside, I became the great author I longed to be; and the right listener was in for some pretty highflown theories of literature and of genius. If the listener were drunk enough, the lecture might go on through several martinis, which I was glad to pay for. If he were still sober, chances are that very quickly I put him down as a Philistine with no appreciation of literary genius; and then I went on to another bar to find a new victim.

So it was that in alcohol I found fulfillment. For a

little while, I was the great man I wanted to be, and thought myself entitled to be just by reason of being me. I wonder if ever there has been a sillier reason for getting drunk all the time. Sobering up, the mind that was ahead of the emotions would impel the question: What have you written or done to be the great man? This question so insulted the emotions that clearly there was only one thing to do, go and get drunk again, and put that enquiring mind in its proper place, which was oblivion.

Depending on the stage of drunkenness, eventually I either fought or went to sleep. Brandishing my "motto," which was "A little man with a stick is equal to a big man," sometimes I varied the literary lecture by a fight with a big man, selected solely because he was big and I was little. I bear a few scars on my face from these fights, which I always lost, because the "stick" existed only in my mind. So did the waterboy on the high school football team attempt to revenge himself on the big brother who was the star quarterback; for I was the waterboy and my brother was the star quarterback, innocent of everything except the fact that he was a star quarterback.

When sleep overtook me, my practice was to undress and go to bed, wherever. Once this was in front of the Paramount Theatre in Times Square. I was down to my shorts, unaware of wrong-doing, before the ambulance got there and hauled me off to a hospital from which anxious friends rescued me, later that night.

Still another friend and temporary host received me at four in the morning from the charge of a policeman who had found me "going to bed" in a garage far from the last place I could remember having been, a fashionable bar and restaurant in the theatrical district of New York, to which I had repaired after my date for that evening, a charming lady of the theatre who had refused my company for obvious reasons. This time, whoever had rolled me, had taken my glasses as well (they were gold). When the policeman released me to my stupefied and exasperated friend at four in the morning, I went to my traveling bag and groped until I found—well, let the officer speak: "Ah," said the policeman, "he's got anuder pair, t'ank God!" Thank *you,* Mr. Policeman, wherever you are now.

I mentioned that this friend was my temporary host. Need I add that such was the case because I had no money to provide a roof over my head? Still, I had had funds sufficient to get plastered because that, of course, was more important than paying my own way.

Once, or even twice, such incidents might be amusing. Repeated year on end, they are horrible—frightening and degrading, a chronicle of tragedy which may be greater because the individual undergoing the tragedy, myself, knew what was happening, and yet refused to do anything to stop it. One by one, the understanding friends dropped away. The helpful family finally said, over long distance, that there would be no more money and that I could not come home.

I say, "refused to do anything to stop it." The truth is, I did not know how to stop it, nor did I want to, really. I had nothing to put in the place of alcohol, of the forgetfulness, of the oblivion, which alcohol provides. Without alcohol, I would be *really* alone. Was I the disloyal sort who would turn his back on this, my last and truest friend?

I fled, finally, after having been fired from my job by a boss who wept a little (since I had worked hard) as he gave notice for me to clear out. I went back home, to a job of manual labor, where for a little while I was able to keep away from alcohol. But not for long; now, for five Friday nights in a row, I went to jail, picked up sodden with beer (which I always disliked, but which was the only drink available); in jail five consecutive Friday nights in the town where I had grown up, where I had been an honor student in high school, where a kindly uncle, bailing me out, said, "Bob, our family just doesn't do this sort of thing." I had replied, "Uncle, give the judge ten dollars, or I'll have to work it out on the county road." I was in hell. I wandered, craving peace, from one spot to another of youthful happy memory, and loathed the man I had become. I promised on the grave of a beloved sister that I would stop drinking. I meant it. I wanted to stop. I did not know how. For by now I had been exposed once to A.A., but I had treated it as a vaudeville and had taken friends to meetings so that they too could enjoy the fascination of the naked revelation of suffering and recovery. I thought I had recovered. Instead, I had gotten sicker. I was fatally ill. A.A. had not worked for me. The reason, as I learned later, was that I had not worked for A.A. I left this home town, then, after I had made a public spectacle of myself in the presence of a revered teacher whose favorite pupil I had been. I could not face the boy and youth I was in the reality of the contemptible man I had become.

Back to the big city, for another year of precarious living, paid for largely by one or two friends I still had not milked dry or worn to exhaustion with demands on their bounty. I worked when I could—piddling jobs I thought them. I was not capable of anything better. I stumbled agonizedly past the theatre where in years gone by a great star had played my play. I had even borrowed money from her, over her protest: "Bob, please don't ask me to lend you money—you're the only one who hasn't." I took her money, though; I had to have it. It paid for a ten-day binge which was the end of my drinking days. Thank God that those days are gone.

On another small borrowed sum, I went up into the country to the home of a doctor I had known since boyhood. We worked in five below zero weather, fixing on an elm tree a wrought iron device which modestly proclaimed that he was indeed a country doctor. I had no money—well, maybe a dime—and only the clothes I stood in. "Bob," he asked quietly, "do you want to live or die?"

He meant it. I knew he did. I did not remember much of the ten-day binge. But I remembered the years of agony preceding the binge, I remembered the years I had thrown away. I had just turned forty-six. Maybe it was time to die. Hope had died, or so I thought.

But I said humbly, "I suppose I want to live." I meant it. From that instant to this, nearly eight years later, I have not had the slightest urge to drink. I choose to believe that the Power greater than ourselves we ask for help, wrapped my shivering body in loving warmth and strength which has never left me. The doc and I went back into the house. He had a shot of brandy against the cold and passed me the bottle. I set it down and made myself a cup of coffee. I have not had a drink of anything alcoholic since that ten-day binge.

Please do not think it ended so simply and so easily. Simply, yes, it did end; for I had changed my mind about alcohol, and it stayed changed. But for the next years, I worked hard and exultantly in A.A. In the nearby little town there was a plumber who once had tried to get an A.A. group going. I went over and met him, and we two started the group up again. It is going strong still, these eight years later, and some of its members have been of great influence for good in state-wide A.A. work. I myself have been lucky enough to help out. I have had the joy of seeing many a human being, down and out, learn to stand straight again, and to proceed under his own power to happiness in life. I learned the true meaning of bread cast upon the waters.

There were debts totaling nearly ten thousand dollars to be paid off. They are almost paid; the end is in sight. I have been allowed to build an entirely new career in a field I had never worked in. I have published a book covering certain aspects of this field, which has been well-reviewed and which is helping other people. I have been appointed to the faculty of my old school, to teach in my new field. All of my family and loved ones, all of my friends, are nearer and dearer to me than ever before; and I have literally dozens of new friends who say they cannot believe that a short eight years ago I was ready for the scrap heap. When I remark that I have been in jail nine times, and in an alcoholic ward twice, they think I'm kidding, or possibly dramatizing for the sake of a good yarn. But I know I'm not. I remember how horrible jails are, how dreadful a thing it is to be behind steel bars. I wish we did not have to have jails; I wish everyone could be in A.A., and if everyone were there would be no need for jails, in my opinion.

For I am happy. I thought I could never be happy.

A happy man is not likely to do harm to another human being. Harm is done by sick people, as I was sick, and doing dreadful harm to myself and to my loved ones.

For me, A.A. is a synthesis of all the philosophy I've ever read, all of the positive, good philosophy, all of it based on love. I have seen that there is only one law, the law of love, and there are only two sins; the first is to interfere with the growth of another human being, and the second is to interfere with one's own growth.

I still want to write a fine play and to get it on. I'd gladly do it anonymously, as I have done this brief account of my struggle with alcohol—merely to present certain ideas for the consideration of the reader. I don't care too much about personal fame or glory, and I want only enough money to enable me to do the work I feel I can perhaps do best. I stood off and took a long look at life and the values I found in it: I saw a paradox, that he who loses his life does indeed find it. The more you give, the more you get. The less you think of yourself the more of a person you become.

In A.A. we can begin again no matter how late it may be. I have begun again. At fifty-four, I have had come true for me the old wish, "If only I could live my life over, knowing what I know." That's what I am doing, living again, knowing what I know. I hope I have been able to impart to you, the reader, at least a bit of what I know: the joy of living, the irresistible power of divine love and its healing strength, and the fact that we, as sentient beings, have the knowledge to choose between good and evil, and, choosing good, are made happy.

The Twelve Steps

1. We admitted we were powerless over alcohol—that our lives had become unmanageable.

2. Came to believe that a Power greater than ourselves could restore us to sanity.

3. Made a decision to turn our will and our lives over to the care of God *as we understood Him.*

4. Made a searching and fearless moral inventory of ourselves.

5. Admitted to God, to ourselves, and to another human being the exact nature of our wrongs.

6. Were entirely ready to have God remove all these defects of character.

7. Humbly asked Him to remove our shortcomings.

8. Made a list of all persons we had harmed, and became willing to make amends to them all.

9. Made direct amends to such people wherever possible, except when to do so would injure them or others.

10. Continued to take personal inventory and when we were wrong, promptly admitted it.

11. Sought through prayer and meditation to improve our conscious contact with God *as we understood Him,* praying only for knowledge of His will for us and the power to carry that out.

12. Having had a spiritual awakening as the result of these steps, we tried to carry this message to alcoholics and to practice these principles in all our affairs.

THE TWELVE TRADITIONS

1. Our common welfare should come first; personal recovery depends upon A.A. unity.

2. For our group purpose there is but one ultimate authority—a loving God as He may express Himself in our group conscience. Our leaders are but trusted servants; they do not govern.

3. The only requirement for A.A. membership is a desire to stop drinking.

4. Each group should be autonomous except in matters affecting other groups or A.A. as a whole.

5. Each group has but one primary purpose—to carry its message to the alcoholic who still suffers.

6. An A.A. group ought never endorse, finance or lend the A.A. name to any related facility or outside enterprise, lest problems of money, property and prestige divert us from our primary purpose.

7. Every A.A. group ought to be fully self-supporting, declining outside contributions.

8. Alcoholics Anonymous should remain forever nonprofessional, but our service centers may employ special workers.

9. A.A., as such, ought never be organized; but we may create service boards or committees directly responsible to those they serve.

10. Alcoholics Anonymous has no opinion on outside issues; hence the A.A. name ought never be drawn into public controversy.

11. Our public relations policy is based on attraction rather than promotion; we need always maintain personal anonymity at the level of press, radio and films.

12. Anonymity is the spiritual foundation of all our Traditions, ever reminding us to place principles before personalities.

THE TWELVE CONCEPTS
(SHORT FORM)

1. Final responsibility and ultimate authority for A.A. world services should always reside in the collective conscience of our whole Fellowship.

2. The General Service Conference of A.A. has become, for nearly every practical purpose, the active voice and the effective conscience of our whole Society in its world affairs.

3. To insure effective leadership, we should endow each element of A.A.—the Conference, the General Service Board and its service corporations, staffs, committees, and executives—with a traditional "Right of Decision."

4. At all responsible levels, we ought to maintain a traditional "Right of Participation," allowing a voting representation in reasonable proportion to the responsibility that each must discharge.

5. Throughout our structure, a traditional "Right of Appeal" ought to prevail, so that minority opinion will be heard and personal grievances receive careful consideration.

6. The Conference recognizes that the chief initiative and active responsibility in most world service matters should be exercised by the trustee members of the Conference acting as the General Service Board.

7. The Charter and Bylaws of the General Service Board are legal instruments, empowering the trustees to manage and conduct world service affairs. The Conference Charter is not a legal document; it relies

upon tradition and the A.A. purse for final effectiveness.

8. The trustees are the principal planners and adminstrators of overall policy and finance. They have custodial oversight of the separately incorporated and constantly active services, exercising this through their ability to elect all the directors of these entities.

9. Good service leadership at all levels is indispensable for our future functioning and safety. Primary world service leadership, once exercised by the founders, must necessarily be assumed by the trustees.

10. Every service responsibility should be matched by an equal service authority, with the scope of such authority well defined.

11. he trustees should always have the best possible committees, corporate service directors, executives, staffs, and consultants. Composition, qualifications, induction procedures, and rights and duties will always be matters of serious concern.

12. The Conference shall observe the spirit of A.A. tradition, taking care that it never becomes the seat of perilous wealth or power; that sufficient operating funds and reserve be its prudent financial principle; that it place none of its members in a position of unqualified authority over others; that it reach all important decisions by discussion, vote, and, whenever possible, by substantial unanimity; that its actions never be personally punitive nor an incitement to public controversy; that it never perform acts of government, and that, like the Society it serves, it will always remain democratic in thought and action.